LOVE'S VISION

Love's Vision

Troy Jollimore

PRINCETON UNIVERSITY PRESS

PRINCETON & OXFORD

Copyright © 2011 by Princeton University Press

Published by Princeton University Press, 41 William Street,
Princeton, New Jersey 08540

In the United Kingdom: Princeton University Press, 6 Oxford Street,
Woodstock, Oxfordshire OX20 1TW

press.princeton.edu

Jacket Art: *Early Hour*, 1935 by Karl Hofer, 1878–1955. Courtesy of the
Portland Art Museum/© 2011 Artists Rights Society (ARS), New York / VG
Bild-Kunst, Bonn.

Excerpt from Goethe: *The History of a Man* by Emil Ludwig, translated
by Ethel Golburn Mayne, copyright 1928, by G.P. Putnam's sons. Used by
permission of G.P. Putnam's Sons, a division of Penguin Group (USA) Inc.

Excerpt from *The History of Love*, by Nicole Krauss. Copyright © 2005
by Nicole Krauss. Used by permission of W.W. Norton & Company.

Excerpt from *Existentialists and Mystics* by Iris Murdoch, copyright 1950-52,
© 1956-59, 1961-62, 1966, 1969-70, 1972, 1977, 1978, 1986, 1997 by Iris
Murdoch. Used by permission of Penguin, a division of Penguin Group (USA) Inc.

Excerpt from *Solaris* by Stanislaw Lem. 1970. Reprinted by permission of
Bloomsbury USA.

Library of Congress Cataloging-in-Publication Data
Jollimore, Troy A., 1971–
    Love's vision / Troy Jollimore.
        p. cm.
    Includes bibliographical references and index.
    ISBN 978-0-691-14872-4 (hardcover : alk. paper) 1. Love. I. Title.
    BD436.J65 2011
    128'.46—dc22   2010050126

British Library Cataloging-in-Publication Data is available

This book has been composed in Sabon

Printed on acid-free paper. ∞

Printed in the United States of America

10 9 8 7 6 5 4 3 2 1

There is always some madness in love. But there is always some reason in madness.

—*Friedrich Nietzsche*

For Sharon

CONTENTS

PREFACE

To live within limits, to want one thing, or a very few things, very much and to love them dearly, cling to them, survey them from every angle, become one with them—that is what makes the poet, the artist, the human being.

—Goethe

The conjunction of the word *love* with *limits* may sound discordant to the contemporary ear. We like to think of love as having no limits, as a force that releases us from limits. We think, or at least we say that we think, that love is eternal, that not even death can end it. At the same time, we have forgotten how to see the value in limits, viewing them only as challenges to be overcome, so that a limit that cannot be overcome and must be lived with is a source of frustration and pain. But as Goethe saw, limits can help make a life meaningful, and part of love's value is to limit a life by giving it a shape, a character, a focus of concern. What one cares about is an important part of who one is. But saying "I care about this" always carries with it an implied "and not that."

This, at any rate, is one of the main thoughts underlying this book. In speaking of love in terms of vision, I will suggest that love is, in a very real way, a kind of perception, a way of seeing the world. And perception is always a matter of being limited because a perceiving agent is situated in a particular time, place, and situation. There is foreground, and there is background; there is what is before one's eyes, and there is what is behind one's back. Seeing one thing always means not seeing something else. In large part we choose what we see, by moving around, taking certain positions, opening (or closing) our eyes, and so forth. But we cannot fully determine how the world appears to us; its contribution to our experience vastly transcends our will. So perception, like love, is both active and passive; it is a matter of interacting with the world, not of determining it or being completely and helplessly determined by it.

In this preface I indicate, or perhaps confess, a few of the idiosyncrasies that characterize my approach to the inexhaustible topic of love. One peculiarity of my approach is that I am especially, indeed exclusively, concerned with love for *persons*. It is undeniable that we use the word *love* in other contexts, too. After all, one can be said to love a great many things: Thai food, Bach's concertos, playing or watching baseball, one's country, and even life itself. And some philosophers have treated the matter as if there were no deep or essential difference between these usages. But I cannot agree. Nor does the crucial difference lie in the fact that love for nonpersons—"love" for Thai food, baseball, and so on—generally tends to be less intense and, over the course of a lifetime, less significant. After all, there are important exceptions to this tendency: it is not at all impossible for a person to structure her life around her love of her country or even her love of baseball. The crucial and deep difference has to do with the nature of the love object: the fact that a person, unlike other objects of love, possesses a profound and complex inner life and exists as a subject in the world. Indeed, we might almost say that each person is a world unto herself; for each person, there is an experienced world that is not identical to anyone else's and that is metaphysically isolated from everyone else's (in the sense that only *I* can have *my* thoughts, *my* desires, *my* experiences, and so forth). I will say more about this as we proceed. But one can get an initial sense of the difference by noting the obvious but nonetheless crucial fact that loving a person is unlike loving a sport, a cuisine, a pastime, a cause, or a country, in the crucial sense that when one loves a person, one loves something that can care whether it is loved; one loves something that can, if one is fortunate, love one back.

Although there are a variety of objects about which people may care greatly, then, and that they may sometimes be said to love in a nonmetaphorical sense, it is love for and between *persons* that people tend to care about most, and that is the love that will concern us in this book. My approach to understanding this kind of love involves the thought that the essential characteristic of such love objects is their possession of an inner life—loving, indeed, is in large part the longing to somehow come into contact with that inner life. Of course, one wants to make contact with the beloved's outer life as well; in fact, it often seems that what one wants is to unite one's life with hers. As Proust writes, "Our belief that a person takes part in an unknown life which his or her love would allow us to enter is, of all that love demands in order to come into being, what it prizes the most, and what makes it care little for the rest."[1]

Love for persons, then, is a type of love that, despite our frequent and regrettable carelessness in using the word, forms a quite distinct phenomenon that is well worth keeping apart from other, related notions. One might be tempted to proceed by attempting to come up with a precise definition of this sort of love. This would be a typically philosophical approach, but it is one I have chosen to avoid. It is hard to come up with a precise definition of love, and if the proposed definition had any flaws at all, they would be likely to throw us off course or constrain the investigation from the outset. Besides, the fact is that we all have a fairly good idea about what the word *love* refers to in this context and how it is used, despite the fact that it is difficult to formulate a precise definition and despite the fact that we may disagree in a great many of our claims about it. I will proceed, then, on the assumption that it is enough to say, by way of identifying the object of our concern, that it is the positive emotion people in certain intimate relationships—romantic lovers, friends, and in many cases family members—tend to feel toward one another; that it is taken to be, at least in part, constitutive of such relationships; and that it seems by its nature to involve at least a degree of passion, affection, or both. (Because it is the sort of love people feel for each other, *agape*, that is, God's love for us, is excluded. Of course, some Christian thinkers and others have thought that humans are capable of feeling agape, or at least that striving to do so is a worthy ethical pursuit. For my part, and for reasons that will probably be clear by the end of the book, I am quite skeptical about the former claim and at least somewhat skeptical about the latter.)

I mentioned "romantic lovers, friends, and *in many cases* family members." But in my view it is a good idea to keep the latter category somewhat separate. The love that obtains between family members may differ in significant ways from that which tends to exist between friends and romantic partners. Love for relatives is frequently regarded as being determined by one's identity in a way that lies largely beyond one's control. It is not uncommon, for instance, to think that love for one's close relations, at least in ordinary circumstances, is to a quite large extent obligatory. To love one's parents, to love one's children, to love one's sisters and brothers—these are frequently seen as simply part of the natural order of things, and perhaps as being morally required, in ways that loving the particular persons who happen to be one's friends, or one's romantic partners, is not. Of course, as a relationship of friendship or romantic love persists, it begins to feel more and more like a family relationship; and, indeed, part of the social function of marriage is to grant one's partner legal status as a member of one's family. Family-type obligations may arise, then, in the later stages of such relationships. But in their early stages matters are quite otherwise. In particular, one tends to pursue relationships with certain potential friends and lovers and not others precisely because one finds oneself *attracted* to some and not to others. And we tend to think, too, that if one does not continue to be at least somewhat attracted to a friend or lover, then something in the relationship has gone badly wrong.

This is not to say that attraction or such related evaluative notions as admiration or esteem are entirely irrelevant in the context of family relations. One would like one's parents, siblings, and children to think highly of one, and not simply because they are obliged to do so. Still, the situations are very different, and so it will almost certainly make a dramatic difference to the account of love we develop which of these types of love we take as paradigmatic. Indeed, these may be so deeply different that it is an error to take *either* as paradigmatic; to develop an account of love on the basis of either of these divisions and then insist that it also apply to the other type would be a Procrustean maneuver that would almost inevitably require us to distort, perhaps beyond recognition, whichever branch of the tree we did not begin by taking as fundamental.

At any rate, I resist the urge that some philosophers have felt to see romantic or sexual love as an impure, deviant, or otherwise secondary form of love, particularly as compared with the sort of love one finds between family members. Harry Frankfurt has written:

> It is important to avoid confusing love . . . with infatuation, lust, obsession, possessiveness, and dependency in their various forms. In particular, relationships that are primarily romantic or sexual do not provide very authentic or illuminating paradigms of love as I am construing it. Relationships of those kinds typically include a number of vividly distracting elements which do not belong to the essential nature of love as a mode of disinterested concern, but that are so confusing that they make it nearly impossible for anyone to be clear about just what is going on. Among relationships between humans, the love of parents for their infants or small children is the species that comes closest to offering recognizably pure instances of love.[2]

Admittedly, "infatuation, lust, obsession, possessiveness, and dependency in their various forms" are phenomena that are quite distinct from love; but it would be a mistake to conclude that any form of love in which they might be involved is not *genuine* love, and so ought to be ignored, or at best taken as secondary, by love's philosophers. Indeed, at least one of these phenomena, dependency, is a deep element of just the sort of parent-child relationship Frankfurt suggests that we take as paradigmatic, and it will be at least as common in such contexts as in sexual or romantic relationships; and infatuation, obsession, and possessiveness— particularly, perhaps, among those who have only recently become parents—are far from unknown. The separation between the two types of love is not as deep, and the love of parents for their children not as pure, as Frankfurt seems to assume.

Moreover, to the extent that they *are* similar, and both can be treated by a single account, there are a number of reasons for thinking that it is friend/lover love, rather than family love, that should be taken as paradigmatic. First, given that we are interested not just in love *for* but in love *between* persons, the friend/lover model is probably more relevant, and almost certainly more interesting, than the family relation model. As noted earlier, part of what distinguishes personal love from other forms of love is the fact that the object can reciprocate in kind; but in fact this is not a feature of all relationships in the family-relation category.[3] Very young children can return a certain degree of affection and attention, but it is not until they begin to mature that they can direct back at their parents the kind of appreciation that constitutes love—an appreciation that, by that point, the parents will have been directing to them for some time. Indeed, many parents at least claim to begin loving their children even before birth. This sort of love may, given Frankfurt's presuppositions, be more "pure" than the love that holds between adults, but it is for that very reason far less distinctively *personal*.

There is another reason, already hinted at, for thinking that if we must choose whether family-relation or friend/lover love constitutes our paradigm of love, we ought to choose in favor of the latter. This is that both romantic love and friendship seem to involve a free or autonomous response in a way that the sort of love directed toward family members may not. It is common to think that we are to a certain degree obligated to love our children, our parents, and our various relatives. As a result, forming love attachments for these individuals may be considerably less likely to reflect or express spontaneous feelings about those individuals. This is not to deny that such feelings are genuine but only to point out that they play a very different role in the psychic economy of the individual than do feelings that are not regarded as in any way obligatory but that occur as unmeditated, spontaneous reactions to individuals toward whom one has no (initial) obligation.[4] The love a person feels for her friends or lovers might for this reason tell us a good deal more about her identity as an agent—and may, for that very reason, be more important to her, or important in quite different ways—than the love she feels for those to whom she bears relations that were fundamentally unchosen.

This book will be more concerned with the sort of love that tends to obtain between (previously) unrelated adult human beings—in particular, the love that occurs between romantic lovers and, to an only slightly lesser degree, between friends—than with the sort that typically obtains between parents and children, siblings, or other persons related by blood. This need not prevent us from wondering whether the claims I advance about love hold in the family context as well as the friend/lover context, and, if they do not appear to, what *does* hold true in that realm. But for the reasons given earlier, I will do my best to avoid the assumption that there must be a single account of love that applies equally well to all of its instantiations.

Then again, it is probably clear by now that I consider the love that obtains between friends to be very similar to that which obtains between romantic lovers—so much so that I think we are justified in providing a single unified account that treats them as essentially the same phenomenon. Some philosophers would disagree. Frankfurt, again, thinks the influence of sexual passion so distorting that it corrupts and threatens to render unintelligible (or at any rate, highly mysterious) any relationship into which it enters. I doubt this. Not, of course, that sexual attraction is without its bizarre aspects. But love is always idiosyncratic to some degree; it attaches to particular features that might leave others cold, and because of this a particular instance of love says as much about the lover as it does about the object of the lover's attention. At any rate, it seems to me that romantic love is simply a particular form of friendship, and that friendship at its best can be as passionate and committed as romantic love. (People speak these days about "friends with benefits," but all friendships have benefits, and a great many of these—affection, passionate commitment, even the sharing of sensual pleasures—are the same benefits we find in romantic relationships.) "*Philia,*" as Alan Soble writes, "is actually a variety of *eros.*"[5] I will not attempt to argue for this but simply take it as a presupposition. Those who do not share it will, in all likelihood, find much else to disagree with as well.

I should say something regarding my choice of pronouns. There is a lot of talk about lovers and their beloveds in this book; I have randomly determined, section by section or sometimes paragraph by paragraph, which one is "he" and which one is "she." The pairing of "he" with "she" is not meant in any way to deny that the love of a man for another man or that of a woman for another woman is as real and legitimate as that of a woman for a man or a man for a woman, and this is so whether the lovers in question are romantic partners or just friends. I tried using "he/he" and "she/she" in places, but the result was nearly always confusing, and in the end I chose clarity of meaning over fairness. It is far from the worst thing I have done in my life, and I hope readers will not be seriously offended.

Finally, let me say a word or two about method. I work in the tradition of analytic philosophy, so this will be a book with arguments. I do not think, though, that the book contains anything that could be considered a proof. I am too much inclined toward skepticism to think that genuine proofs are encountered often, and besides, the nature of the topic makes the very idea of a proof seem, here, especially inappropriate. And not all of the persuasion in the book is even meant to take place by means of argument, at least not if we understand the word *argument* in the narrow sense that philosophers frequently have in mind. Thus the reader of this book will find thought experiments, literary examples, appeals to intuition and to the reader's experience, and other such things in addition to straightforward arguments. All of these methods are meant to do what philosophy paradigmatically aims to do, which is to appeal to the reader's reason; but not all of them fall within the narrowly circumscribed bounds of rational proof or rational argument, as some people insist on understanding them.[6] Rather than providing a proof or even an argument in the standard sense, I have often thought of myself as doing what Wittgenstein suggested philosophers do: painting a picture.[7] Accordingly, the account I propose does not pretend to be an exact, comprehensive, and final theory. Still, I hope that readers will find the picture I offer in this book compelling, enlightening, and true to their own experiences of love.

ACKNOWLEDGMENTS

Much of *Love's Vision* was written during the academic year 2006–2007, which I spent as an External Faculty Fellow at the Stanford Humanities Center. I owe many thanks to the SHC for this fellowship and to my employer, California State University, Chico, for the sabbatical leave that enabled me to enjoy it.

During the writing I was also assisted, encouraged, and/or entertained by Bob Barrick; John Bender; Jerrold Blain; Zoe Bower; Michael Bratman; Stephen Burns; Sarah Buss; Marcel Daguerre; Laird Easton; Dan Edelstein; Andy Flescher; Harry Frankfurt; Eric Gampel; Anthony Grafton; Christopher Grau; Joe Hwang, Roger, Judy, and Taryn Jollimore; Robert Jones; Niko Kolodny; Randy Larsen; Maggie Little; Duncan MacIntosh; John Mahoney; Alexander Nehamas; Richard Parker; John Perry; Christy Pichichero; Robert Pinsky; Ed Pluth; Karen Rapp; Rob Reich; David Riggs; Dennis Rothermel; Ken Taylor; Rob Tempio; Brian and Maryam Wagner; Becky White; Jonah Willihnganz; Wai-hung Wong; George Wright; Zanja Yudell; and Linda Zerilli.

An early version of some of the material in chapters 2 and 3 was published in *Les ateliers de l'éthique* under the title "The Psychology of Exclusivity" (volume 3, number 1, Spring 2008).

This book is dedicated to Sharon, to whom I owe more than I can say.

LOVE'S VISION

one

"Something In Between":
On the Nature of Love

Love's Promise

Is it necessary to begin a book about love by arguing for love's centrality, if not its supremacy, among the values at which human beings aim and by which they order their lives? This fact seems to be acknowledged on nearly all hands. If anything, it may be that we place too much emphasis on love—or, at any rate, that we expect too much of it. In his memoir *Kafka Was the Rage*, the essayist Anatole Broyard recalls telling his analyst that what he wanted was what many people want and think it reasonable to expect: to be utterly transformed. "In novels, I said, people are transfigured by love. They're elevated, made different, lifted out of their ordinariness. . . . It's not so much to ask, I said. I just want love to live up to its publicity."[1]

But love's publicity is impressive indeed, and it would be difficult for any emotion or experience to live up to that. John Armstrong announces on the first page of his book on love: "Love is one of humanity's most persistent and most esteemed ideals."[2] Robert Solomon writes that "love is the most exhilarating—and sometimes the most excruciating and destructive—experience that most of us have ever had, or will ever have," and suggests that it is perhaps "even more profound and basic to our being than most of our talk about it would suggest."[3] The notion of love as transformative, the idea that love initiates a new stage of life and that after falling in love things will never be the same again, is also common. Consider the following description, from a contemporary novel, of the process of falling in love:

> But now she seemed different to me. I became aware of her special powers. How she seemed to pull light and gravity to the place where she stood. . . . At the same time that I was becoming conscious of her body, I was becoming aware of my own. A tingling feeling caught fire in my nerves and spread. The whole thing must have happened in less than thirty seconds. And yet. When it was

over, I'd been initiated into the mystery that stands at the beginning of the end of childhood. It was years before I'd spent all the joy and pain born in me in that less than half a minute.[4]

Perhaps it is inevitable that we will find ourselves expecting great things of love, particularly in the midst of a society that is so obsessed with it, a society whose pop songs insist that "all you need is love" and whose romantic comedies, patterned after the novels of Jane Austen, nearly always view a marriage union with the beloved as a guarantee that the partners will live happily ever after. It is, moreover, a society deeply and profoundly shaped by the Christian faith and its particular conception of love. As Armstrong writes, Christianity's "account of existence places love at the center of life. We live in order to grow in love—that is the meaning and purpose of each individual life. Nothing matters as much as this."[5]

One need not be religious, of course, to place great importance on love. Indeed, in the absence of God, love may well become *more* significant, for what, if not love, can be expected to make us into complete, fulfilled human beings? Consider the following passage from a memoir by J. M. Coetzee:

How long before he will cease to be a baby? What will cure him of babyhood, make him into a man?

What will cure him, if it were to arrive, is love. He may not believe in God but he does believe in love and the powers of love. The beloved, the destined one, will see at once through the odd and even dull exterior he presents to the fire that burns within him. Meanwhile, being dull and odd looking are part of a purgatory he must pass through in order to emerge, one day, into the light: the light of love.[6]

Nor need one adopt a spiritual point of view to see love as some sort of fundamental force or principle of nature. In his book *Love and Its Place in Nature,* Jonathan Lear attributes to Freud the view that "love [is] a basic force in nature," identifies love as a "cosmological principle," and even claims that "the world exists because we love it."[7]

The idea of love as a cosmic force has been part of Western thinking for centuries. Contemporary philosophers such as Iris Murdoch pick up on the metaphorical links drawn by Plato between love, the sun, and the Form of the Good. Love, Murdoch writes, "is the energy and passion of the soul in its search for Good. . . . It is a reflection of the warmth and light of the sun."[8] Dante ended his *Divine Comedy* with a reference to "the Love that moves the Sun and other stars." Pierre Teilhard de Chardin wrote that "love is the most universal, the most tremendous and the most mysterious of the cosmic forces."[9] And it is part of our contemporary stock of clichés, of course, that love makes the world go round.

These metaphors capture several elements of love as we experience it—its being active, powerful, fundamental, and at times irresistible. (Ortega y Gasset explicates Saint Augustine's remark "My love is my weight; where it goes I go" with the comment "Love is a gravitation toward that which is loved.")[10] Along somewhat similar lines, the references to the stars, like Murdoch's metaphorical linking of the Good with the sun and Coetzee's mention of "the light of love," may remind us of the famous moment in *Romeo and Juliet* when Romeo identifies his beloved with that celestial body: "But soft! What light through yonder window breaks? / It is the east, and Juliet is the sun!"

This solar metaphor, which sometimes identifies the sun with love itself and at other times with the beloved, has pervaded popular thought, especially popular song, as titles like "Sunshine of Your Love," "You Are the Sunshine of My Life," and "Ain't No Sunshine When She's Gone" attest. A version of the metaphor is also implied in Martin Buber's claim that "every actual relationship to another being in the world is exclusive. Its Thou is freed and steps forth to confront us in its uniqueness. It fills the firmament—not as if there were nothing else, but everything else lives in *its* light."[11]

The metaphor is resonant and profound. Indeed, my approach to love in this book will be guided both by the thought that part of the effect of love is to place a person at the center of one's life—one might well be pictured as revolving around one's beloved as the earth does around the sun—and by the thought that love functions as a source of illumination, in the sense that it helps us to see what we could not see otherwise, so that the rest of the world must present itself to us in its light (or, what seems equally correct, in the light of the beloved).

Let me expand a bit on the latter thought, as it will be very important in what follows. There are many things that make you the particular person you are, but one of the most fundamental, surely, is your particular way of seeing. That you have a certain perceptual perspective that is occupied by no one else distinguishes you from all other individuals, and it would distinguish you even from a qualitatively exact duplicate of yourself. Thus, to say that love can transform one's way of seeing the world is to open up certain possibilities for understanding how love can transform a person, and in doing so, to open up some possibilities of how love might live up to the promise of which Broyard speaks. If the world quite literally does not look the same to the lover as it does to the nonlover (or, for that matter, to the lover who loves somebody else), then there is a sense in which love causes the lover's world to be transformed. But since the root of the transformation, the love itself, lies within the lover, it is equally correct to say that the lover has been fundamentally changed. What looks to the lover like a transfigured world is really the result of a transformed eye.

My view is not merely that love alters one's way of seeing but that that love itself *is*, in large part, a way of seeing—a way of seeing one's beloved, and also a way of seeing the world. On the level of common sense, this seems to me unassailable. One does not see one's beloved, or anyone about whom one has significant feeling, in the flat, distracted manner in which one tends to see most strangers. She occupies a special place at or near the center of one's attention; she has one's attention from the moment she enters a room. (If she does not, then we must wonder whether the love is still alive.) The lover notices things about his beloved—tiny, easily overlooked, but meaningful attributes—that would escape the notice of others. Yet at the same time there may be things about her that escape *his* notice or that he positively refuses to notice or dwell on. He appreciates, fully and generously, her better qualities and ignores, refuses to acknowledge, or at the very least deemphasizes her less-than-ideal attributes. Like any way of seeing, love is perspectival, meaning that some things are focused on and placed at the center of one's field of view, whereas others, if they are perceived at all, are relegated to the periphery.

Love and Immorality

I propose an account of love that holds it to be largely a matter of vision and to be in large part guided by reason, while at the same time allowing that love is not *purely* a matter of reason. It must immediately be acknowledged, though, that holding love to be reason-guided in any deep sense runs counter to a view of the matter that has played a deep and influential role in Western thinking about the passions. The same can be said of the ideas, which I will also defend, that love is in an important sense a moral phenomenon and that it encourages accurate perceptions of reality rather than badly skewed perceptions or even illusions. Before launching into a defense of my view, then, it will be useful to start by laying out some of the reasons why people have doubted that love can be morally, epistemologically, or rationally justified or endorsed.

Let us start with the immorality; we will come back to the illusion and the irrationality.

Is love moral? We sometimes imagine, idealistically, that because they care so much about their beloveds, lovers will inevitably treat their beloveds better than they treat anyone else. "The lover not only wishes to see the beloved flourish and is pleased to see her happy," Ilham Dilman writes, "he is prepared to take responsibility for her welfare, to care for her. These are natural, moral impulses that belong to love."[12] Such a view naturally suggests that at least within the context of a given relationship, love is a moral rather than a nonmoral, immoral, or antimoral force.

Against this, though, is the knowledge that events in the real world do not always proceed in this manner. That love for a person does not necessarily involve wishing the best for that person—that at least in some cases it could instead involve wishing the worst—was known to Plato. Socrates says in the *Phaedrus*:

> No one can be in any doubt—least of all the lover—that his dearest wish is for the one he loves to lose the closest, most loyal and most divine possessions he has. He would be happy for him to lose father and mother, relatives and friends, since he regards them as people who will obstruct and condemn that association which brings him most pleasure. . . . And further, in his desire to enjoy the sweet fruits of his own pleasure for the longest time possible, a lover would wish upon his boyfriend a life that was unmarried, childless and homeless for the longest time possible.[13]

Passionate love, at least sometimes, seems to involve the desire to have the beloved all to oneself, to remove him from society and put him in some isolated place to which only the lover has access. And it is natural to wish, alongside this, that one's beloved be weakened or rendered vulnerable so as to become dependent on oneself. Thus, while some philosophers have suggested that an essential element of love is a commitment to treating the beloved well and protecting and advancing his interests, it must be acknowledged that in the real world love—or what is at least claimed to be love—sometimes motivates people to inflict various sorts of harm or violence on those they claim to love.

At any rate, it is certainly not unheard of—perhaps it is not even uncommon—to find partners in long-term marriages treating each other with unkindness, hostility, and disdain. Long-term commitments often generate resentment; perceived reliability and constant togetherness can cause one to be taken for granted; and the very emotional intimacy that is, during the good times, love's greatest glory makes possible especially damaging and painful forms of cruelty. (We are frequently in an especially good position to help, but also to hurt, the ones we love, and the reasons why this is so are the same in each case.)

More common, though, and thus perhaps more worrying, is the thought that by requiring *excessive* kindness to, and an excessively narrow focus on, the loved individual, love leads lovers to ignore and neglect other people and perhaps even to harm them. It cannot be denied that love very frequently draws people into much smaller communities—privacies of two from which all others are excluded. (As Murdoch writes in her novel *A Word Child*, "The assertion made by a happy marriage often alienates, and often is at least half intended to alienate, the excluded spectator.")[14]

Love's potential to draw people out of public life and to entice them to turn their backs on their larger communities causes many moralists to regard it with considerable suspicion. If morality demands a thorough-going impartiality—a common view in modern times—then love, which seems to demand nothing if not a powerful and uncompromising species of partiality, must be viewed as morally suspect. Martha Nussbaum, for instance, voices the worry that

> love's partiality . . . seems to threaten any ethical approach involv-ing the extension of concern. Intense attachments to particular in-dividuals, especially when they are of an erotic or romantic sort, call attention away from the world of general concern, asking it to rivet itself to a single life that provides in itself no sufficient reason for this special treatment, as it imperiously claims all thoughts, all desires.[15]

The novelist Milan Kundera goes so far as to suggest (via one of his characters) that in this respect, at least, love may be less admirable—less social, less inherently democratic—than lust: "The gaze of love is the gaze that isolates. Jean-Marc thought about the loving solitude of two old persons become invisible to other people: a sad solitude that prefigures death. No, what she needs is not a loving gaze but a flood of alien, crude, lustful looks. . . . Those are the looks that sustain her within human soci-ety. The gaze of love rips her out of it."[16]

Jean-Marc's position is, of course, a bit unusual; those whose moral-ity leads them to be suspicious of love do not frequently hold up lust as a preferable alternative. Lust, after all, is commonly thought to be wild and uncontrollable and therefore dangerous. Yet Jean-Marc has a point: compared with love, lust is more widely and equitably distributed, more evenhanded, and therefore more democratic. My feeling lust for one per-son need not prevent my feeling an equally strong lust for someone else, but my loving a romantic partner may well prevent me from feeling that sort of love for anyone else. And, if it cannot make it impossible, it is at least supposed to make it *impermissible*. Although lust has often been the target of moral opprobrium, it is the demands of love that, in the long run, may prove to pose the more serious moral danger.

Love and Illusion

I have suggested that love should be understood as largely a kind of vision in that it involves, and is largely constituted by, an appreciative attention directed toward the beloved's positive qualities. But this will immediately strike some people as false and possibly even as outrageous. It is an item of common wisdom that love is blind; it obscures one's vision, making it impossible to see the beloved in the cold, objective, dispassionate light of

reason. If so, then the idea that love is largely a matter of the lover's noticing and valuing the beloved's qualities may seem misguided. For what is
really going on, at least if the most extreme version of this suggestion is
correct, is not that the lover is noticing the beloved's qualities, but rather
that she is *imagining* that he has certain qualities. She is projecting onto
him the qualities she wishes him to have, and then she is valuing those.

As I am now interpreting it, the suggestion is that we should hold a
version of what we might refer to as the imagined qualities view.

> *The imagined qualities view:* A central and highly significant part
> of love is that the lover imaginatively projects certain positive
> qualities onto the beloved and values him for those qualities that
> she imagines him to have.

What philosophers sometimes call the quality theory holds that love is
justified by the attractive or desirable qualities of the beloved.[17] The imagined qualities view holds on to the idea that this is what *seems* to be going
on to the lover, jettisoning the requirement that her love be in any way
an accurate response to the beloved's properties. And of course, if the
qualities that are taken to be the justification for her love are not really
possessed at all but only projected, then talk of any actual justification
would seem to be out of place. The imagined qualities view, then, does
not hold love to be a phenomenon of reason at all.

A classic statement of this sort of view comes from Stendhal, who uses
the metaphor of crystallization to describe the way in which the lover's
original perceptions of her beloved become laden with interpretations
and projected properties to the point where the original can no longer
be seen.

> The first crystallization begins. If you are sure that a woman loves
> you, it is a pleasure to endow her with a thousand perfections and
> to count your blessings with infinite satisfaction. In the end you
> overrate wildly, and regard her as something fallen from Heaven,
> unknown as yet, but certain to be yours.
>
> Leave a lover with his thoughts for twenty-four hours, and this
> is what will happen:
>
> At the salt mines of Salzburg, they throw a leafless wintry bough
> into one of the abandoned workings. Two or three months later
> they haul it out covered with a shining deposit of crystals. The
> smallest twig, no bigger than a tom-tit's claw, is studded with a
> galaxy of scintillating diamonds. The original branch is no longer
> recognizable.
>
> What I have called crystallization is a mental process which
> draws from everything that happens new proofs of the perfection
> of the loved one.[18]

In the most extreme version of this phenomenon, it is an imagined object and not an actual person that is loved; the person one loves does not even exist, literally speaking, since no one in the real world possesses the qualities one has attributed to one's beloved.

But perhaps focusing on this extreme, as the imagined qualities view does, somewhat overstates the point. Surely cases in which the beloved bears *no* resemblance to the lover's image of him—cases in which the qualities attributed to him are entirely the products of the lover's imagination—are somewhat unusual. (And such cases are, moreover, surely doomed to end in disappointment once the reality of the situation begins to assert itself.) More common is the situation in which the lover is able to see with at least some accuracy the qualities possessed by the beloved, but in which her love for him causes her to evaluate these properties in a more positive manner than she would otherwise. Stendhal suggests that after what he calls "the second crystallization," "the original, naked branch is no longer recognizable by indifferent eyes, because it now sparkles with perfections, or diamonds, which they do not see or *which they simply do not consider to be perfections.*"[19]

The testimony of lovers gives evidence of the reality of this phenomenon. Dorothy Tennov quotes a subject who says that "once I fall, really fall, everything about her becomes wonderful. . . . I abhor the sight of toothmarks on a pencil; they disgust me. But not *her* toothmarks. Hers were sacred; her wonderful mouth had been there."[20] This form of misperception seems, perhaps, less threatening than the original form suggested by the imagined qualities view. It allows, after all, that the lover does perceive the beloved more or less accurately, at least in factual terms; he is not, that is, deluded as to the qualities she possesses. Still, there is a serious epistemic concern here, since the lover seems to be deluded about something else: the *value* of the beloved's qualities. To regard someone's pencil, let alone the toothmarks on that pencil, as beautiful or "sacred" is not quite a form of insanity, but it is surely a species of delusion.[21]

As with the worry about morality, the epistemic worry that arises here accompanies not just romantic love but friendship as well. For friendship, like romantic love, demands of us that we believe certain things about our friends and that we see them in certain ways. As Simon Keller writes, "Good friends believe in each other; they give each other the benefit of the doubt; they see each other in the best possible light." And this commitment, Keller goes on to claim, has clear and perilous epistemic implications: "When good friends form beliefs about each other, they sometimes respond to considerations that have to do with the needs and interests of their friends, not with aiming at the truth, and that is part of what makes them good friends."[22]

If Keller is right, there is a second reason for thinking that romantic love and friendship are unreasonable and dangerous. Not only do these forms of attachment pose moral dangers, insofar as they can monopolize our concern and divert our attention away from the broader social world; they can also slant and skew our perceptions of reality and demand that we form and maintain certain beliefs about our beloveds even in the face of countervailing evidence. Love, then, might be beginning to seem not only morally risky but epistemically irrational.

Love and (Un)Reason

Both from a moral and from an epistemic point of view, then, there are reasons to be somewhat wary of love. If love's moral critics are correct, love is dangerous insofar as it can inspire bad, selfish, and perhaps even evil behavior. If love's epistemic critics are right, love is dangerous insofar as it distorts our perceptions of the world—particularly those of the beloved—and encourages us to live in a substitute reality constructed from our own fantasies. These worries both encourage and are encouraged by what is in some ways the more fundamental thought that love, as one of the passions, is fundamentally irrational—perhaps even a kind of madness.

Socrates, in the *Phaedrus,* calls love "the irrational desire which gains the upper hand over the judgment which guides men towards what is right."[23] George Bernard Shaw, for his part, refers to love as "the most violent, most insane, most delusive, and most transient of passions."[24] And Shakespeare writes in *A Midsummer Night's Dream*: "The lunatic, the lover and the poet / Are of imagination all compact."[25] Marilyn French, Shirley Eskapa, and many other recent writers have picked up on this theme; in doing so they have reiterated the idea that love is a passion, a type of madness, destructive, chaotic, and in no way amenable to reason.

The idea that love has little or nothing to do with reason is closely connected to the idea that love has nothing whatsoever to do with *reasons*. Reasons, in the context of love, are frequently regarded as simply irrelevant. It is common to think both that one does not need reasons for love and that it is a misguided enterprise to try to provide them. Perhaps the easiest way of appreciating the impulse behind this thought is to imagine what would be involved if love did involve reasons in this way. Our first reaction to this thought experiment might be that love's involving and relying on reasons in this way would surely rule out the very possibility of *unconditional* love—or, at the very least, it would make such love automatically objectionable. For how could an attitude that is genuinely unconditional and that will therefore be felt and endorsed under any conditions (thus, regardless of what one's reasons are) leave room for reasons to play any substantial role whatsoever? To say that love ought to be supported by reasons, and that its justification depends on these reasons, seems to be just another way of saying that love is justified only under certain conditions and therefore ought to be offered only conditionally. If, for instance, Alighieri's reason for loving Beatrice is his belief that Beatrice possesses property P, then his love for her will be reasonable and justifiable only if it is offered conditionally on her *really* possessing, and continuing to possess, property P. And might this not lead Beatrice to worry that she might one day *lose* P, or that she already might not possess it to the extent that the love-struck Alighieri (whose perceptions are quite possibly warped by love) believes her to possess it?

Thinking about what is involved in offering reasons for love, and in making love conditional upon these reasons, may also make such love seem objectionably self-centered or the lover seem objectionably cold and dispassionate. At least a few attempted appeals to reasons in the context of love go wrong in this way. Consider, for instance, Mr. Collins's proposal to Elizabeth Bennet in *Pride and Prejudice*:

> My reasons for marrying are, first, that I think it a right thing for every clergyman in easy circumstances (like myself) to set the example of matrimony in his parish; secondly, that I am convinced it will add very greatly to my happiness; and thirdly—which perhaps I ought to have mentioned earlier, that it is the particular advice and recommendation of the very noble lady whom I have the honor of calling patroness. . . . Thus much for my general intention in favor of matrimony; it remains to be told why my views were directed to Longbourn instead of my own neighborhood, where I assure you there are many amiable young women. But the fact is, that being, as I am, to inherit this estate after the death of your honored father (who, however, may live many years longer), I could not satisfy myself without resolving to chuse a wife from among his daughters, that the loss to them might be as little as possible, when the melancholy event takes place.[26]

Admittedly, this is a particularly inept attempt to appeal to reasons, and it seems to me that we ought to resist drawing any general conclusions about the appropriateness of "reasons talk" in the context of love on the basis of such examples. What is striking about Mr. Collins's proposal to Elizabeth is how little it has to do with *Elizabeth*. She seems to appear only as a placeholder, a vessel for a set of properties that might just as easily, and just as appropriately, have been attached to someone else. Indeed, the first three reasons Mr. Collins offers do not refer to properties of Elizabeth at all—or at least they refer to properties Elizabeth would share with any other single woman of marriageable age. His final reason at least succeeds in narrowing the class down to Elizabeth and her sisters, but he offers no reason to distinguish her from her sisters, and the general implication of his remarks seems to be that any of them would do just as well. This is insulting, and Elizabeth, of course, takes it as such.

The deep question, though, is, does Mr. Collins err by concentrating on the wrong sort of reasons, or does he err by attempting to offer reasons at all? If we take the former view, we might think, for instance, that he would do better by referring to properties that distinguish Elizabeth from other potential marriage partners, and (hopefully) properties Elizabeth herself would regard as important elements of her identity as an individual. As Neil Delaney has plausibly suggested, a necessary element of romantic love is that "a person A wants a romantic partner B to love him for properties that A takes to be central to his self-conception."[27]

The opposing line of thought is that Mr. Collins's mistake is not offering the *wrong* reasons for loving (or at any rate, marrying) Elizabeth but rather offering any reasons at all. On this view, love is not a matter of appreciating the beloved's valuable qualities; indeed, one need not be able to point to any valuable or attractive property of the beloved in explaining or justifying one's love, for after all love is simply a brute psychological phenomenon that does not stand in need of explanation or justification. This is not to say that we cannot sometimes provide a thoroughly psychological explanation of one person's attraction to or interest in another. The point, though, is that the explanation need not and presumably will not be normative: its function is not to render the lover's attitude reasonable or justifiable, but simply to explain by citing the causal mechanism responsible for his emotional response. Moreover, on this view there is no requirement that a lover be able to provide at least the beginning of a justification, and there is not necessarily anything wrong with the lover who cannot make a list of her reasons for loving.

Harry Frankfurt is an example of a recent, and influential, philosopher who has held a version of this view. In Frankfurt's view, love may sometimes be aroused by the lover's belief that her beloved has attractive or valuable properties. She is mistaken, however, if she takes her love to be justified by those properties (or to be rationally dependent on them or to constitute a rational response to them). Moreover, there is, in Frankfurt's view, no reason why a person could not love someone who was perceived to have no such valuable properties at all:

> Love does not require a response by the lover to any real or imagined value in what he loves. Parents do not ordinarily love their children so much, for example, because they perceive that their children possess exceptional value. In fact, it is the other way

around: the children seem to the parents to be valuable, and they are valuable to the parents, only because the parents love them. Parents have been known to love—quite genuinely—children that they themselves recognize as lacking any particular inherent merit.

As I understand the nature of love, the lover does not depend for this loving upon reasons of any kind. Love is not a conclusion. It is not an outcome of reasoning, or a consequence of reasons. It *creates* reasons. What it means to love is, in part, to take the fact that a certain action would serve the good of the beloved as an especially compelling reason for performing that action.[28]

But if this is so, then the question of justification referring back to the beloved's value simply does not arise. On such a view, love might be considered a response to the beloved in a very minimal sense—it is, at the very least, directed toward the beloved. But it is, in a sense, a predetermined response, one that is determined to emerge with a positive evaluation, no matter what it finds (which suggests, of course, that there is no genuine evaluation going on at all). On this view, then, the lover's valuing is not genuinely responsive to preexisting values: the lover creates value rather than recognizing it, and so there is no question of creating it inaccurately or wrongly.

The suggestion is, then, that the whole enterprise of trying to find or give reasons that justify one's love for another is misguided, if not thoroughly corrupt. Love is simply not dependent on reason in this way. Love is, rather, an attitude that is held for no reason at all and that therefore cannot be rationally defended or, for that matter, rationally criticized. Moreover, we need not see this as any sort of deficiency or problem for love. Indeed, many supporters of this position will insist that it is one of love's strengths to be unreasonable in this way. Who, after all, would want a rational lover? Who would want his lover to love him because she *ought* or had *good reason* to? Who would want his lover to be able to give *proof* that her love was justified and appropriate? Is not love precisely the context in which the part of the human being that acts without reasons and thus beyond reason, which does not demand explanations or justifications for what it does, ought to be allowed the full range of freedom? From a certain perspective—the perspective that tends to regard reason as cold, sterile, and dispassionate—the idea that love is not governed by the dictates and strictures of reason may strike us as a point in its favor. In providing possibilities for passion and spontaneous action, love may be seen as an enriching and liberating force.

Indeed, an account of love that made it out to be excessively reasonable and rationalistic would surely deform love and almost certainly rob it of some of its most vital attractions. Frankfurt's claim that "parents have been known to love—quite genuinely—children that they themselves recognize as lacking any particular inherent merit" is meant to be supported in part by the plausibility of the thought that the ability of parents to love in this way is a good thing, particularly from their children's perspective. Especially in the parent-child context, a love that bases itself on a clear-sighted and objective assessment of the recipient's worth, and is committed to withdrawing itself should that worth be judged to be insufficient, strikes us as ungenerous and judgmental.

I will use the term *antirationalism* to denote the position that denies that there can be justifying reasons for loving a person and thus holds that loving someone is not the sort of thing we do, or ought to do, for reasons. Strictly speaking, then, *rationalism* ought to refer to any position that affirms that love can be justified by reasons. The most common and, in my view, most plausible versions of this position hold that the attractive and otherwise valuable properties of the beloved are the most important and most powerful sources of reasons for love; they are, moreover, what the beloved is most typically loved *for*. In this project, then, when I use the term *rationalism*, it is this position I will have in mind.

Problems for Rationalism

Antirationalism has struck many philosophers as a plausible, even necessary, position, one that seems to accord with certain basic intuitions about the nature of love. Love, as we have noted, strikes many as inherently unreasonable or irrational, an arbitrary matter of the heart. It is a matter of passion, and passion is understood by many philosophers and by nonphilosophical laypeople alike as something very close to the opposite of reason.

There are other reasons, too, for thinking that antirationalism must be true. As the example of Mr. Collins illustrates, it is all too easy to find instances of inept and insulting attempts to appeal to reason in order to justify romantic or marital desire. But such examples are not enough to establish the truth of antirationalism; it might just be that people like Mr. Collins are appealing to the wrong sorts of reasons. There are, though, more general arguments available. In particular, it is frequently felt that rationalism—again, the view that reasons *can* typically be given to explain or justify one's love (and thus that there is presumably something wrong with a love for which reasons cannot be given)— seems to require us to say things about love that strike us as wrong or inappropriate or to think about love in a way that seems untrue to its nature.

For instance, it is sometimes thought that rationalism of this sort leads to the implausible view that love is a matter of obligation. After all, to give reasons for doing something is to provide considerations in the light of which one ought, rationally, to do that thing (if the reasons are strong enough). This suggests that if it were possible to give reasons for loving someone, then it would be possible, at least in principle, to have reasons for loving that person that are strong enough to generate a rational obligation to love him. But to speak of love as a matter of obligation—particularly in contexts of friendship and romantic love—seems to go deeply counter to our experience of it.[29] This may be truer when speaking of positive obligations rather than of negative ones; perhaps we *can* think of cases, most likely involving a prudential interpretation of the word *ought,* where a person could reasonably, understandably, and sincerely say, "I ought not to love him." (Of course, in our imperfect world, such statements are all too frequently followed with "but God help me, I do.") But the idea of a positive *ought*—a requirement to love—strikes most of us as deeply wrongheaded. No matter how many of the beloved's attractive or otherwise valuable properties we cite, they will never add up to an *ought.* I may be perfectly aware of the attractive qualities that Sally possesses and that Harry would cite in response to the question, what is it you find so attractive about Sally? Yet my awareness of these properties does not in any way obligate me to love Sally—not even as a friend, and certainly not romantically. As Adam Smith puts the point, "Our imagination not having run in the same channel with that of the lover, we cannot enter into the eagerness of his emotions. . . . We never think ourselves bound to conceive a passion of the same kind, and for the same person for whom he has conceived it."[30]

The claim, of course, is not that I most certainly *will not* develop feelings of attraction or love on the basis of my understanding of what attracts my friend to his beloved, but that I *might* not and am not in any sense obligated to; my failing to develop such feelings does not indicate that my understanding of why he loves her is deficient or imperfect. As Frankfurt writes, "A declaration of love is a personal matter [in that] the person who makes it does not thereby commit himself to supposing that anyone who fails to love what he does has somehow gone wrong."[31]

I will refer to this claim about the nature of love as the incompleteness thesis. For my purposes, the incompleteness thesis can be defined as follows:

> *The incompleteness thesis:* Any list of properties identified as putative justifiers for loving some particular individual B will necessarily be incomplete, in the sense that no matter which or how many justifying considerations are cited, their totality will not *rationally obligate* a person to love B. That is, no list of attractive or otherwise valuable features of B is such that a person cannot admit that B possesses all of those features and yet fail to love B without being irrational.[32]

The incompleteness thesis at least suggests that love is not a matter of rational obligation. Moreover, it is frequently taken as suggesting that love is not a matter of rationality or reasons at all: whatever it is that explains why I do, in fact, love this particular person, it must not be any set of reasons, for no set of reasons could obligate me to love her. Thus, the incompleteness thesis is commonly taken to provide strong evidence for antirationalism. After all, the move from "B's properties do not obligate anyone to love her" to "B's properties do not provide reasons for anyone to love her" may seem so straightforward as to be irresistible. If q (the set of D's attractive properties, which B cites in "explaining" his friendship with D) is insufficient on its own to force me to love D, then how can they explain B's doing so? The real explanation, then, must not be q, but q-plus-something else. It is for this reason that we may seem to find ourselves pushed very quickly from the denial that we can be obligated to love to the conclusion that, in speaking of love, it makes no sense to attempt to offer reasons at all.

The view that love can and should be supported by reasons and is justified in terms of those reasons—the view that I have been referring to as rationalism—thus seems to some to be vulnerable to a reductio ad absurdum, for it seems to require us to deny the incompleteness thesis, and that thesis seems undeniable. I will refer to this as the universality problem.

> *The universality problem:* If Alighieri loves Beatrice for her valuable properties (if, that is, his love for her is grounded in an appraisal of her value), then anyone who accepts that Alighieri is justified in doing so is obligated to love Beatrice also.

This constitutes a "problem" for rationalist accounts for the very straightforward reason that love simply does not seem to work this way. If it did, we would not find the incompleteness thesis plausible and would not agree with Adam Smith that in accepting another's account of his love, we do not "think ourselves bound to conceive a passion of the same kind, and for the same person for whom he has conceived it."

This problem, that love's "reasons" seem to fail the universality test in applying to some persons but not to others, is intimately connected with, and indeed mirrors, another problem: the considerations that provide "reasons" for a lover's love—the attractive or otherwise valuable properties of the beloved—may show up in other people and yet *not* provide the lover with reason to love those people. As Nussbaum writes with reference to *Remembrance of Things Past*: "Erotic love is based on unequal concern, an unequal concern not explained by reasons: Marcel knows that there really is no rational basis for his choice of Albertine over the other cyclists."[33]

The absence of such a rational basis is indicated by the fact that any feature of Albertine that might plausibly serve as a justification for Marcel's love will be a feature that is also possessed by others whom he does not love and so will not be able to serve to differentiate her from them. If we say, for instance, that it is Albertine's beauty that serves as Marcel's reason for loving her, we leave ourselves unable to explain why he does not love some other beautiful person—or, worse, love them both, and indeed *all* beautiful people. Thus, rationalism seems not only to require too many people to love a worthy beloved (the universality problem), but also to require each lover to love *every* worthy beloved.

> *The promiscuity problem:* If Alighieri loves Beatrice for her valuable properties (if, that is, his love for her is grounded in an appraisal of her value), then rationality will require him to love anyone and indeed *everyone* who possesses those properties.

But rationality does *not* seem to require this; those who refuse to extend their love in this manner are not, in general, regarded as less than perfectly rational. As Roger Scruton has written, "Although there is, no doubt, some feature of James which is a reason (perhaps even *the* reason) why I love him, I am not obliged to love William as well, just because he shares that feature."[34] Those with antirationalist inclinations may wonder, though, whether Scruton's claim is coherent and will take the fact that we are not obligated to love those who resemble our beloveds as evidence that our beloveds' attributes do not, in fact, function as reasons for loving them at all; for if they did, then rationality surely *would* require us to respond in the same manner regardless of where the relevant feature was encountered.

A special version of the promiscuity problem is what we can call the replica problem. According to rationalism, it is sometimes claimed, the lover ought to love an exact duplicate of her beloved (an indistinguishable clone, for instance) in precisely the way she loves her beloved himself, given that the duplicate possesses *all* of the qualities, and exactly those qualities, that ground her love for the original beloved.[35]

There is a maneuver by which we might attempt to avoid the promiscuity problem. Suppose that it is psychologically impossible for the typical human lover to love very many people, and suppose that the word *ought* implies *can*. Then, it might be argued, the typical lover *cannot* love everyone who possesses the properties she values in her beloved—and so, since *ought* implies *can*, it follows that it is false that she ought to do so. The maneuver, though, falls well short of being fully satisfactory. For one thing, it is deeply and objectionably ad hoc. It would be better to come up with an account of love that did not entail the objectionable thesis to begin with and not have to resort to the statement "*ought* implies *can*"— and to what ultimately are contingent facts about human psychology—in order to defuse the objection.

Moreover, the suggested appeal to "*ought* implies *can*" would only open the rationalist up to a similar and, it may seem, equally damning objection:

> *The trading-up problem:* If Alighieri loves Beatrice for her lovable properties and along comes Carmen, who has all of Beatrice's lovable properties plus a few more, then reason will require Alighieri to abandon Beatrice in favor of Carmen (on the assumption, at any rate, that he cannot love them both).

The trading-up problem cannot be avoided through an appeal to "*ought* implies *can*" without committing ourselves to the very implausible view that human lovers cannot transfer their love from one person to another. But the thesis that is implied here—that one ought to trade in one's lover for a better model as soon as the latter becomes available—is surely as counterintuitive, and indeed as objectionable, as the one that gives the promiscuity problem its teeth, for again, love does not seem to work in this way. Although lovers may sometimes transfer their love from one person to another, it seems false and objectionable to say that they are rationally required to do so wherever doing so picks out an object of greater value, let alone that such a requirement follows from the nature of love.

Why does the thought of a lover who is prepared to switch her allegiances in this way seem so objectionable? In part it seems to suggest that what the lover in question is really attached to is not his beloved at all but rather his beloved's *properties*—properties that may turn up in greater abundance in somebody else. As Robert Nozick writes, "Love is not transferable to someone else with the same characteristics, even to one who 'scores' higher for these characteristics."[36] Or at least, love does not seem to be transferable in this sense, and we do not want it to be. What we want, rather, is that a lover's commitment be, if not thoroughly unconditional, at the very least quite robustly resistant to her objective assessment of her lover's value. Indeed, the very use of the word *commitment* in this context seems to demand as much: the person who loves me only as long as she judges me to be the most valuable person in the vicinity is not really committed to me—and, I think we can safely say, does not really love me.

Even putting aside the worry about being cast off for someone else, the worry about being abandoned if the properties for which one is loved are changed or lost is sufficient to merit consideration as an independent problem for rationalism.

> *The inconstancy problem:* If Alighieri loves Beatrice for her valuable properties, then rationally he ought to stop loving Beatrice when she loses those properties.

Once again the thesis is clearly at odds with our understanding of how love works and ought to work. "Eventually," as Nozick writes elsewhere, "one must love the person himself, and not *for* the characteristics. . . . If we continue to be loved 'for' the characteristics, then the love seems conditional, something that might change or disappear if the characteristics do."[37] Of course, just what it is to "love the person himself" might not be immediately apparent. But Nozick is surely correct to say that if Alighieri's love of Beatrice for her attractive characteristics—her beauty, her charm, her intelligence, or what have you—requires that he stop loving her as soon as there is any change in that set of characteristics, then love, as we understand it (and again, as we want it to be), simply does not seem to be a matter of loving a person for her characteristics. As Shakespeare famously wrote in Sonnet 116, "Love is not love which alters / when it alteration finds."[38]

These four problems—the universality problem, the promiscuity problem, the trading-up problem, and the inconstancy problem—comprise a phalanx of challenges that the rationalist must meet. It is no surprise, in light of these difficulties, that many have turned to antirationalism, and in doing so they have rejected the idea that reasons can be given to justify love. We should not conclude prematurely, however, that the abandonment of rationalism will solve all of love's difficulties, for antirationalism, as attractive as it may be in some respects, faces its own set of problems.

The Limits of Antirationalism

I have tried to construct a plausible and to some degree compelling case for antirationalism. I want now to start *de*constructing that case—not because I think that antirationalism is completely wrong—for I do think it gets some important things right—but because I think that rationalism also gets some important things right, and that what is ultimately needed is a more sophisticated and nuanced account that can somehow render these apparently opposed impulses compatible with one another. What is needed, that is, is an account that makes love rational in just the right ways while allowing it to be arational, perhaps even to some degree irrational, where *that* is appropriate.

Antirationalists typically claim that when a person is asked why she loves her beloved, it is completely appropriate for her to respond, "I just do, and that's all there is to it." And they often go on to claim that this fact provides strong evidence in favor of antirationalism. But both claims are disputable. It is true that "I just do" is *sometimes* an appropriate response. It is highly doubtful, however, that this response is *always* appropriate, let alone fully adequate.[39] And the fact that it is sometimes an appropriate response does not provide clear support for antirationalism.

To see why, let us start with the following formulation of the point by another antirationalist, O. H. Green. In support of his claim that love is most frequently not grounded in the desirable properties of the beloved, Green cites a song by Jerome Kern and P. G. Wodehouse that has the singer confessing, "'I love him because he's . . . I don't know . . . because he's just my Bill.'" "The fact is," as Green goes on to write, "the girl evidently has no beliefs which provide reasons for her loving Bill and connect Bill with her love as its object."[40]

The sentiment the Kern-Wodehouse girl expressed (I will hereafter call her KW) seems to me perfectly intelligible. It is not, at any rate, wholly perplexing. It is the same sentiment Montaigne expressed in his famous passage from "Of Friendship": "If someone were to urge me to say why I loved him, I should feel it could not be expressed except in the reply: 'Because it was he; because it was I.'"[41] It does not seem to me, though, that Green has captured what we find compelling about such examples, which seem to express the *particularity,* the *complexity,* perhaps even the *inexpressibility,* of one's reasons for loving another, without necessarily suggesting that there is no reason present.

Let us leave aside, for the moment, the difficult question of whether the lover in the Kern-Wodehouse song must have "beliefs which provide reasons for her loving Bill"; the question of what makes a particular consideration a *reason,* after all, is complex, and it is not clear that the fact that a consideration does not count as a reason must mean that it is completely irrelevant. Let us consider, then, the broader formulation: must the girl have at least some "beliefs which . . . connect Bill with her love as its object"?

It is fairly clear that she must. Given that her love is the love of a person, and that she herself conceives it as such, KW must at the very least believe that Bill is in fact a person. If she thought he was not a person but a lump of coal or a cleverly constructed robotic simulacrum in possession of no inner life, she would not love "her Bill" in the same way at all. Of course, it is doubtful that the sentence "Bill is a person" functions as one of her *reasons* for loving Bill; at any rate, it certainly is not a reason she is likely to cite. But it is precisely this sort of issue about what counts as a reason that led me to put that aside in favor, for the moment, of the broader formulation. Moreover, the fact that there exist certain considerations that *are* relevant to her loving Bill, but that are so basic and obvious that she would probably not think to cite them, at least suggests that there may also be certain reasons that similarly are too basic to cite.

Admittedly, "Bill is a person" is a very basic, and very minimal, consideration. It is for precisely this reason that such considerations tend to escape our notice; they are simply taken for granted as part of the context when we speak about love. But a consideration that tends to be taken for granted and relegated to the contextual background does not for that reason cease to count or to matter at all; indeed, sometimes it is precisely these most fundamental considerations that matter most. And there are, after all, a good many other fairly basic beliefs about Bill that must also form part of the context if KW is to love him in anything like the ordinary way: that Bill is not conspiring against her, has not been paid by her father to pretend to like her, is not secretly a serial killer, and so on. No one, of course, would think to cite these facts in explaining her love for someone else; they are, rather, considerations whose obtaining *allows* for love, in that they would invalidate love if they did *not* obtain.[42] Nonetheless, they are real considerations about which lovers, including KW, will hold beliefs (though for the most part the beliefs will be implicit rather than explicit).

Let us press the point further. If the young woman truly loves Bill, then presumably she sees him as attractive in one way or another. Perhaps it is possible to love someone, even romantically, whom one does not see as physically attractive.[43] One might instead believe him to have an attractive personality. But suppose the young woman claims to believe that Bill has neither an attractive appearance nor an attractive personality. Her claim to love him might begin to seem somewhat less than plausible— unless, of course, she can cite some other aspect of Bill that she finds attractive or admirable or impressive. The point is that there must be *something* that she can cite as a relevant consideration. And indeed, now that we are dealing with, as we might say, the positive aspects of Bill's nature—considerations that are somewhat less basic than Bill's being a person and somewhat less negative than his *not* being a serial murderer— the case for considering such considerations to be *reasons* for loving Bill begins to seem somewhat stronger as well.

Responsiveness to properties is a salient feature of many of our love-related experiences and behaviors. One is attracted to and falls in love with certain people rather than others largely on the basis of what they are like, and the stories that lovers tell reflect this. Of course, it might well be difficult, even with respect to the beloved's attractive appearance or personality, to capture the nature of the attraction in words. It might be difficult, that is, to state these reasons in propositional form. We should acknowledge that capturing what is valuable about the individual Bill might be particularly difficult if we are not acquainted with Bill or if we are acquainted but do not see him at all in the way his lover sees him. If, however, we *are* acquainted with him and *do* see him in at least somewhat the same way, then Bill's lover will be able to communicate her reasons (unless, of course, she is inarticulate) simply by saying things like "I love his sense of humor, especially the playful way he teases me," or "I love his kindness—how he treats his mother, for instance." Such statements do not fully capture the reasons involved. But *fully* capturing the reasons, in a way that would make them comprehensible to people who were not acquainted with Bill, would perhaps require the skills of a novelist, and even these might not be sufficient. That the reasons are difficult to capture in language does not mean that they do not exist or that they play no role in KW's emotional responses to Bill.

Within the circle of people who *are* acquainted with Bill, however, such statements serve adequately as shorthand for one's reasons—in much the same way that "he's just my Bill" can serve perfectly well as an even more concise shorthand statement for people who already know Bill very well indeed. In fact, it is difficult to see how "he's just my Bill" could function at all, or constitute an appropriate thing to say in the imagined circumstances, if there were not a fuller account of this sort on which the shorthand must be assumed to be, so to speak, parasitic. (What does "my Bill" even mean, if there is no meaningful statement that could be put in its place?)

At the same time, what we must not be led to think is that the phrase "my Bill" could be completely cashed out in neutral descriptive terms such that anyone who loved Bill—or, worse still, anyone at all—would be rationally obligated to love anyone who satisfied the terms of the description. This is simply the incompleteness thesis again. Another way to put the point, perhaps, is that it does indeed matter that Bill is not just Bill, but "*my* Bill"—there is an irreducible relational aspect present, so that no list of Bill's properties will get us to the point where love for Bill is not only justifiable but obligatory. What I insist on, however, is that we can accept this without accepting Green's implausible claim that people typically love one another without having, or thinking they have, any reason for doing so. Indeed, I do not think Green has given us any reason for supposing that this *ever* happens.

KW's resort to "I don't know, he's just my Bill," then, might be diagnosed as serving a number of functions. It may be an expression of her doubt—in the light of her inarticulateness—as to her ability to make herself understood to an audience that, presumably, does not know Bill. It may also express her suspicion that some version of the incompleteness thesis is true: that she will not be able to make a case for her love that will not leave others entirely unmoved. What is not at all likely is that the claim is literally true, that the girl truly has no idea of what she finds lovable, attractive, or desirable in "her Bill."

Related problems afflict Frankfurt's view—a view that nevertheless embodies and expresses some important truths. We all understand what a parent might mean when saying such things about his children as this:

> If I ask myself whether my children are worthy of my love, my
> quite emphatic inclination is simply to reject the question as inap-

propriate and misguided. This is not because it goes without saying that they *are* worthy. It is because my love for them is in no way
a response to or based upon any evaluation. . . . It is not because
I have noticed their value that I love my children as I do. It is really the other way around. The reason they are so precious to me is
simply that I love them so much. It is as a *consequence* of my love
for them that they have acquired, in my eyes, a value that otherwise
they would quite certainly not possess.[44]

But at the end of the day, this cannot be quite right; such a view would
justify too much. If Frankfurt's view of love is right—that it really need
not have anything to do with the value of the love object—then it should
not matter *what* the object of love is. Frankfurt has indicated on occasion that he is willing to bite this bullet and accept that love *can* be
directed toward any object whatsoever without becoming inappropriate
or unjustified.[45] But he shies away from the implications of this extreme
position, and thus avoids its most unpalatable consequences, in his choice
of examples. His central example is of his love for his own children—a
case where most people, including myself, would agree that his love is
reasonable and justified. It is all too easy, however, to imagine less attractive examples. Consider, then, the following rewrite of the passage above,
which I will ask you to imagine being spoken by a man who in fact does
not love his children very much—he could not care less what happens
to them, actually—but who does have something in his life he loves very
much, say a 1959 *Oklahoma Today* Mickey Mantle baseball card:

If I ask myself whether this baseball card is worthy of my love, my
quite emphatic inclination is simply to reject the question as inappropriate and misguided. This is not because it goes without saying
that it *is* worthy. It is because my love for it is in no way a response
to or based upon any evaluation either of it or of the consequences
for me of loving it. It is not because I have noticed its value that
I love my favorite baseball card as I do. It is really the other way
around. The reason it is so precious to me is simply that I love it so
much. It is as a *consequence* of my love for it that it has acquired, in
my eyes, a value that otherwise it would quite certainly not possess.

We must imagine that the speaker is entirely sincere and that his feelings
are manifested in his behaviors. We must imagine, that is, that he spends
more time caring for the baseball card than for his children; that the
thought of its being damaged is more upsetting to him than the thought
of their suffering some harm; that if his house were to catch fire, he would
rescue the card from the burning building before attempting to rescue
them; and so forth. Clearly there is something deeply wrong with this

person, but we do not seem to have the resources to say what it is unless we allow ourselves to think that in fact the baseball card is *not* a worthy object of his love; it is a trivial thing, and to love it or care about it in any significant way (particularly in preference to his children!) just shows bad judgment or perhaps bad character. Indeed, this baseball-card lover seems to be making two mistakes: first, he loves his baseball card *too much*; second, he does not love his children *enough*.

Both mistakes seem to consist of a lack of correspondence, or a lack of fit, between the person's attitudes and the objects of these attitudes. The man's baseball card does not merit such passionate appreciation and devotion, and so he should not love it *that much*. His children do merit such responses, and as their father, he should love them more. This is a commonsense statement to make about such cases. But if it is right, then we must reject the antirationalist's radical separation between, on the one hand, the value of the object of love and, on the other, the reasonableness or justifiability of love.

"Something In Between": Love and Vision

Still, antirationalists are surely right in much of what they claim. They are surely right, for instance, to insist that Alighieri's love for Beatrice ought not to obligate him to love anyone with Beatrice's qualities, that it ought not to obligate him to replace her with an available beloved with better qualities, and that our acknowledging his reasons ought not to obligate *us* to love her. They are right, then, to demand that we reject what I call hyper-rationalist accounts of love—accounts that combine the thought that love is a response to the beloved's valuable properties with the claim that a rational lover must behave as a rational economic agent would behave. A rational economic agent who values x for x's valuable properties ought to be willing to trade x in for y if y has similar but better properties. She ought to be prepared to value those properties wherever she may find them. She ought to be willing to give x up if x loses the properties in virtue of which it is valued. And so forth. All of this makes perfect sense in the sphere of economics. All of it seems deeply inappropriate in the realm of love.

Antirationalists are correct about this. They are wrong, however, to claim that we must therefore deny that love is in any substantial way a response to the beloved's properties, for not all valuings are like the valuings of the rational economic agent. There are other types of response to value that are far more appropriate when what is valued is a human being. An account of love built on *these* sorts of valuings avoid the excesses of hyper-rationalism and capture all of the plausible insights of antirationalism; at the same time it avoids the inherent flaws of *that* sort of view by preserving the idea that love is a response to value and is guided by reason.

Or so, at any rate, I argue. As my guide in this endeavor, I take a passage from Plato's *Symposium*. In this dialogue, Socrates feels compelled to correct the overenthusiastic praise of love—or rather of Love, since the emotion is personified—offered by the speakers who have preceded him, and in particular that of Agathon, who has held forth that Love is perfect and divine.

> It will be easiest for me to proceed the way Diotima did and tell you how she questioned me. You see, I had told her almost the same things Agathon told me just now: that Love is a great god and that he belongs to beautiful things. And she used the very same arguments against me that I used against Agathon; she showed me how, according to my own speech, Love is neither beautiful nor good.
>
> So I said, "What do you mean, Diotima? Is Love ugly then, and bad?"
>
> But she said, "Watch your tongue! Do you really think that, if a thing is not beautiful, it has to be ugly? . . . Don't force whatever is not beautiful to be ugly, or whatever is not good to be bad. It's the same with Love: when you agree he is neither good nor beautiful, you need not think he is ugly and bad; he could be something in between."[46]

Love, Diotima goes on to explain to Socrates, is indeed "something in between"; neither divine nor human, neither mortal nor immortal, Love is a spirit, or *daimon,* that functions as an intermediary between mortals and gods. Indeed, Diotima goes on to identify Love as the offspring of a coupling between two deities, Poros (or "Resource") and Penia (or "Poverty").[47]

I suggest that we take advantage of Diotima's metaphorical scheme and explore the notion that love is, indeed, "something in between." This will allow us to avoid the false dilemmas that tend to lead many thinkers astray with regard to love. It will allow us to say that love involves a special species of clear-sightedness that is nonetheless capable of propagating illusions; that it is a type of moral phenomenon nonetheless capable of inspiring immoral actions; and, most fundamentally, that love is in some important respects arational and yet involves reason in a fundamental way.

It will take some time to build the complete picture that establishes how these claims fit together. We can make a start, though, by returning to an observation I made in the first section of this chapter, that love is in large part constituted by a certain way of seeing: the lover sees the world in a different light from that in which other people see it. We should take note right away that this view of love makes much of the connection between the two persons bound by the love relationship. Some philosophers treat love in a way that emphasizes the lover, almost to the exclusion of the beloved; after all, love is an emotion the lover feels and so might be viewed as a fact only about her. But love is a way of seeing, and, more than anything, what is seen is the beloved; it is a mistake, then, to allow him to drop from the equation. Indeed, a love that ignores the beloved, or substitutes its own fantasies for his reality, is not a genuine love; it is a fantasy emotion and nothing more. Love must be a genuine response to the beloved, and moreover a largely accurate and *reasonable* response. Indeed, I argue in this book that despite its various potentials in certain contexts to encourage illusion and inspire unreasonable behavior, love is fundamentally a reason-guided phenomenon.

It is worth noting, too, that other elements of the world are also brought into this picture: loving a person involves a change not only in how you see your beloved but also in how you see the parts of the world that affect or are affected by him. To see with love's vision is to see the world with the beloved at the center and to see his attributes in a certain generous light; but it is also to see the rest of the world, to some degree, through his eyes, to allow his values, judgments, and emotions to have an effect on *your* perceptions, similar, in important ways, to the effect they have on *his*. His concerns become, to a significant degree, your concerns; his hopes, your hopes; his fears, insecurities, and anxieties, yours. That love requires us to see things in this way is part of what people mean when they say that love demands that we identify with the beloved. And this element of identification is a very large part of what makes love the profound and potentially life-changing experience that it is.

The core of the account of love I will defend is thus made up by the following eight theses:

1. Loving someone is, in large part, a kind of positive, appreciative response to her in virtue of her attractive, desirable, or otherwise valuable properties. The way of seeing the beloved, and the world in which the beloved lives, places her at the center of the lover's field of vision.

2. Loving, then, is in large part a matter of opening one's eyes to the beloved and thus of opening one's eyes to the world. Yet at the same time, love requires us *not* to see, notice, dwell on, or be moved by certain aspects of the world.

3. The properties in virtue of which the beloved is loved are in large part attractive qualities such as charm, intelligence, humor, physical

beauty, moral virtue, and so forth—the sort of universalizable qualities in terms of which a person's attractiveness or desirability is typically assessed.

4. Love is also a response to a nonuniversalizable, nonassessable property, that of *being a subject in the world*. The lover's response to this property takes the form not of assessment but of *identification with* the beloved; it is an attempt to make contact with the beloved's inner life, to unite her perspective on the world with one's own.

5. Love is thus a matter of reason, insofar as it is a response to something external that attempts to be adequate to the nature of its object. (And there is, at least in principle, the possibility of failure; one might love an object—the Mickey Mantle card, for instance—that does not possess the right qualities to make it worthy, in which case one's love will be inappropriate and unjustified.)

6. Alighieri's love for Beatrice is thus about Beatrice, in the sense that it is a response to her qualities; but it is also, in an important sense, about Alighieri: the fact that he values and cares for her says something significant about *him*, and in particular about how he sees the world. Since love is largely a matter of how one person sees another, both parties play crucial, irreducible roles in the relation. Moreover, love is constituted by the fact that not only does the lover see the beloved in this way but that to a substantial degree she is *committed* to seeing him in this way.

7. Indeed, love can be seen as an expression of the lover's identity. Part of the reason love matters to us is that our loves express and to a degree even constitute who we are. This makes love an important arena of freedom—an opportunity to make ourselves into certain sorts of people and to allow our identities and values to shape our lives and the world—and it is in part because love is not a matter of rational requirement that it is able to play this role. Love involves forming and expressing an identity by coming to value certain individuals rather than others, in a way that does not simply amount to choosing to maximize impartially determined value or to do what one has the most reason—as determined from a detached perspective—to do.[48]

8. Loving a person constitutes a specifically *moral* way of seeing, insofar as it is an attempt to recognize a person in her full individuality and involves a kind of generous attention. This is not to say, however, that love's way of seeing is the *only* way of seeing that counts as moral. Nor is it to say that love is always, on balance, morally good.

I will refer to this view of love as the vision view. I take the vision view to be a form of rationalism, as (5), in particular, suggests. But I will argue that it can be developed in a way that avoids making it a form of hyper-rationalism and avoids the various problems I outlined above. We can summarize the need to avoid these problems as follows:

1. The view must be compatible with the incompleteness thesis: no set of qualities or properties possessed by the beloved ever generates a rational obligation for anyone to love her. Thus it must not be the case that my recognition of Alighieri's justification for loving Beatrice obligates me to love Beatrice, on pain of irrationality. (This is just to say that the universality problem must be avoided.)

2. Similarly, the promiscuity problem must be avoided also. That Alighieri loves Beatrice for properties A, B, and C must not obligate him to love *everyone* who also has A, B, and C.

3. The trading-up problem must be avoided. That Alighieri loves Beatrice for properties A, B, and C must not obligate him to abandon Beatrice in favor of someone who turns out to have A, B, and/or C to an even greater degree.

4. Finally, our account must avoid the inconstancy problem. That Alighieri loves Beatrice for properties A, B, and C does not mean that he is rationally required to stop loving her if these properties change.

The attempt to develop the vision view in a way that achieves these desiderata will proceed via a number of stages. First, we must come to understand the sense in which love involves, and can even be said to be, a kind of vision. This is the task of chapters 2 and 3. Second, we must clear away false assumptions and misperceptions involving the nature of practical and evaluative reasoning. This is the task of chapters 4 and 5. Chapter 6 assembles the complete view and attempts to answer lingering questions about the nature of love's rationality. And in chapter 7 I will say something about the relation between love's demands and those of morality, which I hope will make clear why, in spite of its moral dangers and its potential to inspire evil, love can be considered a moral phenomenon.

What we want is an account of love that can capture its various and to some degree conflicting aspects: its being both a moral emotion and a potential source of immorality, an emotion that encourages clear-sightedness in some contexts and delusion in others, and an emotion that involves, in significant ways, both reason and unreason. The vision view lets us have all of this, in a way that matches our fundamental pretheoretical intuitions about the nature of love.

two

Love's Blindness (1): Love's Closed Heart

> She's kept her love for him as alive as the summer they first met. In order to do this, she's turned life away. . . . Once Uncle Julian told me how the sculptor and painter Alberto Giacometti said that sometimes just to paint a head you have to give up the whole figure. To paint a leaf, you have to sacrifice the whole landscape. It might seem like you're limiting yourself at first, but after a while you realize that having a quarter-of-an-inch of something you have a better chance of holding on to a certain feeling of the universe than if you pretended to be doing the whole sky.
>
> —Nicole Krauss, *The History of Love*

> A passionate wife necessarily has a closed heart, for it is turned away from the world.
>
> —Albert Camus, "The Myth of Sisyphus"

Introduction

I will develop the vision view in a way that avoids the four problems of rationalism delineated in the previous chapter: the universality problem, the promiscuity problem, the trading-up problem, and the inconstancy problem. Not everyone agrees that these are genuine problems; hyper-rationalists, after all, are prepared to bite the bullet by allowing that reasons for loving should be universal; that lovers should be promiscuous or else prepared to trade in their beloved for a better model; and that lovers ought to abandon their beloveds when they lose their love-grounding properties.

In Plato's *Symposium*, Diotima (via Socrates) describes what she takes to be the proper progress of love:

> A lover who goes about this matter correctly must begin in his youth to devote himself to beautiful bodies. First, if the leader leads aright, he should love one body and beget beautiful ideas there; then he should realize that the beauty of any one body is brother to the beauty of any other and that if he is to pursue beauty of form

28

he'd be very foolish not to think that the beauty of all bodies is one and the same. When he grasps this, he must become a lover of all beautiful bodies, and he must think that this wild gaping after just one body is a small thing and despise it.[1]

Two broad movements are described in this passage: from the concrete particular to the abstract universal and from the singular to the plural. The lover who begins by loving a beautiful body eventually becomes wise enough to "realize that the beauty of any one body is brother to the beauty of any other and that . . . the beauty of all bodies is one and the same." Thus in the end the lover must abandon "this wild gaping after just one body" and "must become a lover of all beautiful bodies." But this seems to require a universalism incompatible with love by prompting the lover to cast his gaze beyond the particular person who is the object of his love. It seems to require him to do the opposite of what love requires, which is to focus his attention all the more fully and intently on the beloved.

There are things to be said in favor of this attitude. In asking us to appreciate and value not one individual but as many people as possible, it constitutes a stance that may be much easier to reconcile with morality than traditional romantic love, which is often seen as posing a danger to morality rather than as encouraging it or even standing comfortably alongside it. But although I intend to defend a form of rationalism, I have to agree with the anti-Platonic tradition that holds that such an attitude bears little resemblance to friendship or romantic love as we understand it. Love, by nature, involves a species of *special* attention and concern and so cannot be directed equally toward all.[2]

As I wrote in chapter 1, I aim to develop the idea that by viewing love in large part as a matter of perception—a matter of how one views and interprets the world in which one lives—we can account for many of the prima facie contradictory features that love for persons seems to display: most centrally, the fact that we seem to love people for reasons, even though love seems in many ways an unreasonable emotion. In this chapter and the next I develop an account of the lover's psychology that is based on the central insight that loving a person is a way of seeing him and, at the same time, a way of seeing the world that puts the beloved at its center. This picture emphasizes what I will refer to as the *blindness* of love.

The statement that love is blind has become a cliché. But this cliché contains a high degree of philosophical insight. Love is largely a matter of paying close attention to a person, and paying attention to one element of the world always involves a comparative lack of attention with respect to other elements; focusing on one object means that other objects are *not* in focus. Just as a person at a loud party must make himself deaf to the many conversations that are going on in order to hear a single voice, a lover, in focusing his attention on his beloved, must turn away from a great deal else that is going on in the world.

"One Thought Too Many"

Loving a person, I suggest, is in large part a matter of seeing her in a special light and paying her a special sort of attention. Let us start to fill in this picture by invoking an example that sets these issues in a life-or-death context. I am referring to a much-discussed example that Bernard Williams describes in his paper "Persons, Character, and Morality." I paraphrase the example as follows:

> *Drowning Wife.* Two people, Daniel and Andrea, are drowning. Sam is nearby, standing on the beach. Sam is Andrea's husband; theirs is a committed, loving, and quite passionate relationship.[3] Sam and Daniel, on the other hand, are strangers to each other. Sam is a strong swimmer and could rescue either Daniel or Andrea with little risk to himself; there is, however, insufficient time for him to rescue both.[4]

Williams's primary concern is what he sees as the tendency among philosophers to overestimate the importance of impartial morality in situations such as Drowning Wife. Of course, few moral philosophers will insist that the agent follow some randomizing procedure, such as flipping a coin, to give every endangered person an equal chance of being saved. But there is another, less obviously implausible way of recognizing the claims of impartiality in this situation, and that is to insist that the permission for Sam to save his wife must refer back to impartial morality. Charles Fried, for instance, writes that so long as Sam does not occupy any official position (lifeguard, ship's captain, etc.), then "the occurrence of the accident may itself stand as a sufficient randomizing event to meet the dictates of fairness, so he may prefer his friend, or loved one."[5]

Fried's reference to a "sufficient randomizing event" reveals that he is committed to a fairly demanding form of impartiality at a quite deep level. And it is precisely these philosophers—those who claim that an agent in a Drowning Wife situation should think of himself as justified, in the terms of impartial morality, in saving his wife—who are Williams's primary target in section 3 of "Persons, Character, and Morality." For why, Williams asks, should the question of moral justification even enter the agent's mind in such a situation? And what does this tell us about the character and motivations of the agent whose mind it *does* enter?

Williams argues that standard moral theories are objectionable insofar as they involve

> the idea that moral principle can legitimate his preference, yielding the conclusion that in situations of this kind it is at least all right (morally permissible) to save one's wife. . . . But this construction provides the agent with one thought too many: it might have been hoped by some (for instance, by his wife) that his motivating thought, fully spelled out, would be the thought that it was his wife, not that it was his wife and that in situations of this kind it is permissible to save one's wife.[6]

Many people share the feeling that there is some sort of problem with having "one thought too many." But what exactly *is* the problem? Suppose we take "motivating thought" to mean, quite literally, the thought that explicitly runs through the agent's mind before he acts and that leads to his action, so that we are assuming that the action would not have occurred had he not had that thought. The occurrence of the thought in the agent's mind does seem problematic, since it seems to suggest that the agent would *not* have saved his wife if he had not had the complete thought (in particular, the part that concerns impartial morality). And although there are at least two ways of interpreting this idea, neither interpretation seems to yield a morally unproblematic result.

The first interpretation states that *given that a thought about impartial morality occurred*, the thought had to be that saving his wife was permitted in order for him to be at liberty to save her. This interpretation leaves it open that if it had not occurred to the agent to think about impartial morality *at all* in that moment, he might have saved his wife. Had he not stopped to inquire about what impartial morality might demand of him, the thought "My wife is in danger" would have been sufficient to motivate him.

The second and more disturbing interpretation holds that the thought "My wife is in danger" is not, on its own, sufficient to motivate the agent; rather, the agent cannot bring himself to perform *any* action unless his perception of the situation includes the thought "and so acting is supported by impartial morality." Such an agent would be obsessed with impartial morality. Similarly, as Michael Stocker observes, there is something wrong with the motivations of the agent who cannot be motivated to visit his alleged friend in the hospital in order to cheer him up, except by the thought that impartial morality requires him to do so.[7] As Marcia Baron writes, "A person is morally deficient if she is so motivationally depleted that, for actions to which most of us would be moved by sympathy, fellow feeling, or affection for a particular person (the list is not exhaustive), the only sufficient motive she has is her belief that the action is morally called for."[8]

Things do not appear to be quite as bad with respect to the first sort of agent, who, while not needing moral requirements to act as sources of motivation for taking care of her loved ones, is nonetheless prepared to refrain from taking care of them in cases where morality forbids doing so. And particularly in an example like Stocker's hospital visit case, where there is not all that much at stake from the friend's point of view, this may seem perfectly reasonable. Morality does sometimes demand sacrifices, after all. Of course, if the friend's life were at stake, things might seem different. But this is precisely the situation in Drowning Wife: one is not merely taking care of one's wife here or cheering her up; one is *saving her life*. As a result, some, including Williams, have thought that while the first sort of agent is not as seriously deficient as the second, she is nevertheless flawed: she seems to place too much emphasis on morality as opposed to the other significant aspects of her life.

From Andrea's perspective, surely the fact that her husband was prepared to let the demands of morality keep him from saving her would indicate something lacking in his character or in his commitment to her. This is so even if he *did* save her, and even if he did not stop to ask himself whether saving her was permissible. The problem, after all, is simply that if he *had* asked himself that question, and the answer was no, he would *not* have saved her. The problem, then, is not what the agent did, nor even what he thought, but what he would have done had his thoughts been other than what they were. If Sam truly loved Andrea, one might say, he would care more about her than he would about doing the morally right thing; the danger to her would render moral prohibitions irrelevant.

Such an understanding of the problem avoids the implausible idea that we can literally count the number of thoughts in a person's head. This implausible idea is taken to its extreme in Harry Frankfurt's amusing response to Drowning Wife:

> I cannot help wondering why the man should have even the one thought that it's his wife. Are we supposed to imagine that at first he didn't recognize her? Or are we supposed to imagine that at first he didn't remember that they were married, and had to remind himself of that? It seems to me that the strictly correct number of thoughts for this man is zero. Surely the normal thing is that he sees what's happening in the water, and he jumps in to save his wife. Without thinking at all. In the circumstances that the example describes, any thought whatsoever is one thought too many.[9]

Frankfurt has a point, but of course the plausibility of his claim depends on an ambiguity in the verb *think*, which we frequently use as if it meant "*stop* to think." In this sense, to say that an agent thought about what he was doing implies that he paused to consider it, suggesting that he acted only after a process of deliberation, rather than immediately, and that he would have acted differently had the outcome of the thought process been other than what it was.

Taking the words *think* and *thought* in this sense, Frankfurt is indeed correct to write that "any thought whatsoever is one thought too many." But this is not what Williams intended. To say that the agent had a thought, in Williams's sense, is simply to say that the agent formed a certain conception of the situation and was responding appropriately to it. And this can hardly be objectionable, since an agent could not respond to a situation *at all*—except perhaps utterly randomly and arbitrarily—without forming a conception of it.

In other words, we do understand what it is to "act without thinking," and this understanding seems perfectly consistent with the idea that even in such cases there nevertheless is a "motivating thought" that can be identified. This motivating thought has less to do with what literally went through the agent's mind than with the question of what retrospective justification might be offered or of counterfactuals concerning what the agent *would have done* under different circumstances. There is, then, a danger here of taking the claim about the agent's having "one thought too many" too literally; the real worry concerns the structure of the agent's commitments and the order of priority in which he places them, as reflected in the facts about what he was prepared to do.

Nonetheless, it is doubtful that everything that might bother us about the man with "one thought too many" can be captured in terms of such counterfactuals; a certain level of attention to the agent's deliberative processes seems required by the nature of the situation. Indeed, it might be that the agent's wife would have a legitimate complaint about her husband's motivation even if all the relevant counterfactuals were in place. Consider a man who does stop to think but then decides that saving his wife is permitted, and so he saves her. Suppose that this agent loves his wife and would have saved her no matter what the outcome of his deliberation regarding permissibility had been. Still, his wife might object to the fact that he did not *know* this about himself. Even if it was inevitable that he would save her, he himself did not *know* that it was inevitable. And this, one might say, is something he should have known. Under this interpretation, then, the objection is not to what he would have done under other conditions, but to the fact that it was not obvious that his wife meant more to him than did the demands of morality.

This brings us back to a more literal interpretation of the phrase "one thought too many," for after all what is now found to be problematic is what went through the agent's head. Admittedly, we need not literally count thoughts. It is enough to know that the agent paused to think things over. But in this sense, we might find ourselves somewhat more likely to agree with Frankfurt's claim that "the strictly correct number of thoughts for this man is zero."

Holism and Silencing

Just what *do* we want an agent in Sam's position to think? The question is surprisingly difficult. It is much easier to say, in a general way, what we do *not* want him to think. He should not be thinking about impartial morality or the permissibility of his saving his wife. And most certainly he should not be thinking about trivial reasons. If the fact that he will ruin his favorite pair of dress pants if he dives in to save her receives serious attention during his deliberative process, something has gone badly wrong indeed.

This much we seem to be able to say. As we have seen, though, it is very difficult to get much more precise than this about just what we think Sam should think or not think. What makes it particularly difficult is a false assumption that we need to overcome: that Sam's thoughts, including the one that is supposed to be objectionable, ought to be treated as propositions that pass through Sam's head. While it is sometimes reasonable to treat thoughts as propositions, there is reason to think that in this case the proposition-centered approach might prove to be inadequate in coming up with an acceptable positive picture of what the loving agent's thoughts should be in this situation.

The main problem with the proposition-based approach is that it is untrue to the very nature of the perception that is involved in decision making. Perception is an unavoidable part of decision making; one cannot respond to a situation without first looking to see what it is. But such a perception is not composed of an orderly series of isolated propositions. Rather, we tend to take a perceived situation in as a whole, under a certain description or conception; the propositions are not experienced as isolated, and the logical connections and relations between the propositions are embodied in our grasp of the situation. Perception, then, is fundamentally holistic; we do not perceive the individual constituents of a situation but rather grasp the whole under some description or conception.

Conceiving of perception as holistic allows us to draw a fruitful comparison with what some neo-Aristotelian theorists have written about the manner in which virtue manifests itself in the thought and behavior of a virtuous agent. A virtuous person, like a lover, is committed to a certain project and set of values in a way that shapes her conception of practical reason and of what ought to be done.[10] On many neo-Aristotelian views, the perception of a crucially important reason-generating consideration often functions by masking other potentially relevant considerations—considerations that in other situations would have demanded considerable attention and might even have successfully moved the agent to act.

Consider, then, John McDowell's way of conceptualizing the nature of a perfectly virtuous agent. Such an agent, McDowell argues, is not someone who resists the temptation to do wrong but someone who does not feel that temptation and therefore need not resist it at all. An agent of this sort embraces "a specific conception of *eudaimonia*," and to do this "is to see the relevant reasons for acting, on occasions when they co-exist with considerations that on their own would be reasons for acting otherwise, as, not overriding, but silencing those other considerations—as bringing it about that, in the circumstances, they are not reasons at all."[11]

This mode of operation, it seems to me, is *precisely* what Andrea would like to see in the psychology of her husband. For Sam to see the danger to her as a reason for action is necessary but not sufficient; it is also necessary that he perceive this consideration as possessing such overwhelming importance that *it simply drives everything else from his mind*. If the danger to Andrea does not strike him with this sort of force and practical import, then his love for her is shallow or not entirely genuine. The "good" husband and lover, then, is one for whom certain considerations, which he acknowledges may very well serve as legitimate sources of reasons for action for *other* agents, are not seen as giving rise to reasons *for him* at all. Such considerations are simply irrelevant to the question of what action he is to undertake. And to fail to see them as irrelevant—to conceive of the moral permissibility of saving one's beloved as relevant, for instance—is precisely to have "one thought too many."

It is important to say, of course, that in Drowning Wife we do not expect Sam to be blind to the fact that Daniel is in danger. The point is not that he does not notice this aspect of the situation, but that if it does explicitly cross his mind, it will not strike him with the sort of compelling urgency with which the fact that Andrea is in danger will strike him. Indeed, Sam may well be aware not only that Daniel is in danger but that the danger to him will count for *other* agents as a generator of reasons. But if he genuinely loves Andrea, this fact will not be one that he regards as especially important, certainly not important enough to cause him to suspend his efforts on behalf of Andrea. Daniel, after all, is a stranger, and Andrea is his beloved wife.

In general, it is not one's intellectual awareness of the facts that is silenced by virtue, love, or other forms of commitment so much as the practical and emotional import of certain facts of which one might well remain aware. Moreover, it is important to be clear that which facts have their import silenced in this way will vary from one situation to another; if Andrea were not present and only Daniel were in danger, Sam would surely regard that fact as giving rise to a compelling reason for action.

Silencing shapes one's deliberations; an agent subject to it need not deliberate extensively to figure out that the silenced considerations are not reason-generating. She certainly need not weigh them against the competing reasons to see which overpowers the other. Her grasp of the relative priority of the reasons presented to her is not something she needs to work out after perceiving the situation; rather, it is expressed in her perception of the situation. To form a perception that reflects these relative priorities is, as Margaret Little writes, to grasp what neo-Aristotelian theorists often refer to as the "shape" of the situation.

> Propositional knowledge can survive shifts or losses in experiential gestalts. One can suddenly lose the ability to find the face in the pointillist painting—to see the dots *as* Marilyn Monroe's visage—without thereby forgetting that it is indeed a painting of Marilyn Monroe. . . . The virtue theorist's claim is that [the] notion of "taking as morally salient" is not reducible to believing or knowing the proposition that a given feature or set of features has such-and-such moral significance. Rather, they argue, "taking as salient" is akin to having a kind of experience. Analogous to the way in which certain features occupy the foreground in a perceptual gestalt, certain features are experienced or taken as occupying a moral prominence; and, analogous to the way in which the individual elements of a gestalt come together to form a certain shape, the individual elements of the situation are experienced or taken as adding up to form a given moral whole.[12]

The idea that "not all cognitive differences can be captured as differences in propositional content" is important because it helps us understand the distinction between an agent's valuing *x* and her judging *x* to be valuable. To say that A judges C to be an appropriate object of love and yet does not love him is much like saying that a person knows (accepts the proposition) that the picture is of Marilyn Monroe and yet does not see it as such.

But why is the distinction between valuing *x* and judging *x* to be valuable crucial? For the moment it is sufficient to observe that in large part this distinction will allow us to understand how a lover can value, and respond appreciatively to, her beloved's valuable and attractive properties without being rationally obligated to extend that valuing attitude to those properties whenever and wherever they appear. Sam recognizes that Daniel's existence is fundamentally as significant and valuable as Andrea's. But his being a lover of Andrea implies that he values her existence in a special way. That valuing will be inextricably incorporated into Sam's perceptions of situations involving Andrea; situations involving threats to her life, for instance, will have an entirely different character from situations involving threats to other persons. (Again, this is not to say that the latter situation will present itself to Sam as making no pressing claim on his attention but only that the nature of the claim will be of a quite different sort.)

For neo-Aristotelians, being virtuous involves a tendency to see situations in a certain light and to see certain considerations as giving rise to reasons for action in a particularly compelling way. Precisely the same can be said about being a lover. A stranger walking into a room is just that: a stranger walking into a room. The entrance of one's beloved, however, constitutes something far more: it is, one might say, an event to which one cannot respond with mere indifference. One's feelings, one's expectations, one's very perceptions—all these are markedly different when the person in question is one's beloved.

Blindness and Temptation

Cases like Drowning Wife unavoidably raise the possibility of conflicts between love and morality. Let us consider instead a type of situation, involving marital fidelity, in which morality's demands (at least as typically conceived) might coincide with those of love. Consider Juliet, who loves her husband and who is presented with an opportunity for infidelity. Here, as in Drowning Wife, love will be thought by many to demand a sort of silencing. Many will say it is not enough for Juliet to decide not to cheat on her husband; what is also wanted is that she not even be *tempted* to cheat. The woman's love and commitment are supposed to prevent her from even considering the choice between faithfulness and infidelity in the cost-benefit manner that might seem entirely appropriate elsewhere.

In such situations, writes McDowell, "the dictates of virtue, if properly appreciated, are not weighed with other reasons at all, not even on a scale that always tips on their side."[13] A silencing reason is not simply one that is stronger than, and thus *outweighs*, some other reason; it is perhaps better to think of it as somehow undermining the opposing reason, thus preventing it from counting as a reason at all.

> "What shall it profit a man, if he gain the whole world, and lose his soul?" Obviously we are not meant to answer "The profits are outweighed by the counterbalancing losses." The intended answer is "Nothing." At that price, whatever one might achieve does not count as profit. Or, in the terminology of reasons: the attractions of whatever wickedness might bring do not constitute some reason for wickedness, which is, however, overridden by the reasons against it; rather, given that they are achieved by wickedness, those attractive outcomes do not count as reasons at all.[14]

Some find McDowell's claim that the truly virtuous person would not even be tempted by immorality implausibly, perhaps insufferably, high-minded.[15] But we must keep certain points in mind. First, the view represents a moral ideal: thinking the perfectly virtuous person will never feel

tempted is compatible with recognizing that no one is perfectly virtuous all the time. McDowell's neo-Aristotelian view allows for a range of
levels of virtue. There are agents who occasionally, but only rarely, feel
temptation. There is the *continent* individual, who feels temptation but
resists it. And so forth. McDowell's ideal, then, does not imply that an
agent's feeling some small amount of temptation must necessarily mean
that she is deeply immoral. I will return to this point, with respect to love
in particular, in the following section.

Second, it is important to acknowledge that McDowell's position does
not hold, in such cases as this, that the agent is so virtuous that she would
not *enjoy* the infidelity. The typical moral agent is neither a robot nor a
saint, and even a virtuous agent is well aware that she would gain significant pleasure from her act. What separates her from the continent or
incontinent individual (both of whom are tempted by the immorality but
differ in how they respond to it) is not this, but rather her finding the fact
that she would enjoy it irrelevant to her reasons for acting. "The temper-
ate person need be no less prone to enjoy physical pleasure than anyone
else," he writes. "But her clear perception of the requirement insulates
the prospective enjoyment—of which, for a satisfying conception of the
virtue, we should want her to have a vivid appreciation—from engaging
her inclinations at all."[16]

The difference between the virtuous and nonvirtuous person, then,
lies not in whether the person would enjoy the infidelity but in how she
interprets the fact that she would enjoy it. The nonvirtuous person sees
this fact as a reason for going ahead, and so feels tempted, whereas the
virtuous person does not. Again, this fact is registered not merely propo-
sitionally but emotionally; in the agent's overall gestalt perception of the
situation, a perceived reason manifests itself as a motivational tug or urge
and thus as temptation. The imperfectly virtuous person, of course, can
still think there are stronger reasons *against* going ahead; the point is that
she sees the whole situation as providing fairly strong reasons in favor
of doing the immoral thing, and so she must resist a temptation that the
fully virtuous person does not even feel.

The third point is that McDowell's view is perhaps most implausible
when considered in relation to the demands of impartial morality, with
respect to such virtues as courage. Consider a virtuous soldier on the
battlefield. The demand that this soldier not regard the possibility of her
being killed as a reason for running away—not even as a reason she
might regard as being outweighed by compelling reasons for standing her
ground—may indeed seem excessively demanding. Surely it is no blemish
on the moral character of the soldier if she does, in fact, feel afraid at the
prospect of her imminent violent death. Indeed, a soldier who felt no fear
whatsoever might well strike us as inhuman or a kind of maniac, and thus
not morally admirable.

In the context of personal relations, however, the neo-Aristotelian silencing view strikes many people as both appropriate and plausible, for it is quite common to regard the lover who is not even *tempted* to cheat on her partner as the better or truer lover than the one who is tempted but resists. Again, this is fully compatible with her being fully cognizant of the fact that were she to cheat, she would greatly enjoy it. (Admittedly, some people will not think that sexual fidelity is an important part of love and so may not feel the force of the claim with respect to this example. Skeptics about sexual fidelity, though, will almost surely still regard *some* forms of behavior toward loved ones as constituting betrayal. So the same point can still be made, simply by substituting a form of betrayal that is recognized as such by the skeptic for the commonly but not universally recognized example I have chosen.)

This interpretation can help us understand a related part of the view, which even McDowell's sympathizers have sometimes found implausible.[17] This is McDowell's claim that the virtuous agent, in regarding gains of immorality as being irrelevant to the question of her reasons for action, ought not only to regard those gains as irrelevant but to regard those gains as *not really being gains at all.*

> If someone really embraces a specific conception of human excellence, however grounded, then that will of itself equip her to understand special employments of the typical notions of "prudential" reasoning—the notions of benefit, advantage, harm, loss, and so forth—according to which (for instance) no payoff from flouting a requirement of excellence, however desirable by ... [ordinary] canons ... can count as a genuine advantage; and conversely, no sacrifice necessitated by the life of excellence, however desirable what one misses may be by those canons, can count as a genuine loss.[18]

Again, this might seem implausible with respect to the soldier on the battlefield: no matter how highly she might prize the notions of courage, honor, and stoicism, the idea that she would save *nothing* of value by saving her life seems hard to accept. It is more plausible in such cases, perhaps, that the agent recognizes the potential loss as genuine but refuses to see it as generating reasons for action in the usual manner. Indeed, we might hesitate to go even *this* far. Perhaps, we might think, a context of this sort is one in which silencing simply does not apply; it is perfectly permissible, here, for the agent to *feel* a reason, and thus be tempted, and to need to exert her willpower to resist that temptation.

But to many people things appear to be different in the sphere of personal relationships, and here McDowell's controversial claim about value may seem considerably more plausible. It is too much to ask, and indeed seems wrong to ask, that a soldier see her life as possessing no value.

But it is not, perhaps, too much to ask a potential philanderer to see the pleasure she would gain from her infidelity as possessing no value. Why is this? Part of the answer lies in the fact that the latter involves mere pleasure, whereas the former concerns survival itself. But the more significant part of the answer lies in the fact that the latter case concerns a *relationship*, and this alters the way in which various possible outcomes must be evaluated.

Many writers on love suggest that the formation of a love relationship involves, among other things, a kind of unity of interests between the two lovers. Unification views of love have a long and distinguished history, stretching back at least to Aristophanes' account in Plato's *Symposium*, according to which the lover's desire is to unite with the individual in the world who quite literally constitutes one's other half. And the idea that romantic lovers merge to form a single entity with a single set of interests goes back at least to Kant, who writes that the two partners in a marriage "constitute a unity of will. Neither will be subject to happiness or misfortune, joy or displeasure, without the other taking a share in it."[19] The point of asserting that this involves a genuine *unity* is to go beyond the obvious fact that lovers' fortunes have causal effects on one another, to the stronger claim that love creates a genuinely new subject, distinguished, among other things, by its possession of *joint* interests that are not reducible to the interests of either partner.

It is possible, surely, to overstate the degree of unification that is required by love, and some have expressed reservations about unification views on this score.[20] Still, there is something very plausible about the idea that lovers share each other's interests. Moreover, the fact that a sufficient degree of unity of interests must obtain in genuine love fits very well with the claim I am borrowing from McDowell, that the lover, in her practical reasoning, will make use of "special employments of the typical notions of 'prudential' reasoning—the notions of benefit, advantage, harm, loss, and so forth." What is special about these particular employments is that they are defined relative not to the individual who is doing the reasoning but to the *we* that encompasses both that individual and her love partner.

What love demands, then, is that the pleasure of infidelity be measured not relative to the lover herself but relative to the special entity that she and her beloved together make. The relevant question is not "Will this be good for me?" but rather "Will this be good for *us*?" And from *this* standpoint the pleasure will indeed be found to possess no value whatsoever. Love transforms the agent's conception of her own self-interest, dissolving potential conflicts between her self-interest and the we-interests she and her lover share. There is, for such an agent, "no payoff from flouting a requirement of [love]," since "no sacrifice necessitated by the life of [love], however desirable what one misses may be by [ordinary] canons, can count as a genuine loss." This explains why the occurrence of felt temptation seems to indicate a problem: it shows that the lover is not fully occupying the perspective of love, that there are deep and serious gaps separating her from her beloved.

Obsession and Uniqueness

> A person in love is unremittingly and uninterruptedly occupied with the image of the beloved.
>
> —Stendhal

> When a man loves a woman
> he can't keep his mind on nothing else
> —Percy Sledge

The courageous or otherwise virtuous agent, McDowell suggests, finds that considerations that would be seen as generating reasons from perspectives whose authority she rejects—the perspective of pure self-interest and self-preservation, for example—do *not* generate reasons from the perspective she actually occupies. It is not that the rejected perspective generates *weakened* reasons that are easily overruled, but rather that it is not taken to generate reasons at all, which is why the agent is not even tempted to act badly. The competing perspectives are incompatible: a commitment to one value perspective prevents the attractions and reasons of competing perspectives from being motivationally effective. The competing values cannot be weighed against one another from a neutral standpoint, for there is no standpoint from which they all may be fully appreciated; rather, an agent who is in the position to fully appreciate the reasons for behaving uncourageously arising from the perspective of self-preservation is guaranteed not to also possess a full appreciation of the reasons for being courageous.

Similarly, the loving agent's commitment to a particular person shapes her habits, motivations, and responses so as to prevent her from being motivated or even mildly tempted to act in unloving ways. Thus the loving wife might be intellectually aware that infidelity would be pleasurable and yet not be tempted to betray her husband. Moreover, even her intellectual awareness of the possibility of such pleasure will to some degree be attenuated; if she is truly in love, her mind will be too full of thoughts centering on or relating to her beloved to admit such thoughts as these.

As before, we are clearly speaking of an ideal here—few, if any, actual lovers are *so* full of loving and appreciative thoughts directed toward their partners that they will have no room for *any* such thoughts about others. But the ideal I am describing here is one that has been hugely influential in shaping the way Western society, at any rate, thinks about love. Indeed, it is probably impossible to understand our culture's emphasis on the *uniqueness* of the beloved without grasping the importance, to this conception, of love's mind-filling, quasi-obsessive aspect. Elaine Scarry writes:

> Usually when the "unprecedented" suddenly comes before one, and when one has made a proclamation about the state of affairs— "There is no one like you, nothing like this, anywhere"—the mind, despite the confidently announced mimesis of carrying out the search, does not actually enter into any such search, for it is too exclusively filled with the beautiful object that stands in its presence. It is the very way the beautiful thing fills the mind and breaks all frames that gives the "never before in the history of the world" feeling.[21]

The beloved's attractive properties "fill the mind" of the lover, leaving no room for her to appreciate similar properties possessed by others. An infatuated person becomes blind to the attractions of everyone but his beloved. ("I only have eyes for you," he says.) And what many people hope for from love is precisely the continuation of this state of affairs— that one's lover will remain blind to the attractions of others. Indeed, an intense state of being in love not only impedes the lover's attraction to other persons but also interferes with her ability to think about anything other than the beloved.

The hope that this obsessive state will persist indefinitely is quite unrealistic in the light of what is known about human psychology, namely that infatuation tends not to persist for more than a couple of years at most. Still, it is common in our society for lovers to attempt to behave, for the duration of the relationship, *as if* they were still infatuated and to pretend, at any rate, not to notice the existence of other attractive individuals; any temptation that might be felt is supposed to be suppressed, resisted, and as far as possible denied. Nor should it be assumed that, after the initial period of infatuation, all such behavior must be nothing more than pretense; it is surely true, at least with respect to those long-term relationships in which the partners may really be said to still love each other, that such lovers remain biased in favor of one another at least to a significant degree insofar as the appreciation of positive and attractive qualities is concerned.

Romantic love has always tended, at least in Western society, to be regarded as an essentially exclusive relationship; a hallmark of a genuine romantic commitment is thought to be that the lovers are faithful to one another, and this is most frequently understood as requiring that the lovers be bound by mutual sexual attraction and experiences of intimacy that are not felt for or shared with other individuals. The idea is not simply that one's lover, when compared with other individuals, must always come out on top; rather, the idea is that such comparisons are to a large extent to be avoided. Love involves seeing one's beloved in a certain light, thinking of her in positive terms, and so on, but the question of how she ranks against other persons, considered objectively and impartially, simply should not arise.

In chapter 1 I quoted a passage from Martin Buber in which Buber claims that the object of love's attention "steps forth to confront us in its uniqueness. It fills the firmament—not as if there were nothing else, but everything else lives in *its* light." About this passage, R. M. Adams remarks that as Buber intends it,

> other objects are in view, but only insofar as they illuminate the nature or the meaning of the Thou or the object of love. To ask seriously whether the beloved is more (or less) excellent than some other object is to shift the focus of attention, demoting the beloved from being *the* focus to being at best one of two or more coordinate foci. Such a question is therefore no part of the fullness of appreciation.[22]

It is not only other potential lovers, of course, who are expected to be excluded from the lover's awareness and practical deliberations. As Drowning Wife suggests, it may be that love is expected to silence various *moral* claims arising from others as well. And there are other considerations, too, that are to be silenced, other forms of valuing or ways of thinking about value, in which a genuine lover will not engage. In particular, there are certain emotional or otherwise affective responses that one not only ought to have with respect to the individuals one loves, but also ought *not* to have with respect to those whom one does *not* love.

Let us return for a moment to Scarry's observation that the thought that a beautiful object is unique is not formed as the result of a sincere attempt to see whether the beautiful object is, indeed, genuinely unique. The point is not that one has looked and turned up nothing, but rather that this sort of encounter renders one uninterested in looking; the urge to keep looking could be only an expression of dissatisfaction and so a sign that the object immediately before one has not, in fact, entirely captured one's attention and filled one's mind.

Actual, literal uniqueness, then, does not matter in such contexts; seeing someone as unique is a way of seeing her, so that the uniqueness is the effect of a certain way of seeing rather than its cause. On this point, the antirationalists seem to have come quite close to the truth. I have urged, of course, that we should reject Frankfurt's following claim about value:

"It is not because I have noticed their value that I love my children as I do. It is really the other way around. The reason they are so precious to me is simply that I love them so much. It is as a *consequence* of my love for them that they have acquired, in my eyes, a value that otherwise they would quite certainly not possess."[23]

But if we replace "value" with "uniqueness," we get—with a little rewriting—a claim that seems quite correct: "It is not because I have noticed their uniqueness that I love my children as I do. It is really the other way around. The reason they are unique, in my eyes, is simply that I love them so much. It is as a *consequence* of my love for them that they have acquired, in my eyes, a uniqueness that otherwise they would quite certainly not possess."

Of course, in certain trivial senses any child will be unique: there are, in fact, no exact duplicates of persons. But precisely because everyone is unique, being unique is the furthest thing from a unique property. It does not *matter* much that one is unique. One's love for a person is not based on that, for as Frankfurt has correctly pointed out elsewhere, even if it turned out that an exact replica of one's beloved *did* exist, this would not suggest that one had been mistaken in loving her.[24]

The thought that uniqueness does not matter much may seem to run contrary to common sense. Most of us tend to place a great deal of value on the qualities that make our beloveds unique and distinguish them from other individuals. But we must be careful here. We do, of course, value many qualities that, in the world as it is, render individuals unique. But we do not value these properties *because* they render their bearers unique. Such properties would still be important even in a world in which each of us had several qualitative replicas. Admittedly, there is something creepy about this thought experiment, and it is difficult to know exactly how our love for persons would be affected in a world so different from the one we know. Still, there is little reason to think that love for individuals would be *impossible* in a world of replicas. What matters, if I love you for your beauty, is simply your beauty, in and of itself; the existence of another individual who happened to be beautiful in just the way you are would not make you any less beautiful or suggest that valuing your beauty is somehow unreasonable or unjustified.

What matters, then, is not that one's beloved is unique, but that one's way of seeing picks him out *uniquely*, which means making him the subject of a special level of attention that is not directed toward others, and appreciating his value as a human individual in a way that does not involve a neutral comparison of his various valuable properties with those of other individuals—not even with individuals whom one might have come to love instead had circumstances been different.

Conclusion

In this chapter I have attempted to describe certain elements of the psychology of the lover. I have for the most part avoided normative argument; my intent has been only to describe the sort of psychology love encourages and demands and not to argue that these encouragements and demands are admirable, reasonable, or even permissible. Indeed, since my overall position is that love is something in between—between the purely moral and the deeply immoral and between reason and utter unreason—it would not be to my purposes to claim that these demands are purely admirable or reasonable. However, I do think there are compelling things to be said in their favor. But I have not, as yet, attempted to say what these are.

Chapters 4 and 5 will be largely devoted to articulating and making intelligible the view of practical reason that underlies the view of love I am discussing. The discussion of these chapters, if successful, should support the claims that such love is, first, a matter of reason and, second, a response to real and independently existing values. Before taking on that task, however, I must consider an additional type of blindness that forms an essential element of love. The current chapter has concentrated on the effect of an agent's love on the way in which she perceives (or fails to perceive) persons other than the beloved—the way in which the passionate wife's heart is, as Camus writes, "turned away from the world." Chapter 3 will take as its focus the question of how the lover perceives her beloved. For here, too, not only is it true that love calls for a certain kind of attention, it is also true that love's attention must involve, again, a kind of blindness—in this case, a blindness to certain flaws, deficiencies, and limitations in the beloved, with the result that such vision involves a kind of generosity of perception. Both with respect to the beloved and with respect to others, then, love's vision—like all vision—is characterized not only by what is seen but by what one's way of seeing renders invisible as well.

three

Love's Blindness (2): Love's Friendly Eye

A friendly eye is slow to see small faults.
—Shakespeare, *Julius Caesar*

Introduction

According to the vision view, love is a unique and very particular way of seeing. As noted in chapter 1, the process of falling in love can feel like a transformation—a transformation in, among other things, how the beloved is seen. The kind of attention paid to the beloved is distinguished in part—but only in part—by its being more intense and of a higher degree than the attention paid to other things. Consider the following description of first love, from Nicole Krauss's novel *The History of Love*:

> But now she seemed different to me. I became aware of her special powers. How she seemed to pull light and gravity to the place where she stood. I noticed, as I had never before, the way her toes pointed slightly inward. The dirt on her bare knees. The way her coat fit neatly across her narrow shoulders. As if my eyes had been given magnifying powers. I saw her more closely yet. The black beauty mark, like a fleck of ink above her lip. The pink, translucent shell of her ear. The blond down on her cheeks. Inch by inch she revealed herself to me. I half expected that in another moment I'd be able to make out the cells of her skin as if under a microscope.[1]

The beloved, now that she *is* beloved, will be scrutinized with a level of attention she had not been subject to before. Yet one might wonder how much this is a matter of seeing what is already there and how much of a contribution the lover's imagination is making. Presumably he really sees "the black beauty mark" and "the blond down on her cheeks." But what of "her special powers" or the way "she seemed to pull light and gravity to the place where she stood"? And what of his expectation that he would soon "be able to make out the cells of her skin as if under a microscope"? Even as he finds himself seeing his beloved more closely, and in more detail, than he ever has before, the lover in this passage seems simultaneously to be caught in the grip of a fantasy, an act that is not one of perception at all but rather a *projection* of certain ideas, certain ideals, certain hopes and longings, onto his beloved.

It is the influence of imagination of this sort in the lover's perceptions of the beloved that leads Stendhal and his followers to insist that love is not a matter of seeing at all but rather a process of "crystallization"—a projection of fantasy onto the beloved that obscures, rather than reveals, her true nature. Although I will argue that views like Stendhal's are, at the end of the day, exaggerated and excessively cynical, I will acknowledge— as I think any proponent of the vision view should—that the fundamental contention of such views is not entirely false. There are elements of imagination, idealization, and even falsification and delusion in love. In most cases, I believe, these elements are present only to a limited degree, and relationships in which they have come to dominate—relationships in which the lover cannot even *see* his beloved—are not instances of genuine love at all but of something else that may in relatively superficial aspects resemble love. At the same time, though, we need to acknowledge the existence of one phenomenon, very closely related to these others, that will feature in *all* instances of love, including "true" love at its very best. This is the lover's tendency to view the beloved in the best possible light, to see her flaws but interpret them in a way that renders them insignificant or irrelevant (and perhaps manages to see them as not genuine flaws at all), the tendency, to borrow Shakespeare's phrase, to see the beloved with "a friendly eye."

We have already seen how love encourages the lover to be effectively blind to a great many properties of and facts about people other than her beloved—facts and properties that if attached to her beloved, would command her attention and in many cases matter a great deal. The suggestion we are now considering is that there is a second sort of blindness, which stands alongside and functions simultaneously with the first. Both species of blindness raise issues in both moral and epistemic contexts. Love, because it might seem to encourage these forms of blindness, may be accused of a tendency to cause lovers both to perform immoral actions and to form or accept false or misleading beliefs. Indeed, some writers have suggested that we see love's requirements as fundamentally opposed to requirements of morality and of epistemic rationality. I will discuss the moral issue in chapter 7; in this chapter I will consider the epistemic issue. What I will argue is that love, rather than representing a challenge to epistemic standards, is best understood as embodying epistemic standards of its own.

Idealization and Delusion in Love

> The question is not whether I can love someone who is *in fact* ugly—
> for better or worse, most people do—but whether I can love some-
> one I *find* ugly, and I believe that's impossible.
> —Alexander Nehamas, *Only a Promise of Happiness*

The natural presumption is that any form of blindness is epistemically perilous. What is it to close one's eyes to any aspect of the world if not to refrain from forming as complete and comprehensive a picture of the world as might be formed? Thus if, as suggested in the previous chapter, love calls on us to turn our attention away from those existing at the periphery of our field of vision—in particular, those individuals whose attractive features or claims and interests might compete with those of our beloveds—then love might already seem to pose a serious epistemic danger; it might seem to constitute, in epistemic terms, a kind of disability, a cognitive impairment. We might find ourselves agreeing with Ortega y Gasset, who called love "an abnormal state of attention which occurs in a normal man," a state that diminishes the consciousness of the lover, rendering one's attention "fixed and rigid, the captive of one person alone."[2]

The dangers posed by this obsessiveness, it might seem, are exacerbated when we add the second form of blindness we are now considering: love's tendency to have us idolize our beloveds by turning a blind eye to those personal qualities that might be less than perfectly lovable and that might even be positively *bad*. Love, as we have already seen, involves privileging some aspects of the world—those belonging to or having directly to do with the beloved—more than others, which are removed from the focus of the lover's attention and so fall away to the peripheries. But not all of the beloved's characteristics are equally privileged. Love, it is charged, requires not only a certain blindness toward elements of the world *other* than those connected to the beloved in the right way, but also a certain blindness toward some of the beloved's own characteristics, particularly those that would threaten, challenge, or stand in the way of love. A lover, that is, must be at least somewhat blind to the beloved's faults. She will insist on seeing her beloved in the best possible light, magnifying his virtues and accomplishments and minimizing, if not entirely ignoring, the same weaknesses, faults, and discreditable actions that she criticizes or finds intolerable in others. "Love," as George Bernard Shaw put it, "is a gross exaggeration of the difference between one person and everybody else."[3]

Studies by psychologists lend considerable support to the idea that romantic lovers tend to idealize their partners—to find, as Stendhal wrote, "new proofs of the perfections of the loved one" in "everything that happens." In "When Love Is Blind: Maintaining Idealized Images of One's Spouse," Judith Hall and Shelley Taylor write that available evidence suggests that a very strong positive bias underlies the typical spouse's evaluations of her partner.[4] Although such idealization effects are sometimes assumed to be most pronounced in, if not exclusive to, the early "infatuation" stages of a love relationship, Hall and Taylor, along with other researchers, have found evidence to suggest that these persist throughout the duration of even long-term relationships. Sandra Murray, John Holmes, and Dale Griffin, for instance, write in their 1996 study that "even as these [romantic] relationships progressed, intimates' impressions of their partners were still largely constructions, reflecting the projection of self-images and ideals."[5] Other research provides evidence that nonromantic love may involve blindness of this form as well. Indeed, a recent study by Andreas Bartels and Semir Zeki finds that parts of the brain connected with the formation of negative social judgments about other persons are deactivated in mothers who look at photographs of their own children.[6]

Several distinct levels and forms of falsification can be distinguished. Perhaps the most disconcerting one occurs when love leads a lover to accept claims that are plainly false or to deny facts about the beloved that are plainly true. ("I can't believe that she would do that," the lover insists, even though a room full of witnesses saw her do it.) A somewhat less extreme and presumably far more common form of falsification involves the *indirect* influence of love on the lover's grasp of the facts. Since a lover will be inclined to seek out evidence that supports his positive view of the beloved and be very disinclined to seek out evidence that would challenge or undermine that view, it is likely that over time a lover will end up with a set of beliefs about the beloved that exhibits a selection bias, which fails to be representative of the "objective" set of facts concerning her. Even if all of his beliefs about her are true, he may still have a misleading or inaccurate picture of her nature if the positive facts about her are disproportionately represented in comparison with the negative facts.

Other forms of falsification concern not so much the facts themselves but one's interpretation of them. "To love," writes John Amstrong, "is to interpret another person with charity. It is to believe the best about them which is consistent with the facts."[7] It is clear that believing the best "consistent with the facts" is one thing, and falsifying the facts is something else. Consider the loving mother presented with evidence that her son has committed an unspeakable crime. If the evidence is strong enough, she would have to be very irrational to continue to insist that her son could not possibly have committed the crime. (I do not claim that such cases do not occur; people are, after all, capable of impressive displays of irrationality.) What is far more likely, however, is that she will continue to cling to certain interpretations of the facts; she is likely to conclude, for instance, that he must have had a good reason for doing what he did, that his intentions were admirable, that the people his action harmed deserved what they got, and so forth. Indeed, Hall and Taylor find considerable evidence to support their hypothesis that "idealization is maintained through a pattern of biased causal attributions, in which the spouse's good behaviors are seen as caused by personal qualities, while bad behaviors are attributed to situational factors."[8] The function of these attributions seems to be "to buffer the idealized image of the spouse against contradictory information."[9]

This phenomenon can be observed not only in cases connected to the moral evaluation of behavior, but also in connection with personal qualities or attributes that are evaluated as good or bad in nonmoral ways. Once in love, a person may come to find various neutral or even ordinarily *unattractive* features or habits to be endearing, adorable, or downright beautiful. We might recall the example from Tennov's *Love and Limerence* quoted in chapter 1 of the man who said, "I abhor the sight of toothmarks on a pencil; they disgust me. But not *her* toothmarks. Hers were sacred; her wonderful mouth had been there." Tennov's book offers a number of other examples, including the following:

> Yes I knew he gambled, I knew he sometimes drank too much, and I knew he didn't read a book from one year to the next. I knew and I didn't know. I knew it but I didn't incorporate it into the overall image. I dwelt on his wavy hair, the way he looked at me, the thought of his driving to work in the morning, his charm (that I believed must surely affect everyone he met), the flowers he sent, the consideration he had shown to my sister's children at the picnic last summer, the feeling I had when we were in close physical contact, the way he mixed a martini, his laugh, the hair on the back of his hand. Okay! I know it's crazy, that my list of "positives" sounds silly, but those *are* the things I think of, remember, and yes, want back again![10]

Such lovers are able to maintain their knowledge of the facts, but their love influences, perhaps obscures, their interpretations or evaluations of the facts. The lover need not deny that the beloved chews her pencil or has hair on the back of his hand; she need only be able to find a way of seeing such habits and attributes as charming. In such cases as this—if, at least, the lover's self-description is to be believed—the lover's reinterpretation of the facts has not extended as far as we might have worried it would. One might have thought, for instance, that love would prompt the lover to *deny* that her beloved drinks too much. What has gone on instead, in this case, is that the lover was aware of this shortcoming but decided that it *did not matter*; it was taken not to be a serious problem, nor a revealing indication of the beloved's character. The fact was simply not "incorporate[d] into the overall image."

Of course, the line between the facts and interpretations of the facts is not one that love can be expected always to observe. After all, if the lover has managed, in this and similar cases, to get the individual facts right, the same cannot be said of her overall image of the beloved, which may seem to be quite inaccurate indeed. Love's effect on the lover, then, will not amount merely to a clean and clinical subtraction of certain beliefs—which she is prohibited to have—from her belief set, leaving the remainder of the belief set incomplete but otherwise untouched. Rather, since belief is a holistic matter—the content of one's beliefs depends, in part, on what other beliefs one accepts—this grasp can be expected to be, in certain respects, inaccurate. The elimination or suppression of true beliefs changes the character of one's other beliefs and can lead to the formation of beliefs that are straightforwardly false. For instance, the refusal to acknowledge bad features about the beloved's character or to acknowledge their importance may lead one to form the false belief that one's beloved has an excellent moral character or is morally better than most of the people around her.

It is no wonder, then, that some go so far as to claim that love prohibits the lover from seeing the beloved at all. Indeed, at this moment the reader might well find somewhat more plausibility than was initially apparent in Stendhal's claim that ultimately it is a created substitute image rather than the actual individual that is the true object of love.

There is an obvious threat here to the vision view—indeed, two threats. The first creates difficulties for the basic idea that love is a matter of vision—of opening one's eyes to the beloved and paying her a special degree of attention that allows one to see her as she is and to notice and appreciate things about her that no one else can. This idea might be fully compatible with the kind of blindness discussed in chapter 2, but it does not sit at all comfortably with the notion that love involves blindness *about the beloved*. For if love involves this sort of blindness to any significant extent, then it would seem to be a distorting phenomenon: an emotion that discourages, rather than encourages, the formation of a complete, fair, and accurate picture of one's beloved. The more skeptical we allow ourselves to become regarding the lover's ability to see, interpret, and evaluate the beloved accurately, and the more convinced we become that love ordinarily, if not necessarily, involves, at least to some degree, the substitution of an idealized fantasy for an actual beloved, the more we find ourselves pushed away from the vision view and toward the imagined qualities view. Indeed, one might find oneself wanting to say that what love involves is not *vision* but a constant process of *revision*.

The second threat is to the idea that in loving the beloved, the lover is responding to real, preexisting, and independent values. The idea that love involves a significant form of blindness regarding the beloved seems to imply that the lover is incapable of perceiving the beloved's valuable features clearly, which makes it implausible to claim that her love for the beloved is a response to those features. We seem to find ourselves being pushed toward either the imagined qualities view (which holds that the lover takes himself to be responding to valuable qualities, but that the qualities are imagined rather than real), or the type of antirationalism that holds that love, insofar as it concerns value at all, *creates* a value that it bestows upon the beloved, to which the lover then takes herself to be responding. Rather than seeing and valuing the beloved, what the lover sees and values is, in one sense or another, her own creation.

Epistemic Partiality and the Virtues of Engaged Perception

> "What do you do when a friend writes a book?"
> "Try to give it a favorable review. If you don't like the way his mind works, why is he your friend?"
>
> —John Leonard, *This Pen for Hire*

As is my practice throughout this book, I will defend love against the objections I have been considering—but not completely. My view, again, is that love is best understood, in relation to the various objections, worries, and puzzles that arise in connection with it, as "something in between." I will not argue, then, that love does not involve certain forms of epistemic bias. Nor, for that matter, will I argue that love can *never* lead to unreasonable or even harmful idealization. Indeed, I will acknowledge that love does, by its nature, involve epistemic partiality and that such partiality can on occasion go too far and end up posing an epistemic danger. Moreover, its critics are even correct to point out that love can sometimes lead us to substitute a set of wished-for or longed-for beliefs for reality.

Nonetheless, we must be careful not to conclude too much from these facts or to exaggerate the role that bias and delusion play in love. After all, it has not yet been shown that epistemic partiality is objectionable, even in epistemic terms; the fact that various forms of partiality, including tendencies to ignore or reinterpret facts and traits that initially present us with a negative appearance, can sometimes lead us astray does not show that such partiality is generally, let alone inherently, harmful. We might consider an analogy with the moral virtues: courage, for instance. Courage, if allowed to govern one's behavior in an extreme manner rather than in moderation, can cease to be a virtue and even become a vice by inducing a person to perform reckless or foolhardy acts. But the fact that courage carries this potential for becoming a vice does not stand in the way of our calling it a virtue in ordinary cases in which it is functioning properly or even judging it to be generally good or even good by virtue of its nature.

My view is that the epistemic dangers described in the previous section, although real, have been somewhat exaggerated and do not reflect or express the true nature of love as we ordinarily experience it, let alone love at its best. These dangers tend to be most prominent in cases of extreme passion and obsession—cases that resemble love in some respects but not in others—and are not nearly as apparent in the ordinary (let alone proper) workings of romantic love or friendship. Indeed, the view that love typically stands in the way of our coming to true beliefs about the world is not only false but, in an important sense, the opposite of the truth. For part of what love offers is a way of seeing the world that makes possible insights and understandings that cannot be achieved through less involved, more dispassionate modes of engagement. Rather than standing in opposition to proper standards of epistemic rationality, then, love offers its own epistemic approach, one that is apt to be mischaracterized as epistemically faulty precisely because it poses a genuine challenge to the allegedly objective standards that are sometimes, wrongly, assumed to represent epistemic rationality itself.

What we need to determine, then, is what sort of role epistemic partiality *does* play in love. It will be useful to start by looking at two recent attempts by analytic philosophers to defend the idea that love for persons makes demands on the lover that frequently and perhaps necessarily conflict with the demands of epistemic responsibility. In her article "Epistemic Partiality in Friendship," Sarah Stroud has defended the claim that friendship demands a kind of epistemic partiality that "is contrary to the standards of epistemic responsibility and justification held up by mainstream epistemological theories," thus requiring us to ask, "What if friendship goes against not just our moral ideals, but our epistemic ideals?"[11] Similarly, Simon Keller has argued that "the fact that a person is someone's friend can sometimes explain why she is inclined to believe certain sorts of falsehoods," and that "sometimes, the norms of friendship clash with epistemic norms."[12]

I will return to Stroud's article in the following section; for the moment I will concentrate on the argument as developed by Keller. In elaborating his position, Keller offers the following story:

> Rebecca is scheduled to give a poetry reading at a café. She is ner-
> vous about reading her poetry in public, but has decided to do it
> on this occasion because she knows that a certain literary agent
> will be present and she hopes that her work might catch his atten-
> tion. She lets her good friend Eric know that she will be giving the
> reading, and asks whether he would mind coming along to be in
> the audience.
>
> Eric, as it happens, is a regular visitor to the café, and has over
> time accumulated strong evidence for his belief that poetry read
> there is almost always mediocre, and that it is very unlikely that
> anything read there would make any literary agent take notice. He
> had not known that Rebecca fancies herself a poet, and has no fa-
> miliarity with her work. But he is her friend, and he makes sure that
> he is there for the reading[13]

According to Keller, Eric's friendship with Rebecca requires two things
of him that are epistemically unreasonable. First, *prior* to hearing the
poetry read, his friendship requires him to refrain from forming certain
beliefs for which he possesses strong evidence—in particular, the belief
that Rebecca's poetry will probably not be very good. "If some stranger
were about to give the reading, then Eric would believe that the poetry
he is about to hear will probably be pretty awful, not of the type that is
likely to impress a literary agent—and he would have good evidence for
his belief." As Rebecca's friend, though, "he ought not, before she takes
the stage, have those beliefs about her."[14]

Second, Eric's friendship with Rebecca requires him to approach the
poetry *as it is read* with a different attitude from what he would otherwise manifest.

> If it were a stranger giving the reading, and if Eric were setting out
> to make an accurate judgment about the poetry's quality . . . then
> he would listen attentively and with an open mind, and then form
> critical and dispassionate judgments, informed by such things as
> a hardheaded comparison of this work with others and a set of
> realistic expectations about the average literary agent's psychol-
> ogy. . . . [But] in listening as a friend, he will allow the poetry to
> strike him in the best possible light: he will actively seek out its
> strengths, and play down its weaknesses; he will be disposed to in-
> terpret it in ways that make it look like a stronger piece of work.

In the process of hearing the poetry read, Keller concludes, Eric "should
put himself into a situation under which it is more likely that he will form
certain beliefs, but his reason for putting himself into that situation is not
one that bears upon the likelihood that those beliefs are true."[15]

It is worth noting that most of Keller's claims concern the manner in which Eric ought to form his beliefs, rather than the content of those beliefs. Admittedly, Keller does claim that *before* hearing Rebecca read, Eric ought, as her friend, to believe that her poetry will be good.[16] It is important to acknowledge, though, that Keller refrains from making the much stronger claim that Eric must think Rebecca a good poet *regardless of all evidence* and thus must keep on thinking her a good poet even *after* hearing her read, *regardless* of what the poetry is like. Indeed, he makes it explicit at one point that this is *not* what is required by friendship.[17] The claim that friendship *does* require this would be endorsed, presumably, by someone who believed that love involves the most extreme form of idealization: someone who believed, that is, that since love leads the lover to love an idealized image of the beloved rather than the actual beloved, facts about the actual beloved are simply irrelevant to the lover's perceptions.[18] But merely to state the view in these terms, and to connect it with this sort of example, is to see how implausible it is. If Rebecca reads her poetry, and it turns out to be plainly and obviously bad (imagine that she simply repeats the phrase "I am the Walrus" in a monotone for five minutes), the most heroic act of will will not permit Eric to believe it is good. Idealization to an extent is a psychological possible and, indeed, actual phenomenon; *complete* idealization, where one's beliefs are controlled by one's desires, expectations, and preexisting beliefs, and not at all by the way the world is, is impossible, except perhaps for a human being whose perceptual faculties are simply not functioning. For an ordinary human being, perceptions of reality will inevitably break in at some point and so will constantly threaten to disrupt whatever idealized visions one might be trying to maintain.

What of Keller's claim that prior to hearing her read, Eric must believe Rebecca's poetry will be good? I must confess that I do not, for the most part, share Keller's intuition on this matter. Perhaps at least this much is required: he must believe there is a reasonable *possibility* that it will turn out that she is a good poet. (If he were convinced that there was no such possibility, then he surely ought not to have come in the first place.) Perhaps we can go a bit further and say that Eric must not expect Rebecca's poetry to be bad—doing so would be incompatible with the generous, open-minded, and receptive attention that, as her friend, he ought to be prepared to provide. (Though even this is not clear. Suppose I have a friend who I know is bad at all things artistic—she has consistently proven herself to be so, though she cannot see that this is the case. Am I not justified, after a certain point, in expecting her next artistic endeavor to be inept, and is thinking so really incompatible with my being her friend?)[19] But now we are speaking again in terms of the manner in which he ought to hear her poetry—that is, the manner in which he ought to form his beliefs about whether or not it is good—rather than the question of what he ought to believe about it before being exposed to it. And this question, I think, is the heart of the issue. Indeed, it seems rather unclear why, prior to his being exposed to it, Eric ought to be expected to have any sort of belief about the quality of Rebecca's poetry.[20] Until he has actually heard the poetry, that is, there seems to be nothing wrong with Eric's simply not yet having made up his mind.

Of course, saying that is compatible with saying that he ought to be prepared to listen and respond to her poetry in a certain manner. Here I find Keller's claims to be on the whole fairly plausible. But I think we ought to resist some of the conclusions he draws from them. It seems quite plausible to claim that Eric is required to pay to Rebecca's work a special degree of attention and give it a special degree of sympathy—to give it not only a fair hearing but a hearing that is in a sense more than merely fair. Indeed, if loving is largely a matter of opening one's eyes (and ears) to the beloved, then this is precisely what we should expect. Thus, the claim that Eric's friendship requires him to put himself in a state that renders him somewhat more likely than he would otherwise be to enjoy the poetry and judge it to be good seems quite plausible.

The question, though, is why we should assume, as Keller assumes, that this constitutes an epistemic *fault*. To draw this conclusion is to assume that Eric's *default* state—the state in which he ordinarily approaches poetry or other works of literature or art, in situations in which no personal relationships are at stake—is ideal for making true evaluative judgments. And one might wonder at this point why we should assume this to be so. At any rate, if I think about my own default state, I find it quite implausible to think that this state is ideal for such a purpose. Like a lot of people, I expect, I am more or less constantly inundated with various demands on my attention, and although I would like to think that I somehow manage to respond to all of these demands in a fair manner and according to their merits, my considered judgment is that this is, unfortunately enough, quite unlikely to be true. Poetry, like any art, is difficult—difficult not only to produce but to appreciate. Particularly where the work is unfamiliar, I will be quite unlikely to appreciate its value without making a significant and somewhat strenuous effort to pay attention, to be open-minded and at least somewhat charitable in my responses, and *really to hear* what is there to be appreciated. What is necessary for appreciating most poetry is precisely *not* a state of detachment but a state of engagement. Being open and engaged in the relevant sense is a matter of not being skeptical but of approaching the work as if one already believed that there is something of value to be obtained—or, at the very least, as if one already believes it likely that this is so.

Indeed, many poets and critics have emphasized the idea that the ideal listener or reader must be actively involved and engaged with a poem. Edward Hirsch writes that poetry can accomplish its goals only "with the reader's imaginative collaboration and even complicity," adding that "a common sensation of reading [is] the eerie feeling that we are composing what we are responding to."[21] Theodore Roethke's instructions to the reader of his "Praise to the End" sequence are in a similar vein. "Believe," he writes. "You will have no trouble if you approach these poems as a child would, naïvely, with your whole being awake, your faculties loose and alert."[22] What is immediately obvious is that the psychological activity being called for here is anything but an objective, detached process of evaluation and critical assessment. Rather, the reader must exhibit "imaginative collaboration and even complicity" with the poet; he must "believe" in the poem from the outset and approach it "naïvely"; doing so, far from impeding one's faculties of appreciation, actually encourages them to be "loose and alert."

In this light it seems somewhat misguided to suggest that an ideal evaluator of Rebecca's work would aim at "critical and dispassionate judgments" formulated from a detached point of view, or that to "allow the poetry to strike him in the best possible light" and to "actively seek out its strengths" would be to commit epistemic errors. In fact, it is quite doubtful that a person who did not allow a poem to strike her in the best possible light, or attempt to actively seek out its strengths, would be able to find anything of value in the poem she is reading or hearing. What Keller identifies as epistemic *vices,* in other words, may in fact constitute epistemic *virtues,* at least in the context we are presently concerned with. The sort of interested, involved, predisposed-to-find-something-of-value stance Eric's friendship demands he take toward Rebecca's work is precisely the sort of stance we should take in order to give *any* work a reasonable hearing. Such a stance does not guarantee that we will end up liking the work—since we are still both guided and limited by what is there, our efforts at active involvement may after all come to naught—but it does at least open the real possibility of our finding something of value.

Of course, this might seem just a quibble about the particular example Keller has chosen. Poetry may indeed require a certain active and sympathetic participation on the part of the reader (which may help account for its current cultural status or its lack thereof), but some might wonder whether this must serve as evidence of a *general* worry for Keller's account. In fact, the point is easily extended to other contexts. Consider, for instance, my attitude toward my friends' philosophy papers. Ideally I would not only read every philosophical paper in every journal and even every draft paper, but I would read each with an exceptionally high degree of attention and open-mindedness, doing my best—no matter how far from my own views the author's standpoint or presuppositions might be—to give the argument a fair hearing, to allow myself to be moved by whatever legitimate force it possesses, and to appreciate any potential insights contained therein. But of course this is impossible; there are too many papers for me to read them all, let alone to read them all with this ideal degree of attention. So I am forced to be selective, and in being selective I tend to give preference to my friends' papers, not only by taking the time to read them but also by attempting, as far as I can, to read them with the attitudes described earlier. It would be implausible to complain that in reading my friends' philosophical work in this way I am *less* likely to form an accurate impression of it. (Admittedly, if a friend's work turns out to be *very* bad, it might be difficult for me to admit this, but even here the genuine difficulty will lie in my admitting it to *him*, more than in admitting it to myself.) The problem, then, is not that the nature of friendship requires me to act in a less than epistemically ideal manner toward my friends' papers, but that the limitations of the world permit me to act in an ideal manner *only* with respect to a small set of papers, including those of my friends.

I think something like this will be true with respect to many sorts of activity—though not with respect to all. Where a standard of success and the actions that are judged by that standard are public and relatively objective in the sense of being broadly agreed upon and decidable on the basis of observation, epistemic partiality of this sort will be considerably less pronounced. If one's friend is a lousy baseball player and strikes out or drops the ball every time, it would take a heroic effort to maintain that he is the best player on the field, in a way that everyone else in the stands (not to mention the team's manager) is simply unable to appreciate. The difference between a good baseball player and a lousy one is more or less obvious to everyone; one need not make a special effort to perceive this distinction. But with respect to activities and pursuits where there can be meaningful disagreement regarding what counts as an admirable performance, and where an evaluator who pays too little attention might miss what is genuinely admirable, impressive, or innovative about a given performance, epistemic partiality would seem to demand, with respect to our loved ones, precisely the type of focused, generous attention that an ideal evaluator would lavish on everyone.

In Keller's own words, his example is supposed to make the point that "good friendship can require that you make a special effort—effort that you need not make with regard to just anyone—to see value in your friends' projects before you decide (and say) that you think them misguided."[23] I agree with this completely, but see no reason why *any* reasonable epistemic standard would condemn such a special effort. After all, to call the effort "special" and to assert that one "need not make" it with respect to others is not to impugn it as deficient in any way, nor even to assert that one *ought* not or *may* not make such an effort in the case of others. (What prevents us from making such an effort in every case is not, presumably, any sort of epistemic or moral consideration, but simply pragmatic limitations on our abilities and energies.) The fact that we are in general more likely to reach certain conclusions with respect to our friends' efforts than with those of strangers, then, is not a necessary indicator of epistemic trouble, at least not in the sense that Keller intends. Although it is, in one sense, evidence of a certain epistemic imperfection—a perfect epistemic agent would approach *every* situation with the kind of open-minded, full, and generous attention that we, on the whole, reserve for our friends—it does not follow from this that such instances of special attention are to be condemned in epistemic terms.

Epistemic Partiality and Moral Character

Perhaps, though, this sort of partiality would strike us as more objectionable if what is at issue were not a friend's artistic merit or accomplishment but something like her moral character, or the moral nature of her actions. After all, a display of favoritism with respect to a friend's poetry or her other artistic or professional endeavors might seem a minor matter; whatever false beliefs are arrived at on the basis of our bias will most likely not lead to any serious consequences or have regrettable repercussions. But to ally oneself with a morally bad person, to call a wrong action right, to help justify serious wrongdoings by another, to forgive (or, worse, to praise) what is unforgivable—these might well strike us, at least in the right set of circumstances, as very major errors indeed.

Sarah Stroud's argument is similar to Keller's in that it, too, is largely motivated by the assumption that "mainstream epistemological theories" will privilege objectivity and detachment. But whereas Keller's examples tend to concern judgments of a friend's artistic or professional merit, Stroud's tend to focus on judgments of our friends' characters. The good friend, Stroud writes, "fails to make inferences and to draw conclusions that would come naturally to a disinterested observer. Instead, she gives greater credence to [more sympathetic] construals of her friend's conduct and character."[24]

This is quite right, and perhaps the worry in this context is more pressing than that which arises in connection with judgments about the quality of a friend's verse. Still, in light of the discussion of the previous section, I hope that the reader will be motivated to wonder why we are supposed automatically to think that it is the disinterested observer's practice, rather than that of the friend, that ought to be taken as ideal here. We might wonder, that is, whether there might be reason here, as there is in the poetry case, to think that at least some of the time the friend who approaches with an open mind and involves herself in the situation will in fact be more likely than the detached, dispassionate stranger to reach a correct, accurate understanding and evaluation of an agent's behavior.

After all, the effects of friendship on the practices of moral evaluation, as described by Stroud, bear considerable resemblance to those that seem to affect how one judges a friend's poetry or her performance in some other nonmoral area.

> We tend to devote more energy to defeating or minimizing the impact of unfavorable data [when a friend's behavior is in question] than we otherwise would. To start with, we are more liable to scrutinize and to question the evidence being presented than we otherwise would be; we spend more time and energy doing this than we otherwise would. . . . Furthermore, we will go to greater lengths in the case of a friend to construct and to entertain alternative and less damning interpretations of the reported conduct than we would for a nonfriend. . . . [And] we are also likely to give such alternative constructions greater credence than we would for a nonfriend. And at the end of the day we are simply less likely to conclude that our friend acted disreputably, or that he is a bad person, than we would be in the case of a nonfriend.[25]

As in the nonmoral case, two main trends seem to be involved: first, the friend will work harder than she ordinarily would, putting more energy into the effort to find evidence for a favorable interpretation; second, the friend will be more likely than she would be otherwise to interpret whatever evidence she does find in a favorable way.

It is important here to distinguish between the claim that there is a *morally* problematic issue and Stroud's claim that friendship is *epistemically* problematic. The claim that there is a moral issue might seem to stand on firmer ground, given the existence of apparent inequalities of treatment. But whether the alleged issue is moral or epistemic, it is important not to assume that if there *is* an issue of inequality, we must conclude from this that the demands of love are at fault. After all, it is presumably the people who are *not* on the receiving end of the generous, sympathetic attention mandated by love who have the strongest title to complain. They are the ones getting the short end of the stick, so to speak. And the solution to the inequality—if there is any sort of general solution to be had—might not be to attempt to expunge love's way of seeing from whatever realm we are speaking of, but rather to transform the realm in question so that *everyone* can be seen in this way. Of course, in certain contexts—the judicial system, for instance—it is difficult if not impossible to imagine how this might be brought about. Still, it is important to see that the fact that some overall system is unfair, insofar as it involves unequal treatment, combined with the fact that some of the unequal treatment is motivated by love, does not automatically entail that it is love that is at fault. It might well be, rather, that it is our practices with respect to evaluating and judging strangers that are remiss.

Indeed, as I did in the nonmoral case, I suggest once again that the willingness to work harder to find favorable evidence with respect to one's friends' *moral* behavior, and the generosity manifested in the willingness to interpret available evidence in a positive rather than a negative way, can be viewed as not only justifiable but also admirable practices—practices that we ordinarily refrain from not because they are inherently flawed or less likely to get at the truth (once again, there is considerable reason for thinking them *more* likely to do so), but simply because they are too costly for us to incorporate them into universal policies. As Robert Wright points out, a parent who sees someone else's child misbehave is likely to think "What a brat!"; the same behavior from her own child would be more likely to provoke a thought such as "That's what happens when she skips her nap." But the latter is frequently the more accurate explanation, leading Wright to observe that love "at its best brings a truer apprehension of the other, an empathetic understanding that converges on the moral truth of respect, even reverence, for the other."[26]

Admittedly, there are cases in which such admirable epistemic practices lead us astray, and perhaps this is easier to see in moral cases than in other ones. In moral cases, after all, one person's interests and claims are frequently pitted against another's; the inevitable consequence of being especially epistemically generous to my friend, then, might be that I turn out in a very real sense to be especially ungenerous to those who have been harmed by my friend's behavior and who might have very real claims against him. (Think again of Stroud's observation that the friend will be more critical of the evidence against her friend—and, by extension, of those who present this evidence—than she ordinarily would.) Still, not all cases are of this sort, and not all of those that are involve epistemic wrongdoing on the friend's part. Those in which the friend's efforts are focused not on the prosecution of the prosecutors but on the search for a sympathetic interpretation of her friend's apparently disreputable behavior will, for the most part, avoid this sort of worry.

Moreover, just as in a court of law, it is sometimes important in private life that people be willing to serve as advocates for the accused. Some accusations, after all, are overblown, misleading, or downright false, and some prosecutors therefore *ought* to be prosecuted—or, at the very least, the evidence presented ought to be scrutinized and verified before simply being accepted. Although there would certainly be something wrong with a closed-minded insistence, regardless of the evidence, that one's friend's accusers *must* be misrepresenting the case against him, in many cases one serves an important and useful function by being prepared to advocate for one's friend, to investigate the adequacy of the evidence that is against him, and to communicate to others any inadequacies one finds. To the extent that the motivation for a thorough investigation is provided by one's friendship, friendship may thus turn out to encourage, rather than impede, good epistemic practice.

Still, there is always the risk that friendship will make one *too* inclined to excuse, to forgive, to exonerate, and this perhaps is the deepest danger of the approach to moral evaluation that recommends personal involvement and sympathetic engagement—the determination to understand the reasons of those whose behavior initially strikes us as objectionable, to see the world as they see it and thus come to see their actions as intelligible—as opposed to the approach that recommends the occupation of a detached, impersonal, and objective perspective. If the latter perspective risks encouraging us to be too harsh, to give up the search for sympathetic understanding too early, the former approach risks encouraging us to forgive too easily, perhaps even turning us into dupes. "The fact is that most people act very badly from time to time, and have some more or less serious character flaws," Stroud writes. "So from an objective point of view your friends are very likely to possess these features as well."[27]

This is perhaps true; but it is too quick, I think, to conclude that friendship "involves, if not a blind spot, at least less than perfect vision where your friends' sins and flaws are concerned"—as if the only epistemic error possible here were that of being too generous to people, and *failing to be generous enough* was never an issue.[28] For as before, we must keep in mind the very common human tendency to err in the *other* direction: in Wright's terms, to stop searching for an explanation that would make bothersome behavior (at least somewhat) intelligible and instead to be satisfied with judgments like "What a brat!" (Or, when dealing with the bad behavior of adults, judgments such as "He's just a bad person.") It may be true that most people act at least somewhat badly once in a while. Perhaps Stroud is even correct to say that most people act "*very* badly from time to time." And it may well be that our friend-favoring epistemological bias will sometimes prevent us from seeing these occasional bad actions for what they really are. But it might also be true that most people act quite well, and not at all badly, a good deal of the time, and that even many of their criticizable actions may result from what are fundamentally good intentions, the deployment of faulty judgment in the unsuccessful pursuit of laudable goals. Our grasp of this fact may well be obscured, when the agents in question are strangers, by various sorts of biases and blindnesses toward *them*—most significantly, perhaps, our habitual lack of interest in the large majority of human beings we encounter. The tendency to assume the best of a person may indeed lead us astray in those occasional cases when a person is in fact acting badly; but the tendency *not* to assume the best, to abandon too quickly the effort of seeking an explanation that can rationalize someone's behavior and render it intelligible and even admirable, can also act as an impediment to our efforts to form a truer picture of the world. It is very easy, when thinking about the actions of strangers of whose conduct we disapprove, to conclude that they had no reason whatsoever for their behavior and did what they did simply because they were selfish, insensitive, cruel, or in some other way bad, and that there is nothing more to be said of the matter. It is much more difficult to reach such a conclusion with respect to a person one knows well or whose perspective on life one manages to imaginatively occupy. But explanations like "He is just a bad person," although they do sometimes capture part of the moral truth of a situation, very rarely succeed in capturing all of it.

Attachment, Moral Knowledge, and Trust

Stroud's argument, then, does not justify the conclusion that the belief-forming practices and biases that tend to characterize friendship "do not seem to be ones we could endorse from a purely epistemic point of view. Rather than being truth conducive, they seem to lead [the friend] into a distorted conception of reality."[29] It is not clear that the kind of generous, understanding, and forgiving view that friendship asks us to take of people is on the whole less likely to reveal the truth than is the detached, dispassionate view we tend to take of those we do not know or like. Most people, after all, believe they have reasons for acting as they do at least most of the time; being emotionally intimate with someone and knowing her well may put us in a much better position to appreciate those reasons.

Admittedly, in cases where our friend is self-deceived, there is a chance that we too will be taken in by her deception. But even here we ought to remember that this is not always the case; frequently, in fact, I will be in a better position to perceive the truth of the situation than either my friend (who is, after all, self-deceived) or a dispassionate stranger (who will lack both the necessary knowledge and the motivation to understand the situation). And in more ordinary situations—those in which an agent's reasons for acting are clear to herself but not necessarily to others—friends will surely be better placed to understand than will strangers. What Stroud calls a "blind spot" may in many cases be better characterized as the refusal, in contexts involving our friends, to resort to or rest satisfied with the sort of easy, dismissive, and ultimately cynical explanations we tend to deploy against individuals whose behavior we cannot be bothered to try genuinely to understand.

This is not to deny that Stroud is correct in thinking that the epistemic approach of the detached objective observer will sometimes be most likely to lead to a true understanding of the situation. It is only to say that there is an equally strong case that goes in the other direction, reminding us that the detached approach is sometimes precisely the wrong approach to take if one wants to achieve genuine moral understanding. There are strong reasons, that is, for thinking that when trying to understand and evaluate human affairs, the sort of epistemic standpoint that is called for is frequently not one of detachment but one of engagement. As Margaret Little writes:

> From the valorized position of dispassionate detachment we are often actually less likely to pick up on what is morally salient. Emotional distance does not always clarify; disengagement is not always the most revealing stance. To see clearly what is before us, we need to cultivate certain desires, such as the desire to see justice done, and the desire to see humans flourish; but we must also, more particularly, work at developing our capacities for loving and caring about people.[30]

If the lover is blind to certain explanations and interpretations—those that tend to see the beloved in unflattering or negative terms or that perhaps avoid seeing her as an agent or subject—the detached observer is blind to other, more sympathetic explanations and interpretations. In many cases the detached observer's blind spot will, at the end of the day, be more epistemically disabling—particularly if, as Little and other neo-Aristotelians have argued, correct perception of the world's evaluative properties requires close attention, emotional engagement, and the activation of an agent's affective responses. "If we were to succeed in transcending our affect and occupying a dispassionate epistemic stance," Little writes, "then we would be blind to some of the most important truths there are, namely moral truths."[31]

There are also cases in which occupying an impersonal, dispassionate standpoint simply is not an option. A particularly important case here involves moral testimony and occurs when one is called on to morally evaluate behavior one did not witness. Suppose, for instance, that Agnes is told by a third party that her friend Brad was unacceptably rude to Phil. Brad's account of the event is that he was only responding to some comments Phil made —comments that Brad interpreted as rude and insulting. Had she been present and witnessed the exchange, Agnes would have been able to judge for herself whether Phil's comments were indeed rude and whether Brad's response was reasonable and justified. But Agnes was not present, and so she had to rely on the testimony of those who were—including, of course, the testimony of Brad himself.[32]

In such cases there is no possibility of obtaining a complete and neutral account of what happened. Even a precise word-for-word transcript of the verbal exchange between Brad and Phil (not that any such thing would ordinarily be available) would be insufficient, for when making judgments about rudeness, clues such as body language, tone of voice, and even the details of timing are also essential. In the end, Agnes may well find herself in the position of having to decide between conflicting accounts, one of which finds Phil to have behaved rudely and so puts the major portion of responsibility on him, and the other of which exonerates Phil and so finds Brad guilty of unjustifiable rudeness.

How is an agent like Agnes to make such a choice? If, as we are supposing, she is friends with Brad, her friendship may help her make this decision by suggesting that she has reason to take the side of her friend.[33] Love's epistemic critics might see this simply as the expression of a brute, arbitrary attachment; having committed herself to Brad, Agnes is now determined to stand by him, come what may. But there is another way to see such commitments that makes them considerably more rational. If her knowledge of Brad's character and her experiences with him have given Agnes evidence that Brad is, in fact, a reliable witness and moral evaluator, she will then have reason to trust his account of a disputed situation to a greater degree than she trusts the accounts of those for whom she has no such evidence. To the extent that Agnes's friendship-love for Brad is a response to certain good features she perceives and values in him—in this case, features having to do with moral character and trustworthiness—she will have reason to place substantially more credence in his judgments than in those of strangers, and there need be nothing arbitrary about this.

It is worth noting, at least in passing, that the same can be true in contexts other than the moral. I said earlier that although I did not share Keller's intuition that Eric's friendship with Rebecca required him to believe her poetry to be good in advance of his hearing or reading it, I do acknowledge that Eric might have *some* prior reason to expect it to be good. After all, *Rebecca* must think it is good—good enough to read in public, at any rate—and if part of what he values in Rebecca is her intelligence and good judgment, then Eric will tend to think that her judgment here is at least likely to be correct. (Moreover, it is worth considering the possibility that this sort of reason might, in the right circumstances, be enough to override Eric's *own* judgments; if he admits to knowing little about poetry but thinks that Rebecca knows a great deal about it, then he might continue to believe that her poetry is good even *after* hearing and failing to appreciate it.)

Consideration of this sort of case reinforces the point that being biased in favor of one's friends—where this includes making a special effort of imagination to see the world the way they see it, being particularly open to the accounts and interpretations they provide, and being willing to accept their testimony over the testimony of others—can be a perfectly legitimate and justifiable approach to belief formation, even when judged in purely epistemic terms. Of course, we must yet again admit that this is true only under the right conditions; it is perfectly possible to make friends with and thus put one's trust in the wrong people or to be misled by the "right" people in certain cases. There is no denying that, for all I have said in favor of the epistemic virtues of attachment, agents will sometimes be better off stepping away from or resisting those attachments and attempting to see the situation as a dispassionate, impartial observer would.

What conclusion should we draw from this? Keller's discussion emphasizes the conflicts between various sorts of reasons and in particular the conflicts between reasons arising from our friendships and those connected with good epistemic practice; he writes that "there can be reason not to be a good friend," that "it is desirable that we sometimes assess our commitments to friends in light of other values," and that "the idea that we allow friendships to lead us wherever they may, that friendship is something that we embrace without hesitation, is a philosophical fantasy."[34] I agree with every claim that Keller makes here, including the claim that reasons of friendship or love can *sometimes* conflict with good epistemic practice, and that there is therefore no guarantee that all of our reasons will always point us in one unitary direction. I am not convinced, though, that we should follow Keller in focusing on possible conflicts (which he discusses at length and in detail) while ignoring the ways in which friendship and other love attachments can lead us *toward* the truth. Rather than posing a threat to epistemic standards per se—as if there were only one set of epistemic standards that applied to every situation and could be universally endorsed—love suggests a certain kind of epistemic practice, one centered on close attention, empathy, and generosity of vision, one that tends to conflict with other sorts of epistemic practice, particularly those that take neutrality and detachment as their presiding virtues.

Unlike Keller, who as we have seen wants to emphasize the diversity of values, Stroud is more inclined to think that all of an agent's reasons should point her in one unitary direction, and so she urges us to take seriously the idea that we might modify our epistemic standards so as to incorporate love's demands, at least to an extent. But here I side with Keller, to a degree. Like him, I do not see any reason for assuming in advance that all our reasons must form a unified set. The world is complex and various, and we should expect our reasons to reflect this. We should expect, too, that we may sometimes have to choose one reason or value at the expense of another, without the comforting implication that one of the options must be illegitimate or illusory. This is true even in the case we have been considering, the intersection of epistemic demands and those of love.

But while I want to allow for conflict, I also suggest that Keller may overestimate the amount of *actual* conflict that we will find here, while ignoring the ways in which the demands of love and those of good epistemic practice may coincide and reinforce each other. As I have suggested, the demands of love embody a kind of epistemic practice that will frequently take us closer to rather than further from the truth and so can be commended even in purely epistemic terms. There is, then, little need to amend our epistemic standards, which take truth as the goal, by adding to the goal of truth seeking the additional goal of being good friends or lovers. Being a good friend or lover is already a way of being a good truth seeker—at least in many cases.

Seeing the Beloved as Beautiful

At the beginning of this chapter I mentioned two possible objections to the vision view, based in epistemic phenomena associated with personal relationships. The first, which has concerned me for most of this chapter, was rooted in the claim that love distorts our view of the beloved and so leads us away from a true and accurate apprehension of the world into delusion and self-deception. I have argued that while this can and does happen in individual cases, it does not represent the general trend of love. Indeed, there is a strong sense in which love is epistemically praiseworthy, for it provides a kind of vision of and insight into reality that it is difficult to imagine achieving in any other way.

The second objection, which is related to the first, is more particularly focused on the question of the beloved's value. Like the first objection, it suggests that love may lead us to hold false beliefs about the beloved: here, that the beloved bears a kind of objective value that obtains independently of one's loving him, and that one's love is a type of rational or reasonable response to this value. This objection does not suggest (as the first objection might well do) that the lover's delusion is explained by the fact that the beloved is not as valuable as she takes him to be. Rather, the suggestion here is that the beloved is not valuable *in the way that* she takes him to be. He might, in fact, be very valuable, but the value he bears is subjective—it is the causal consequence, the product, of her love for him—and love encourages her to think of this value as objective, as if it would obtain regardless of her feelings.

The second objection thus supports the view preferred by such antirationalists as Harry Frankfurt, who, as we have already noted, claims that "it is not because I have noticed their value that I love my children as I do. It is really the other way around. . . . It is as a *consequence* of my love for them that they have acquired, in my eyes, a value that otherwise they would quite certainly not possess."

It is easy enough to bring out the deep tension between this view of love and our commonsense view, for it simply does not feel as if this sort of value bestowal is what is going on when one loves someone. Most parents feel that in loving their children, they recognize how wonderful their children are and do not somehow *make* them wonderful by loving them.[35] Few parents think, after all, that their children would *stop* being wonderful if they stopped being loved. (Suppose the parents are killed in a tragic accident; do the children cease to be valuable?) At the very least, the antirationalist account runs counter to the phenomenology of love; if it is correct, then that phenomenology is deeply misleading, and what we think about love, on the level of common sense and daily experience, is profoundly wrong.

The discussion of this chapter has, I hope, undermined at least one reason for thinking that our common thinking about love is wrong in this way. If we viewed epistemic partiality as a matter of holding certain beliefs about the value of the beloved *regardless of* and *in isolation from* all available evidence—a matter, that is, of simply deciding that the beloved is valuable, and then treating him as such regardless of one's reasons for doing so, and in particular regardless of any particular fact about him— then we would have good reason to say that what bears the relevant value, and indeed what is loved, is not the beloved but a projection, and this would be reason for thinking that the causal story must run in the direction that the antirationalist suggests.

But epistemic partiality, as I have been developing it, is not to be understood in this way. It is not a matter of creating values ex nihilo and projecting them onto the beloved. It is, rather, a matter of looking for value. What distinguishes the attention demanded by love from the ordinary sort of attention we give most human beings is not that the lover's attention gives rise to a preestablished conclusion about value in a way that essentially renders the beloved irrelevant (in that case he could not even be said genuinely to *see* the beloved, and the so-called attention would really be no attention at all), but rather that the lover is especially determined to *find* value in the beloved and to appreciate the values that are there (while also being inclined to judge any flaws or other negative elements found there to be nonessential or relatively unimportant). It is this sort of determination that should be understood as constituting the lover's commitment to seeing the beloved in a positive and generous light.

It is important to see that although love does involve a certain blindness toward the beloved's faults, it is not necessary that one be blind to *all* of his faults or that one see him as possessing *only* virtues. In Keller's case of Rebecca and Eric, it does not seem that Eric must necessarily admire Rebecca's poetry or give it a positive evaluation in order to continue being her friend. Love, though it involves a tendency to see one's beloved in the best possible light, does not demand that one completely divorce oneself from reality. Indeed, it is sometimes the place of one's friends to be aware of one's shortcomings and perhaps to encourage one to try to alter or overcome them[36]

Still, it is almost certain that the following is true: if Eric and Rebecca are to have a decent friendship, there had better be *something* about her he admires or approves of. In fact, we might be tempted to go further and hold not only that Eric had better find something of value in Rebecca, but that he had better judge that Rebecca's positive, admirable qualities outnumber or outweigh her negative, regrettable ones if they are going to be and remain friends.

It is difficult to know precisely what to think here. On the one hand, we might think that to be a friend is, in part, to be willing to forgive one for his shortcomings: the fact that a person is imperfect simply does not matter very much when that person is one's friend. On the other hand, this way of putting the point might seem to get things slightly wrong, for even this willingness to forgive seems to be rooted in the recognition that the friend has some sort of *other* virtue in respect of which the deficiencies in question pale in significance. It is still not clear, that is, that true friendship makes *all* personal faults irrelevant; a better description of the situation might be that true friendship involves an attachment to a person, in light of his good qualities, that renders irrelevant, or at least less relevant, what would otherwise constitute problematic shortcomings.

At any rate, we can certainly say that in the ordinary case, people do find their friends attractive and admirable in at least some significant respects. Perhaps a necessary part of truly being in love is seeing the love object as so beautiful, so desirable, so wonderful, that one can hardly imagine anyone *not* loving her—to think that, in the words of lyricist Phil Spector, "To know him is to love him" or, as the Beatles put it in "And I Love Her": "And if you saw my love / You'd love her too."

But this thought seems to go too far; no matter how consumed one is by the intensity of an all-encompassing passion for another, one never expects that everyone else will share that passion—or, for that matter, believes that everyone else *should*.

Perhaps the implicit thought in "And I Love Her" is better understood as something like this: if you saw my love *the way I see her*, you'd love her too. That this seems to me not only very likely correct but correct in a significant way should not be surprising, given that my purpose in this book is to defend the contention that loving is, in large part, a way of seeing. I do not want to say—not quite—that to see someone in a certain way is just to love her. There is more involved in love: the commitments of the will that loving leads to, for instance. But the seeing is primary; the commitments follow from it insofar as, given our seeing the world in a certain light, we find it natural, pleasurable, and fitting to respond in certain ways, and perhaps we cannot keep ourselves from doing so. Love is largely a way of seeing, one that guides both our intellectual understanding of the world and our practical responses to its situations and demands.

When I say that love is largely a way of seeing, I mean *seeing* in an intellectual sense; but I also mean it in a literal one, for I think that loving someone literally alters the way I see her—the way, that is, her physical appearance is presented to me. Here I take myself to agree with Alexander Nehamas, who writes: "It is impossible for us to find our friends ugly: we are always able to find something in them attractive—their eyes, their smile, the way they carry themselves."[37] It is for this reason that love, particularly romantic love but also love for friends, is closely related to beauty, why the two seem so frequently to be inextricably intertwined.

The key to understanding the relation between love and beauty is to see that the influence goes both ways: if Alighieri's finding Beatrice beautiful encourages him to love her (without taking him all the way to love on its own, since for genuine love other types of appreciation must be involved too), it is also true that his loving her encourages him to find her beautiful. Nehamas expands on his suggestion that we cannot find our friends ugly with an example drawn from cinema, David Lynch's 1980 film *The Elephant Man*:

> The film tells the story of John Merrick, a nineteenth-century Englishman horribly disfigured by neurofibromatosis, and Frederick Treves, the physician who gives him asylum in his hospital. Treves, whose original interest may have been only in the disease, gradually realizes that Merrick's grotesque face is not a sign of a psychological wasteland but belongs to an intelligent, kind, and sensitive man. And as Treves comes to like and respect him, Merrick's face seems no longer grotesque to him, and his appearance is no longer an issue. Throughout that process, Lynch identifies the physical point of view of the camera with the fictional point of view of Treves, and as Treves lets his eyes linger on Merrick, the viewer actually watches his transformation; what is more, since that is also the viewers' own point of view, we too undergo the same transformation. At the beginning of the film, our glimpses of Merrick are as short as the camera's, and probably shorter—it is difficult even to parse his face—but his looks are no longer in question by the time we have come to know him better, not because we have be-

come aware of his inner qualities but because his personality—his soul—is manifest in his appearance, which alters when it finds an alteration in us.[38]

The notion that "we are always *able*" to find something attractive in our friends suggests that being a friend involves a commitment to finding that attractive element. This seems to me exactly right. Lest it be thought that this takes us right back into the camp of the antirationalists, we should pause here to remind ourselves yet again that thinking that loving involves a commitment to seeing someone as beautiful is perfectly compatible with thinking that seeing someone as beautiful is a matter not of *creating* beauty or *projecting* it onto someone but of *finding* or *discovering* a beauty that is already there but that may be difficult to see. As John Armstrong writes,

> The kind of attention the lover brings allows less obvious qualities to be seen and appreciated. Just as a muted work of art, like Turner's small sketch, would be quickly passed over by someone alert only to the most obvious signs of artistic bravura, so a muted person (an ordinary person) has attractive qualities which will probably not be evident to a casual observer. In other words, imagination can be allied to acuteness of perception, rather than to distortion. . . . We're not inventing [our beloveds'] charms, we just happen to be responsive to them.[39]

The idea, then, is that the fact that love encourages us to see our beloveds in a different way from the way in which others see them does not suggest that we are seeing them inaccurately—if anything, we may be seeing them more accurately than anyone else. The idea is well captured by the narrator of Coetzee's *Youth*, quoted in chapter 1, who awaits "the beloved, the destined one," who "will see at once through the odd and even dull exterior he presents to the fire that burns within him." We might think, too, of Randall Jarrell's description of Gertrude, the novelist and creative writing teacher, in his novel *Pictures from an Institution*: "Yet when you knew her how different it all looked; Gertrude's spirit shone through her body as though the body were an old pane of glass, and you thought, 'My God, how could I have been so blind!'"[40]

What the narrator of *Youth* wants is to be really seen, seen for what he is; and when this happens, what is there for the seer to say but "My God, how could I have been so blind?" According to the vision view, what love does is precisely to put a person in the position where he is more able than anyone else to appreciate those valuable qualities: qualities that are genuinely valuable but are muted, subtle, or difficult to discern. The view, then, sees love as a response that is something between an appraisal and a bestowal. It is an appraisal insofar as it takes itself to be responding to independent, preexisting values. These values, however, are sometimes difficult to detect and nearly always difficult fully to *appreciate*; recognizing that some feature is valuable is sometimes an easy matter, sometimes not easy at all, but taking the next step and actually *valuing* that feature is more difficult still.[41] Thus love, as a response to the beloved's valuable characteristics, also has some features of bestowal. What is bestowed, however, is not the value itself—again, presumably that was there all along—but rather the sort of close, generous, and imaginative attention that allows valuable features of this sort fully to reveal themselves.

Conclusion

Love's epistemic critics are correct, in principle, to point out that love involves certain methods of belief formation, evaluation, and acceptance; that it can thus be understood as making certain epistemic *demands* of us; and that such demands may, in at least some cases, lead us to engage in unreliable epistemic processes and, perhaps, to form or accept false beliefs. Moreover, it is no exaggeration to say that love is in part constituted by such practices. If Alighieri's thinking and belief formation with respect to Beatrice are not influenced by such demands, then Alighieri cannot be said to love Beatrice. I have argued, however, that it would be a mistake to see love as nothing more than a source of epistemic danger or to conclude that love and epistemic rationality will inevitably or even typically be at odds. Accepting the descriptive claims of love's epistemic critics, then, need not and should not lead us to reject the idea that there is a significant sense in which love constitutes a reason-guided response to the world; in particular, that it constitutes an appreciative response to various real, independently existing values.

Keller is correct to claim that friendship (like other forms of love) "is not to be unreservedly embraced."[42] But this is not for reasons that are in any way peculiar to friendship or to love. Rather, there exists *no* value or commitment that ought to be unreservedly embraced; any value or commitment, no matter how genuine or legitimate when considered in itself, is, at least in principle, capable of coming into conflict with other genuine values and commitments in an objectionable way. A commitment to a friend can indeed make demands that conflict with the demands of epistemic rationality (or, for that matter, with those of impartial morality, etc.). But then again, a commitment to one friend can make demands that conflict with the demands of a commitment to some other friend. The world is a messy, complex place, and it does not offer us a guarantee that all of the things that properly matter to an individual will turn out to be completely consistent with one another and to fit together to form a frictionless, conflict-free whole.

There is more than one possible approach to the formation, evaluation, and acceptance of belief. Some of these approaches are more amenable, others less, to the formation of attachments and commitments to
individual persons. Sometimes those that are more amenable—those that
involve giving certain individuals a privileged place in our epistemic practices—can lead us to form false beliefs or to miss out on important facts.
But the sort of approach that distances itself the most from this, by insisting on the importance of detachment, neutrality, and objectivity, can also
lead us to miss out on important facts, to settle for a less than wholly
adequate understanding, or to accept false beliefs. The fact that the perspective this approach demands is more detached, and even in a sense
more neutral, does not entail that it represents the "objective" view of the
matter and that any other perspective must be considered irredeemably
subjective.[43] Indeed, since different epistemic practices are appropriate in
different situations, and since there is no perfectly reliable neutral method
for determining which practice is most appropriate in any given case, any
possible set of epistemic practices will carry at least some risk that an
agent who adopts and employs it will nonetheless end up doing less well,
in epistemic terms, than she might have had she adopted some other set
of practices.

There is no reason to think that the epistemic approach that makes
room for love for persons by allowing the systematic epistemic privileging of certain individuals over others is, in ordinary circumstances, a
particularly bad approach. Indeed, in the world as we know it—a world
in which the limitations on our time and other resources prevent us from
reaching a deep understanding of most of the people we encounter in
our lives—an openness to and focus on a small number of individuals
can make possible insights and understandings that would not be available otherwise. What Iris Murdoch refers to as "a just and loving gaze
directed upon an individual reality" can be a route to a cognitive grasp of
the world considerably deeper and more profound than any that might
be achieved from the standpoint of a more detached perspective.[44] Or, as
Shakespeare puts it in *A Midsummer Night's Dream*:

> Lovers and madmen have such seething brains
> Such shaping fantasies, that apprehend
> More than cool reason ever comprehends.

four

Beyond Comparison

> When Rilke was dying in 1926 ... he received a letter from the young Russian poet Marina Tsvetayeva. "You are not the poet I love most," she wrote to him. "'Most' already implies comparison. You are poetry itself."
>
> —Robert Hass, *The Selected Poetry of Rainer Maria Rilke*

Introduction: Two Troublesome Ideas about Rationality

William James once wrote that "the very best of men must not only be insensible, but ludicrously and peculiarly insensible, to many goods."[1] In chapter 2 I applied the neo-Aristotelian idea that virtue involves being insensible to certain goods—the potential gains of immorality, for example—to the case of love, and I argued that love, too, involves a lack of sensitivity to certain values. To love a person is to regard her as special: not to believe, implausibly, that she is objectively more valuable and attractive than any other human being, but rather to refuse to objectively compare her merits with those of other persons. It is thus as correct to say that loving Beatrice involves regarding Beatrice *in a special way* as it is to say that loving Beatrice involves regarding her *as special*.

The recognition that people other than our beloveds deserve to be seen as important, valuable, and worthy of love, then, is not taken by most lovers to ground an obligation that they extend their love to everyone. The belief is one thing, the emotional response is something else. And what prevents them from having the emotional response with respect to everyone they judge worthy is precisely the sort of silencing discussed in chapter 2.

However, certain views of rationality seem to suggest that lovers cannot rationally separate their value beliefs from their emotional responses in the way that I have just described. There are two ideas about rationality that are particularly troublesome in this regard. The first is that a rational agent must fully respond to *every* legitimate value. This idea either simply denies the distinction between valuing x and judging x to be valuable or else pressures us to think that valuing x in the fullest possible manner is always the proper response to any perceived value, and that merely to judge x to be valuable, without following through by actually coming to value x, is to fall short of the ideal response. We can call this, then, the full response requirement. Socrates seems to accept the full response requirement in the *Symposium* when he says, following Diotima, that reason requires the person who loves one beautiful body to eventually "become a lover of all beautiful bodies, and . . . think that this wild gaping after just one body is a small thing and despise it."

The second idea is that, when selecting the values to which she *will* fully respond, an agent must do everything possible to try to ensure that she selects the very best values, as ranked by some sort of objective standard. This idea, which we can refer to as the maximizing requirement, would require a lover constantly to compare the object of her love with others and ask whether she really has managed to focus her love on the best possible object. To say that such an attitude is contrary to the spirit of love is not to deny that a certain amount of comparison is appropriate, particularly in the very early stages of a romantic relationship. Why pursue an apparently less intelligent, charming, or beautiful potential partner when more intelligent, charming, or beautiful persons are available? (Then again, one might sometimes prefer a potential partner who scores less highly in these respects, but there will still be some consideration with respect to which she scores higher, even if it is only to say, "I enjoy her company more" or "We have more fun together.") But once the pursuit has turned into an actual relationship, such comparison is expected to dwindle quite drastically and perhaps to disappear altogether. Once again, a form of silencing either prevents the lover from judging others to be more desirable than her beloved or, in cases where that judgment is unavoidable, makes it the case that it does not matter to her that this is so; her affections remain with her beloved even though she is aware that others rate higher. Indeed, the lover who is not subject to such silencing, and who is constantly asking whether her beloved is the funniest, the prettiest, or physically the strongest of the persons in her acquaintance, seems not to be a genuine lover at all.

The maximizing requirement expresses a view of rational evaluative thought that places such thought in the context of an impartial, neutral point of view from which various values are assessed and objectively ranked against one another. In this chapter I will attempt to undermine the assumption that all rational evaluation must take place from such a point of view. (In doing so I will also start laying the groundwork for an understanding of the distinction between valuing and judging to be valuable, though the full treatment of this issue will have to wait for chapter 5.) There are ways of responding to value, I argue, that have little or nothing to do with this sort of neutral comparison, and they are not rationally deficient for that. Although there are certainly contexts in which attempting to take the perspective of an objective evaluator by performing a comprehensive survey of the available options is reasonable, recommended, or even rationally mandatory, we make a mistake if we assume that all contexts are of this sort. Thus, although the conception of evaluative reasoning that identifies rationality with dispassionate comparison and objective evaluation is, in the proper context, a useful and significant one, it is important not to insist that it be held up as our only model or overestimate the extent of the realm over which it has jurisdiction.

The Comprehensive Comparative Survey View

The two troublesome ideas described in the previous section are frequently found in the context of a broader view of evaluative reasoning—one that has exerted a profound influence on the way people think about such reasoning. This picture has a number of elements. Again, my claim will not be that proper evaluative reasoning *never* displays the various features identified by this picture—which I will refer to as the comprehensive comparative survey view, or the CCS for short—but rather that evaluative reasoning, to be adequate, need not always display these features, and indeed in some contexts ought not to do so. The CCS might well give a perfectly adequate picture of, for instance, what the evaluative reasoning of public administrators choosing from among various social or economic policies ought to look like. It does not, however, give a very good picture at all of what a *lover's* evaluative reasoning ought to look like. Or so, at any rate, I will argue.

Consider the following quotation from Descartes regarding what he calls "the true function of reason": "The true function of reason, then, in the conduct of life is to examine and consider without passion the value of [the available options], so that since we are commonly obliged to deprive ourselves of some goods in order to acquire others, we shall always choose the better."[2]

The passage suggests several features that are frequently assumed to characterize proper evaluative reasoning. First, such reasoning is taken to be a fundamentally *comparative* matter. It is to be carried out from a standpoint of detachment and emotional disengagement, across a range of alternatives that are viewed as comparable or commensurable, with the ultimate aim of reaching an evaluative verdict as to which of the available goods is optimal. (Thus, it is not the value bearers themselves who are being compared but their values, where "values" is understood as degrees of value, i.e., something akin to axiological grades or scores.) Moreover, the evaluative process should presumably be comprehensive—it should consider all potentially available goods—and the verdict as to which option is optimal ought to be practical, in that it should issue in action.

The elements of the CCS identified above can be elaborated on as follows:

1. *Comparativeness.* The process of evaluation is pictured as a fundamentally comparative matter: we are to judge the value of a given option by comparing it with other options, and ranking it against them.

2. *Comparability.* Since evaluation is fundamentally comparative, its possibility presupposes that all of the options being evaluated must be capable of being straightforwardly compared with one another *in the same terms.* Again, it is not the options themselves but the *values* of the options that are being compared, with an eye to which one is larger, clearly implying that these values must be expressible in the same terms. At the very least, the following must be true: given any pair of items between which one must choose, it must be, at least in principle, possible to say which of the two is superior to the other or whether in fact both are exactly equally good.

3. *Comprehensiveness.* The evaluating agent must compare the value of the option under consideration with as many other options as possible, ideally with a perfectly comprehensive range of options—that is, one that includes *all* available or relevant options. Otherwise there could be no guarantee that the agent will manage "always [to] choose the better" of those options that were available to her.

4. *Detachment.* The evaluating agent must be sufficiently detached from the various options she is evaluating so that she can "consider [them] without passion," so as to be impartial between them, and to avoid her judgment's being swayed by her attachment to or emotional investment in any one of them.

5. *Optimality.* The point of being provided with a value ranking that meets the criteria identified up to this point—the criteria, that is, of *comparability, comprehensiveness,* and *detachment*—is that it makes it possible for the agent to choose from the range of available options the one that is optimal—namely the one that a fully informed neutral evaluator would regard as the best.

6. *Practicality.* The point of the process is, precisely, the selection of the optimal option. Ultimately it is not the process but the output of the process—the agent's choice of the optimal option—with which we are primarily concerned: the evaluation is meant merely to provide the verdict, to guarantee that the best possible choice will be made.

Together, these claims constitute a certain view about the nature of evaluative reasoning. I should make it clear here that I am not concerned with the question of how many philosophers have endorsed the whole view. Indeed, although I use a single name to refer to the picture of evaluative reasoning that is in question, I do not want to suggest that one well-defined theory is being singled out. My interest is not so much in the theorists who have served as overt and explicit proponents of the view in its most radical forms, as in the surreptitious influence exerted by the view on the thought of many philosophers, including some who would be unlikely explicitly to declare allegiance to such a picture. It is all too common for it to simply be assumed, and indeed taken as obvious and undeniable, that reasoning *must* work in the way here described, and that reasons, therefore, must bear certain features if they are to possess justificatory or normative force at all.

Consider, for instance—to return for a moment to an argument I considered in the previous chapter—the way in which elements of the CCS make covert appearances in Simon Keller's description of how Eric, if he is to be an epistemically ideal agent (i.e., one who is most likely to reach reliable evaluative judgments), ought to experience a poetry reading:

> If it were a stranger giving the reading, and if Eric were setting out to make an accurate judgment about the poetry's quality . . . then he would listen attentively and with an open mind, and then form critical and dispassionate judgments, informed by such things as a hardheaded comparison of this work with others and a set of realistic expectations about the average literary agent's psychology.

Keller does not of course claim that Eric ought, *all things considered,* to adopt this "dispassionate" and "hardheaded" stance; he allows that his friendship with Rebecca gives him reason *not* to occupy such a perspective. He is explicit, however, that in refusing to adopt a detached stance, Eric is refusing to act as epistemic ideals require; he is deliberately functioning as a less-than-ideal epistemic agent in order to meet the demands of friendship. The conception of evaluative reasoning that is in play here has clearly been influenced by the CCS. We may note three elements of the CCS in particular: the emphasis on detachment ("critical and dispassionate judgments"), the centrality of comparison ("a hardheaded comparison of this work with others"), and, above all, the assumption that the concern of the agent lies in, and will be exhausted by, the deliverance of a verdict regarding the work's worth, an "accurate judgment about the poetry's quality."

I argued in the previous chapter that although a detached, dispassionate, and comparative standpoint might be appropriate in some contexts, it was quite inappropriate in the context of judging poetry or other works of art—not only for reasons having to do with the demands of friendship but also, contra Keller, for explicitly epistemic reasons. There are certain insights into art that are obtainable only from an involved and engaged standpoint. The idea, then, that an adequate account of evaluative thought that is to cover *all contexts* must display all or most of these features is a mistake. For there is good reason to think that certain values are not well approached or engaged with by agents whose evaluative thought displays all or most of the features listed above. As might be expected, many of these values will turn out to have to do with individual projects, idiosyncratic goals and commitments, and personal relationships with other individuals—values that comport poorly with the sort of "informed rational shopper" model implicit in the comprehensive comparative survey view.

Incomparability, Neutrality, and Value Conflict

Part of the comprehensive comparative survey view's popularity stems from the assumption that it constitutes a purely formal conception of how agents ought to respond to values and does not embody or express any substantive position about values. The view is assumed to be purely neutral; its central thought, after all, is simply that whatever values there are ought to be regarded from as neutral and impartial a standpoint as possible, and compared against as wide a range of potential competitors as can be cognized, before a decision is made. But it is precisely this claim of neutrality that must be questioned.

As we have observed, the CCS dictates that a choosing agent adopt a detached perspective from which to take as broad and comprehensive a survey as possible of the available candidate goods and that she evaluate these goods as dispassionately as possible. It demands, moreover, that having made her choice, the agent either continue to occupy such a perspective throughout her engagement with the chosen goods or, at the very least, that she return to occupy it relatively frequently. This requirement is necessary to guarantee that the agent remains reflective and self-critical and does not tie herself down, as the result of a mistaken initial evaluation, to a defective set of commitments and policies that would not succeed in maximizing available values.

Indeed, the very thought that rationality involves the goal of maximizing seems to imply that rational choosing must take place from a perspective of this sort. Again, though, this view depends on the assumption that such a perspective will not privilege certain values in a way that would impede the operations of practical reason. It depends, that is, on the assumption that all goods *can* be adequately evaluated from a detached perspective by an agent whose psychology is governed by the dictate to compare and maximize. If, in fact, there exist some goods of which this is not true, then the CCS *itself* incorporates, beneath its apparently impartial and fair-minded surface, a certain substantive view about value that privileges certain goods over others. And if these goods are important enough, then the CCS might turn out to be self-defeating.

To see that such goods do exist, let us begin with the deeply ahistorical nature of the model. Part of the detachment thought to be involved is precisely that of being able to step away from one's own history, and in particular from value commitments that stem from past decisions, as well as aspects of one's situation that were out of one's control. But this rejection of historical contingency strains against the reality of human life. By the time any human being is in a position to reflect on her own values, she has already been brought up within a set of traditions that have shaped her sensibilities in a deep way. This is not to say that she will necessarily be incapable of rejecting or transcending such traditions to a significant degree. Still, the decision-making faculty that results in the intention to do so is largely a product of these very traditions. The traditions, then, will have a role to play even in the explanation of their own rejection.

Moreover, even if a person ultimately comes to fully endorse the value system in which she has been brought up, only the most sheltered individual will be able to avoid noticing that she might well have adopted some other value system had she been brought up under its sway. The importance of the fact that we are situated when reflection begins is that it undermines the detachment implicit in the CSS picture. Let us allow ourselves, for a moment, to imagine what is surely an impossibility: an utterly detached and as yet unencumbered observer—a genuine "blank slate"—who is to come to the plurality of potential life styles available to human beings, to compare and evaluate them. The practical deliberations of such an unlikely evaluator would still fall short of what the CCS demands, for she will have to try out different ways of life in a temporal sequence; that is, she will have to try some before others. And unless we are to imagine her entirely unchanged by each experience (in which case, how can it be possible for her to compare them?), we must acknowledge that the order will matter; changes wrought on her character and preferences by earlier experiences may make her more or less disposed to respond favorably to later ones. A blank slate that undergoes any sort of experience will not remain a blank slate for very long.

But the idea of the agent as a truly blank slate is deeply implausible anyway. Indeed, part of what is absurd about the demand for a truly objective and comprehensive survey is precisely the idea that it is possible to dip in and out of different ways of life as one might sample different courses at a buffet. This goes beyond the point about history—that it matters in what order a person undergoes the various experiences that shape her—to the further point that there exist values that can be appreciated or enjoyed only as a result of a long-term and dedicated commitment to a certain practice or even a certain mode of life. The appreciation of some values involves the acquisition and honing of certain skills, a process of education, or the long-term training of one's sensibilities. Such values demand a degree of commitment over time, where part of what *commitment* frequently involves is a refusal to be absolutely open to whatever other values might come along, no matter how legitimate such values might be, and how enthusiastically we might have responded to them had we encountered them first.

The value of being a Buddhist monk cannot be straightforwardly and neutrally compared with the value of being a classical pianist or a professional chef. Even if certain elements within each may be compared, there will be other elements that cannot. Each of these options constitutes a certain mode of life that must be experienced from the inside in order to be fully evaluated, and there are obviously limits on how many such modes an individual can experience at one time or even in the course of a lifetime. The impossibility of direct comparison is still more marked in connection with differences that occur at more fundamental levels— differences in basic conceptions and value commitments that we might think of as constituting a *total* way of life. For as Stuart Hampshire argues, genuinely total ways of life will tend to exclude alternatives almost completely.

> As children we inherit, and may disown, a particular way of life, and a particular set of prescriptions, which specify, more or less vaguely, the expected virtues and achievements of this particular complete life. ... The ideal of friendship between young males in some ancient Greek cities is thought to have entailed a cost in the ideal of romantic love between men and women, and perhaps also in ideals of married love, ideals that have prevailed in other places and at other times. Individuals inevitably become conscious of the cost exacted by their own way of life and of the other possibilities of achievement and enjoyment discarded. They feel the cost in internal conflict also. Every established way of life has its cost in repression.[3]

My point is not that two very different ways of life cannot be compared at all. A person who has experienced or even successfully imagined both will after all be in a position to make true observations regarding the similarities and differences between them and sometimes to judge their relative merits. The point, then, is not that anything goes, that it is impossible to make value judgments about various ways of life, or that each person's judgments on such matters are automatically true or "true for her." Nor is it to advance a form of relativism. At the very least I agree with Hampshire that "there are obvious limits set by common human needs to the conditions under which human beings flourish and human societies flourish. History records many ways of life which have crossed these limits."[4]

So we should not deny the possibility of comparisons between different modes of life. We must recognize, though, that such comparisons are made not from a neutral, detached standpoint, but rather from positions in which certain values have been accepted and endorsed in preference to others. Even for those who have experienced two deeply different ways of life—former religious believers who have become skeptics, for instance—the order in which the ways of life have been experienced will matter, and it will still not be possible to retreat to a genuinely neutral perspective from which the two may be objectively compared. To the extent that our understandings and assessments of values are gained through experience, certain facts about the nature of experiences—that they occur in temporal sequence rather than all at once, and that each, at the time at which it is had, tends to exclude other sorts of experience—will strongly influence both the process by which such knowledge is gathered and the outcome of that process.

These influences may sometimes hinder our attempts to gain practical knowledge and make good judgments, but it would be a serious overreaction to conclude that human beings can *never* get at the truth about such matters or that we are radically incapable of making such judgments. What is important is that we give up on the myth that there exists a complete and comprehensive ranking of values, which any human being, regardless of where she happens to be situated, can comprehend and internalize—and along with that, that we abandon the myth that such a value ranking is what realism about values, or intelligent evaluative thinking, would require.

Reverence and Contemplation

The argument of the previous section is based in a quite general point about the impossibility of comparing goods from a neutral perspective— an impossibility arising from the fact that to be a human agent is to have a certain perspective on the world, which is shaped by one's experiences. But we must now consider another limit, which arises not from the nature of human agency but from the nature of certain goods; some goods, I suggest, *demand* to be appreciated from a standpoint that is anything but detached and comprehensive and call for a response that is anything but neutral or calculating.

The discussion in chapter 2 strongly suggests that humans are value bearers of this sort and that love takes the form it does in part because of this fact. But the point can also be made with respect to objects, and exploring it in those areas may put us in a better position to appreciate how it works with respect to personal love. As an example of an object calling for such a response, then, consider some majestic artifact such as the Notre Dame Cathedral. The proper response to such an object, it would seem, has nothing whatever to do with promotion or maximization. What would it even *mean* to maximize the value of the Notre Dame Cathedral? To build duplicates in other locations? To add to it so as to make it larger? Either of these, or any other such response, would be *incompatible* with appreciating its value in the proper way; rather than maximizing its value, it would cheapen or diminish it. Whatever the proper response to an object like the Notre Dame Cathedral is, it is a response that is not directly linked to action—not in any straightforward and obvious manner, at any rate. Nor is it a response that seems to be thought from a detached and impartial standpoint. Indeed, the person who stands before Notre Dame thinking thoughts like "How many times more impressive is it, exactly, than the Salisbury Cathedral?" fails to appreciate it as it ought to be appreciated. There is something deficient in the response that insists, in the midst of one's direct experience of such an object, on its being compared with something else—or, indeed, on its being objectively measured, assessed, or judged at all.

Natural objects, too, can provoke such responses. Some of them—the ocean, the earth's ecosystem, or the "starry heavens above" so admired by Kant—cannot be compared in part because they are genuinely singular; there is simply nothing to compare them *to*. But the deeper fact is that even if there were potential objects of comparison, comparison would still be out of place. Whatever the precise basis for one's awestruck response to the starry sky or the ecosystem, such awe does not seem anywhere to contain the thought of that object's being *better*—not even much, much better—than some other, less impressive thing. Nor need an object be singular in this sense in order to demand noncomparative appreciation. A person might find herself regarding a tree, for example, with the same attentive aesthetic appreciation as other people (or she herself on other occasions) regard sculptures or paintings, and the existence of many other trees, even in the immediate vicinity, need be no obstacle to such an experience.

Experiences of such objects seem to involve something like reverence or awe. Objects calling for such a response present themselves as possessing a value that is both objective or independent (insofar as it is not simply the creation or result of our own subjective responses) and intrinsic or final (insofar as their value does not depend on further purposes they can be turned to). The existence of the thing tends to be regarded, on such occasions, as in itself good. Reverence and awe are most typically responses to things that we perceive as being in some significant sense both beyond and larger than ourselves and, frequently, as involving a certain degree of mystery.

In experiences of reverence, the practical element is not nearly as pronounced as the responsive or contemplative element. Of course, in unusual contexts action might be called for. One's appreciation of Notre Dame Cathedral or of the earth's ecosystem would presumably prompt one to action if either were threatened with immediate destruction and one were in a position to prevent the destruction. Still, being prepared to act so as to protect and preserve the objects one reveres does not exhaust one's value response to those objects; indeed, it does not even seem to constitute a central part of that response. Such preparedness is, rather, a consequence of one's valuing, not a primary component of it. The main effect of reverence is frequently to *stop* a person from acting—one is, as it were, frozen in place before the object, "stopped in one's tracks." Love, as J. David Velleman writes in "Love as a Moral Emotion," feels like "a state of attentive suspension, similar to wonder or amazement or awe."[5]

In addition to stopping one in one's tracks, such experiences also bear a feature that we have seen before: they silence one's perception of other attractors of attention. During these experiences the object "fills the mind," so that one's mind is, in Elaine Scarry's words, "exclusively filled with the beautiful object that stands in its presence." When genuinely appreciating some value in this way, one's attention will be entirely focused on the object, and if one's consciousness is scattered or diverted, this must be taken to indicate that one's appreciation has in some sense failed to be wholehearted or complete. Thus, overt comparisons, which would require the simultaneous consciousness and appreciation of two distinct values or value-bearing objects, are frequently precluded in this context.

It is important to understand that this phenomenon is distinct from that described in the previous section. There we were concerned with the way certain values cannot be fully appreciated except by agents who devote a significant portion of their lives to them. Here the point is that even a person who has the necessary background, training, and experience to appreciate a certain type of valuable object may be unable to appreciate more than one instance at a time. Thus, there can certainly be a single person who is capable of appreciating both Notre Dame Cathedral and Salisbury Cathedral, or Beethoven's Symphony No. 5 and Shostakovich's Symphony No. 5. But it is beyond human capabilities to simultaneously enter into, experience, and appreciate two such different works.

Consider the following passage from an essay on George Oppen and John Berryman, by the poet Louise Glück:

> It is valuable, though nearly impossible, to try to read Oppen and Berryman side by side. Nothing in Oppen feels involuntary. And yet nothing feels rigid. *One impression genius fosters is that there is,*

beside it, no comparable mastery: no other way to sound, to think, to be. I admire both Berryman and Oppen to this degree; I regret not knowing what these two thought of each other. Berryman's meticulous need to offend everyone, to be certain that in no mind was he even briefly associated with anything even slightly conservative, mannerly, acceptable, his poignant but extremely wily egotism sometimes seems childish and limited beside Oppen. And sometimes, next to Berryman's feverish wildness, Oppen seems too lofty, too hermetic, too secure. Temperamentally, they seem to cancel one another out.[6]

As Glück points out, when we are in the grip of a work of creative genius we find ourselves unable to imagine any other way of going about things (much as, in the grip of depression, we find ourselves unable to imagine that we will ever feel substantially better). And yet we are able to feel precisely this way about the creations of *multiple* artists, by moving from one aesthetic perspective to another. What we cannot do, however, is to simultaneously occupy two distinct aesthetic perspectives, each with its own set of value commitments and way of seeing the world. From the perspective that appreciates Berryman, Oppen seems deficient; from the perspective that appreciates Oppen, Berryman seems flawed. It will not have escaped the reader that Glück's account is clearly a description of silencing; when one is genuinely gripped by a work of genius, one has the impression that there is "no other way to sound, to think, to be." To be in the midst of a full-fledged episode of aesthetic appreciation—to be genuinely overcome and possessed by a work of art——is to adopt, for the moment, its way of seeing the world so fully that one cannot imagine that the world might appear under any other guise (or, perhaps, that one would be interested in it if it did).

This returns us to the point about contemplation. A feature of the CSS view, noted earlier, is that it regards the purpose of the comprehensive comparative survey undertaken by the agent as being that of delivering a *verdict* on the options considered: either the assignment of a numerical value or at the very least the formulation of an ordinal ranking of options that determines which options are superior to which others. This thought is closely tied to the view that the ultimate purpose of all evaluative thinking is practical; the assignments of value are meant to enable, guide, and provide justifications for the performance of physical actions (and not merely mental responses). In other words, we need to know which options are better than which others in order to know what to do. Moreover, which options are better than which others is *all we need to know*: insofar as the differences between one option and another are irrelevant to their respective value rankings, such differences need not concern us.

Such views are, in the terminology employed by John Broome, *teleo-logical.* "Teleology," writes Broome, "is the view that how one ought to act is [entirely] determined by the goodness of the available options."[7] It is a clear implication of such a view that where there is no difference between the relative values of the various outcomes of one's choice, it cannot possibly matter how one chooses.

> If you are faced with a choice between two options, and they are equally good, it does not matter which you choose. . . . Actually this remark is a mere tautology. To say a choice between two options does not matter—literally, and not simply that it does not matter much—is simply to say the options are equally good, and to say it does matter is simply to say they are not equally good.[8]

But the example of aesthetic thought, and other forms of thought involving objects that evoke reverence or responses similar to reverence, call these assumptions into question. For what such objects seem to call for is a mode of active engagement that is not oriented to some future action or course of action but is an end in itself. Of course, it is possible to take a simpleminded "reviewing" model—the deliverance of a "thumbs-up" or "thumbs-down" verdict in response to a given work of art—as the standard for aesthetic thought, in which case one will indeed be tempted to see such thought as being oriented toward a practical outcome: do I go see the movie or not? But as Nehamas reminds us, this form of critical response represents only one small aspect of criticism, not to speak of evaluative thought more generally.

> We don't read the critics of *Hamlet*, or *Hamlet* itself, in order to determine how good the play is but in order to grasp what it has to offer us, which requires us to understand what it says; what it says may turn out to be truly magnificent, but making *that* judgment is never the purpose of reading. . . . The idea that "having found out about all the components of the work, we put everything together and give a verdict" depends on, and encourages, a deep misunderstanding of both beauty and aesthetic value. It also has little to do with what critics do in real life. . . . Why, then, do we continue to think that the main aim of criticism is to determine the value of artworks and that criticism ends when it has done so?[9]

Contemplation, as a mode of thought, is not primarily concerned with rankings; indeed, it is not inherently practical at all. As Iris Murdoch writes, "Great art teaches us how real things can be looked at and loved without being seized and used, without being appropriated into the greedy organism of the self."[10] Such thought is pursued for its own sake, and for the sake of its object, to which it aspires to be adequate and with respect to which it attempts to be enlightening, enriching, and revealing. That a process of contemplation does not issue in any visible action does not suggest that it must be considered imperfect or incomplete, let alone a failure. If we take the phrase "evaluative thought" in a broad sense, to stand for all thought that responds to and attempts to grapple with instances of value in the world, then to the extent that such thought involves contemplation, detailed description, and the attempt to understand, it represents a cognitive activity that will tend to treat values as irreducible to one another, and quite frequently not mutually reconcilable to a single scheme of ranking or quantification. Indeed, the fact that they are not reducible to one another is the source of much of their interest; within aesthetics, at least, it tends to be precisely what sets the aesthetic object apart from all others, what it possesses and displays that they do not, that lies at the heart of its ability to fascinate us.

It is simply false, then, to assume that the point and purpose of evaluative thought is to find itself exhausted in the deliverance of a practically oriented verdict, for a very large part of our thinking about value is simply not directed toward practical ends at all. Moreover, even where our evaluative thought *is* so directed, we should not make the mistake of agreeing with the view that, in Broome's words, "if you are faced with a choice between two options, and they are equally good, it does not matter which you choose." Far from being a tautology, this claim is simply untrue. We might, perhaps, agree with the considerably weaker claim that if one is faced with a choice between two equally good options, then the choice of either could be justified or regarded as reasonable. But to say this is not to go so far as to say that it *does not matter* which of two equally good options one chooses. For it might, for instance, make a great deal of difference to the future course of one's life whether one chooses to live in New York City or in Napa Valley, and this can be true even if neither of the resulting lives can be said to be clearly better than the other. On a more modest scale, to say that it makes a difference whether one begins the day with Mozart or the Flaming Lips can be perfectly true, even if neither would make one happier or one's day ultimately more successful than the other.[11]

The conception of comparison employed by the CCS, then, is too restrictive. But what matters most is that evaluative thinking in some contexts does not involve comparison *at all*. Some types of value are best appreciated, and perhaps can only be appreciated, from within a practice or set of commitments; to attempt to step outside and regard such values from a more objective, neutral standpoint would be to endanger, rather than to enrich, one's experience. As we have observed, some values, and some value-bearing objects, simply forbid us to regard them from a detached, objective standpoint. And we have seen that it is inevitable, given the nature of human beings, that they will approach many of the valu-able items the world offers from a standpoint that is deeply *non*-neutral. Within certain limited contexts—where goals have already been defined, where both the range of possible alternatives and the types of consider-ation with respect to which they are to be compared are limited in certain respects, and so forth—evaluative reasoning should aspire to the model provided by the CCS. But to take this model as an ideal for all of our evaluative reasoning is a mistake. If we cannot keep ourselves from mak-ing that mistake, we will inevitably misunderstand a great many aspects of human experience, love for persons being, perhaps, chief among them.

Love as an Ethically Ideal Relationship

> The human mind is only capable of absorbing a few things at a time. We see what is taking place in front of us in the here and now, and cannot envision simultaneously a succession of processes, no matter how integrated and complementary. Our faculties of perception are consequently limited even as regards fairly simple phenomena. The fate of a single man can be rich with significance, that of a few hun-dred less so, but the history of thousands and millions of men does not mean anything at all, in any adequate sense of the word.
>
> —Stanislaw Lem

> Among human beings, only the existence of those we love is fully recognized.
>
> —Simone Weil

Individuals are simply not the sort of object one ought, ideally, to take a detached view of. Why not? In part, because individuals, like sublime landscapes or great works of art or architecture, are entities that call for respect, reverence, and awe. The fact that there are so many, and that we are for the most part constantly surrounded by them, may tend to blind us to this fact, but human beings are quite unlike anything else that ex-ists in the world, and the world would be an incomparably poorer place without them.

Moreover, human individuals possess something extraordinary that even the most impressive landscape or the greatest work of art or archi-tecture lacks: a self, an interior life. We might be struck dumb by the Sa-haran sand dunes or filled with quiet joy by Notre Dame Cathedral, but we cannot converse or interact with them, we cannot inquire after their thoughts or wonder whether their experience of the world is like ours or whether it is different in potentially fascinating ways. Such objects have no experience of the world, and the result is that although we can be vastly impressed *by* such things, we cannot identify *with* them.[12] And this is a highly significant fact, for to say that a person occupies a perspective on the world from which the world is experienced, is to say that in a sense there is a world that exists *for* that person, a world that is unique and metaphysically distinct from all the various worlds that exist for other people.

This crucial thought is difficult to get hold of. George Berkeley famously thought that the world existed only when someone was perceiving it, and thus it would go out of existence altogether if all perceivers vanished. This is presumably somewhat of an exaggeration. However, the thought that there is a sense in which an unperceived world would fail *fully* to exist is, I think, intelligible: it is the sense in which a tree falling with no one around to hear it really does not make a sound. And this seems to suggest a sense in which each person, in perceiving the world, *creates* a world relative to herself. But if each person creates a perceived reality for herself, then the death of a person means the destruction of that perceived reality. The ancient Hebraic saying "He who saves a single life saves the world" thus seems to express a version of the elusive but crucial thought. Again, the saying is clearly false in the most literal sense: We all know that the world survives the death of any particular person. We even know that it will survive our own. But there is a part of me that does not feel that the world will survive my death. And if what "the world" means here is *my* world, the world that is perceived by me and so exists for me in that sense, then this feeling is, in its own terms, quite correct.

It is no wonder, then, that we think it important to be loved if to love someone is to place her at the center of one's world. For to be valued in this way, to be installed at the center of a lover's universe, is to have one's reality and individuality truly and fully acknowledged. Only the lover, after all, looks closely, carefully, and generously enough to truly recognize the beloved in all her individuality. The great horror of not being loved is that one ceases to matter, that the mental and emotional events that fill one's days are not really events at all, for they happen *only* in one's own mind and not in any part of the outside world. To put the matter starkly, it is almost as if the unloved person does not exist at all.

In Alice Munro's story "Floating Bridge," a character who is considering leaving her husband reflects on the possible consequences of her decision.

> She felt herself connected at present with the way people felt when they had to write certain things down—she was connected by her

feelings of anger, of petty outrage (perhaps it was petty?), and her excitement at what she was doing to Neal, to pay him back. But the life she was carrying herself into might not give her anybody to be angry at, or anybody who owed her anything, anybody who could possibly be rewarded or punished or truly affected by what she might do. Her feelings might become of no importance to anybody but herself, and yet they would be bulging up inside her, squeezing her heart and breath.[13]

"You're nobody 'til somebody loves you," as the song goes, and the suggestion I am pursuing is that this expresses an important truth. Love matters because it is a way of fully recognizing the value of an individual person, of recognizing her importance in a world that contains so many individuals that the importance of a single one is distressingly easy to lose sight of. To love someone is to place her at the center of one's world, so that, as in the quotation from Martin Buber, the beloved "fills the firmament—not as if there were nothing else, but everything else lives in *its* light."

Of course, the idea is not that *everyone* must recognize a particular individual's value as an individual; it is enough that *someone* does. Consider the moment in Michael Ondaatje's novel *The English Patient* in which the nurse Hana turns her back on World War II and devotes herself to the care of a single person, the "English" patient of the title. "She would not be ordered again or carry out duties for the greater good," Ondaatje writes. "She would care only for the burned patient. She would read to him and bathe him and give him his doses of morphine—her only communication was with him."[14] Having seen what the attempt to act out of concern for the greater good can come to, Hana attempts to establish an ethically ideal relationship in which she will treat one person as, ideally, everyone ought to be treated—and in which her treatment of him will not, if she is successful, be compromised by conflicting obligations to others. Love, the emotion that takes a particular individual as its focus and end, is the guiding principle behind this ethically ideal relationship.

The desire to be loved is the desire to be seen for what one truly is: an individual person for whom a world exists and therefore a thing that possesses a genuine significance regardless of how many other such persons there might be; regardless of how tiny a thing one's existence is relative to the world as a whole; and regardless of how many larger world events might compete for attention and threaten to drown out one's own claims to attention. Such a way of seeing, which is precisely what love offers, is obviously incompatible with the detached, impartial perspective from which the claims of any individual would have to be balanced in a neutral way against the claims of all others and in which, given the sheer number of individuals in the world, no one person's claims could possibly be viewed as having much intrinsic significance at all. From *that* perspective, in the words of *Casablanca*'s Rick (Humphrey Bogart), the problems and concerns of individual people "don't amount to a hill of beans." How awful it would be, though, if there were *no* perspective from which such concerns could amount to more than that!

Loving, then, is justified not because the object of one's love is especially valuable in relation to other persons but because each individual deserves to be especially valued. Such valuing is a response to her value, but it is not the sort of response that justifies itself by insisting on comparing her value with others. It is, rather, a response that justifies its *refusal* to compare *in terms of* her value. In loving a person, one values a thing that deserves not to be subject to comparison, and the nature of one's valuing is determined precisely by this fact about the beloved.

Suppose—to take one especially explicit example that has concerned some people who have thought about the nature of the value of persons—that a person is offered a significant sum of money to abandon, or betray, her lover or friend. I expect that many people would think that the individual in question ought to say something along the lines of, "No thank you, my relationships are not for sale—I wouldn't regard any amount of money as a fair trade for my friend. Indeed my friend is simply not something I am willing to 'trade' at all. I simply don't think in those terms. And I don't think, for that matter, that any true friend does."

At any rate, something along those lines is what I hope *my* friends would say. A "friend" who would not offer such a response but who would be at least willing to consider the trade (even if in the end she rejected the proffered amount as insufficient) would not seem to be committed in the manner necessary to true friendship; she would occupy a perspective from which friendship was, in an important sense, viewed as being on a par with other sorts of value, including the value of money. Part of being a friend to x, then, is to regard one's relationship to x as something for which one would not be willing to exchange *any* amount of money. It is to regard the value of the friendship as inexpressible in monetary terms and thus to regard the two kinds of value as incomparable.

Some writers deny this—Ruth Chang, for instance. "Suppose I am faced with a choice between friendship and a dollar," she argues. "If I judge that the friendship is worth more than a dollar, have I thereby lost all of my friends?"[15] But this argument avoids the crucial issue. One might say, "My friendship is worth more than a dollar," in the same way in which one might say, "My car is worth more than a dollar." In both cases the chosen language strongly suggests that the problem is simply that one dollar is not enough, but that there is some dollar amount that *would* be equivalent in value to the friendship or the car. And if this is one's position, then one endorses the deep comparability and commensurability of money and one's friendship, in which case it does seem questionable whether one really is a friend at all. (If I found out that the person I had taken to be a close friend was willing to betray me for a certain amount of money—even if the amount was large—I would probably conclude that our relationship, whatever it might have been, was not genuinely one of friendship.)

If, however, one's position is that *no amount* of money would be enough, then one would seem to be committed in the right way for friendship. But it is rather misleading to express this by saying, "My friendship is worth more than a dollar." One ought to say, "My friendship is worth more than *any number of* dollars." But to put things this way is to make it clear that although there is a sense in which the *types* of value involved can be compared (friendship as a general value is held to be worth more than money as a general value), the friendship in question is not being compared with the suggested dollar amount at all; rather, one's beliefs about the relative standing of the general values in question renders such comparisons unnecessary and, indeed, objectionable.

This recalls our treatment of the infidelity case in chapter 2, where I argued, along the lines suggested by McDowell's way of understanding virtue, that the truly committed and loving husband would not be the one who was tempted to betray his wife, considered the matter, and decided that fidelity was more important (and so ended up resisting the temptation through an act of will), but rather the one whose love for his wife silenced the attractions of infidelity and so was not moved by temptation in the first place. In both cases a crucial step toward understanding the situation is to realize that the psychology that is expected or desired of the lover in such circumstances reflects the fact that there are multiple standpoints an agent might occupy, and that the standpoint of friendship or love is not the same as that of individual self-interest. The value of the money I am offered is, presumably, its value *for me*. But the value of a friendship is not properly regarded as value *for me*, but rather as value *for us*.

To love, whether romantically or as a friend, is to see a person in a certain light. It is to place him at the center of one's attention, and thus to see considerations regarding his happiness and flourishing, and the flourishing of one's relationship with him, as central to one's conception of value and of what ought to be done. Competing considerations—for instance, those that support actions that conflict with one's friend's interests or with the health or very continuation of the relationship—are not merely overridden or outweighed; they are silenced. This is to say, in part, that friendship requires not only that these interests typically *win* contests with competing interests, but that the contest be typically not be felt as such. That a person feels tempted to betray her friend or lover for her own pleasure or gain may already constitute evidence against the depth and genuineness of her commitment, even if she manages, by falling back on the strength of her will, to resist the temptation. Thus it is not enough, from the standpoint of love, that the interests of one's friend or lover always prevail over competing interests. What is required, in ordinary circumstances at least, is not just that one's beloved's interests win the contest but also that there be *no contest*.

Conclusion

Love seems to demand that we often refuse to compare our beloveds with others, that we allow our appreciation of our beloveds to silence other values, and that we regard our beloveds with a sympathetic, generous attention, rather than from a detached, coldly impersonal perspective. If rationality forbade silencing and demanded constant comparison and dispassionate scrutiny, then love would seem to be deeply at odds with rationality. As I have argued in this chapter, however, although rationality may make these demands of agents in certain contexts and with respect to certain sorts of goods, it does not make them everywhere in connection with all goods. A great many of the values that are most important to people could not be properly appreciated or engaged with by people whose evaluative thinking always proceeded along the lines suggested by the comprehensive comparative survey view.

I have argued in this chapter that values should be understood in a pluralistic manner that allows that not all values can be accommodated from a single perspective or within a single human life; that there is often no neutral impersonal perspective from which choices between different values, value bearers, or even ways of life can be made; and that some values are thus incomparable, in the sense that an agent cannot compare them fully and impartially in the process of choosing between them. Moreover, this incomparability is not just an artifact of human limitations; it is not as if an intellectually superior being could always take in all the relevant values and make an informed, unbiased choice. Some values are such that a full appreciation of them *must* "fill the mind" to the exclusion of other values. A creature who was not able to experience this—one who could not feel awe or reverence or experience true engagement with an object of value—would not be in a *better* position to understand and evaluate such values, but in fact would be in a *worse* position. Such a creature might perhaps be a kind of ideal calculator of certain sorts of values. But to be a calculator is one thing, and to be an agent, and in particular a loving agent, is quite another.

Part of the key to understanding the rationality of love is to avoid misunderstanding the ways reasons work. In particular, it is necessary to understand the way in which values generate reasons that render certain objects or options *eligible* for choice without making it *mandatory* that agents select those particular options[16] Such a conception of reasons leaves an agent free to recognize the existence of certain values and value bearers without being rationally required or compelled always to respond to them in the fullest sense. She may, that is, judge something to be valuable without valuing it herself. This is what makes it possible for a person to love without contravening the requirements of rationality.

In loving Beatrice, Alighieri values her in a way that he values few, if any, others. Yet the fact that he values her in this special way does not require him to judge that she is especially valuable in comparison with others. Rather, to say that he loves her is to say that he is especially appreciative of her value, where "her value" includes both the general kinds of value that tend to be possessed by all individuals (but not by things, which is what makes individual persons as a class especially valuable) and the particular idiosyncratic values that help distinguish her from other persons. There is a good deal more to say, though, about just what such valuing involves and about what the distinction between valuing and judging to be valuable amounts to in psychological terms. Chapter 5 pursues this task.

five

Commitments, Values, and Frameworks

One cannot be capable of commitment on all planes. At least one can choose to live on the plane on which commitment is possible. Live according to what is honorable in oneself and only that. In certain cases this may lead to turning away from human beings even (and above all) when one has a passion for human beings.

—Albert Camus

Introduction

According to the vision view, one person's love for another is a positive response to her value and involves a positive assessment of at least some of her valuable features. Some antirationalists, as we have seen, deny this on the basis that if love were a positive response to the beloved's features, then the lover would be rationally obligated to respond in the same way to those features wherever they were found—and thus, rationally obligated to love anyone who possessed those features. If such consequences really do follow from the vision view, then we should reject it, simply on the basis that love quite clearly does not work in this way. As the incompleteness thesis states, there is *no* set of qualities that rationally obliges a person to love anyone who possesses those qualities, and this is true even if the set of qualities in question is the qualities "that one values in one's beloved." One is not, for instance, rationally obliged to love even an exact replica of one's beloved who possesses every quality one identifies as valuable in the beloved, for no one is ever *rationally* obligated to love anyone. Love is simply not the sort of response that can be rationally required.[1]

Thus, although initially it might appear plausible to say that a certain person loves another for her beauty, antirationalists such as O. H. Green will claim that this cannot be true, for neither beauty nor any other repeatable property can possibly play this role: "Of course Antony's love disposes him to pursue Cleopatra, but why? Once more, it is not just because he thinks she's beautiful. Antony knows many beautiful women in Egypt and Rome, and he doesn't pursue them all."[2]

The antirationalist's case, as we have seen, is based on a certain picture of the way valuable features generate reasons. (The reasons in question might be reasons for acting in certain ways, for having certain emotional responses, or for other sorts of responses; the point is the same regardless of what type of reason is in question.) In particular, the picture assumes that a valuable feature that generates reasons in one context must generate the same reasons in any context. Thus, if Cleopatra's beauty generates reasons for Antony to pursue her, then the beauty of Cleopatra's sister Arsinoe must also generate reasons, and indeed reasons of just the same sort (and, if she is as beautiful, of the same strength), for Antony to pursue *her*.

However, the discussion of chapter 2 suggests that this picture of the relationship between reasons and value bearers must be rejected. For there we noted that values sometimes seem to silence competing values, and that this could happen not only between competing values of different sorts (the way that the demands of morality silence the possible gains of immoral behavior, for instance), but even between values of the same sort. Thus Antony's appreciation of Cleopatra's beauty might act to silence, and thus make it impossible for him to appreciate, the beauty of Cleopatra's romantic rivals. He is, as people sometimes say, blinded by her beauty.

Such blindness can sometimes look a bit like insanity, particularly in melodramatic romantic novels.

> "Philip," she said softly, "come over here to me." She sat up on the narrow shelf and pushed back her hair. "I have helped to ruin your life, Phil," she said. "What can I do to help you now?"
>
> She was prepared for anything, reckless for the moment, touched by old memories, old loves, the hopeless sorrow of his face. But her beauty left him cold—the warm bloom of her cheeks, her full scarlet lips, her black-lashed eyes. Every hope in his being was centered on the slight sleeping figure at the farther side of the room, and he had no thought for anyone else.
>
> "Ask her to forgive me," he said suddenly. "You have done me some ill turns in your life, Vera, but her forgiveness would compensate for everything. I believe she has bewitched me. I care more for her little finger than I have ever cared for the whole body of any other woman. Help me now, Vera, or I shall go mad!"[3]

But while such declarations as Philip's may carry a tinge of romantic excess, they express a phenomenon that is familiar, intelligible, and, in many cases, not at all irrational. The temptation to view love's tendency to pick out and focus on particular individuals—and the silencing and blinding that accompany this—as irrational or arbitrary is based on a misunderstanding of the nature of the realm of values, which fails to recognize that human agents are faced not with a single continuum of comparable values from which rationality commands them to seek as large a share as possible, but with a plurality of frequently incomparable values, and that practical life is largely a matter of selecting and committing oneself to values in such a way as to give rise to the formation of a coherent and consistent identity.

Agents will, then, focus on certain values (or value bearers),[4] and the result will frequently be that competing values are silenced; for these agents, the way to a full recognition of the competitors' values is blocked. To say that a certain value is silenced for a given agent is not necessarily to say that he is entirely unaware of the existence of that value. Nor does it require that he regard it as somehow illusory or illegitimate. He might well admit its existence and presence, and even regard it as a valid source of reasons for action for *other* agents. (Philip is unmoved by Vera's beauty, but he can still see it; and unless he really has gone mad, he will surely be able to understand that other men might value her little finger in just the way that he values Elizabeth's.) To say that it is silenced is simply to say that he does not see it as providing reasons for *him*. He might still be able to recognize in a dispassionate, intellectual way that the value obtains. He might be able to recognize that this value plays the same motivating and justifying roles in the lives of others as the particular values to which he responds play in his own life. And at least in some cases he will be able to recognize the value in question as one that, had circumstances been otherwise, he himself might have come to appreciate and even to love.[5]

There is a distinction, then, between judging something to be valuable and actually valuing that thing oneself. The latter will presumably include the former, for it is hard to see how someone could value a thing without judging it to be valuable. At the very least, such a case of valuing must be unusual.[6] The important point, however, is that valuing x involves more, psychologically speaking, than does judging x to be valuable. It involves not merely a belief-type mental state—more precisely, an intellectual judgment—but various other motivational and emotional phenomena as well.

It is often the case that when an agent judges a certain value x to be valuable without valuing x in the full sense, it is because x has been silenced, for her, by her appreciation of some other value. The discussion in chapter 4 was meant to help us understand why such silencing should be a fairly pervasive feature of our evaluative and practical lives. If, as suggested there, values are pluralistic and sometimes deeply incompatible with one another, so that they may not all be incorporated into a single life or even compared fairly and objectively against one another from some sort of neutral point of view, then it is only to be expected that

evaluative thought will sometimes adopt a posture in which competing
values do not simply weigh against but silence one another. If the occupation of certain perspectives on value makes it impossible to appreciate
other forms of value, then silencing will to some degree simply be inevitable. But as we have seen, there are also cases in which silencing is not
inevitable so much as desirable. There are, that is, cases in which an agent
could conceivably come to recognize some value that is in competition
with the values she is most deeply committed to—that is, where coming to recognize the competing values is a *psychological* possibility—but
where it is better, for one reason or another, that she be the sort of person
who does not feel the full force of those competing values.

The perfectly virtuous agent, for instance, might, if she tried, come to
appreciate the force of the considerations that are trying to push her to
perform some immoral action or other. If she is truly and deeply virtuous,
then it might be hard for her to do so; but I do not think that we should
picture her virtue as a kind of intellectual incapacity that would make it
impossible for her to be able to feel the pull of the goods that immorality
promises, no matter how hard she might try. They are still goods, after
all, and appreciating goods is one of the things that virtuous agents tend
to be good at. But if she is truly virtuous, and if she values being virtuous
(and such valuing is presumably part of being virtuous), then she will not
want to make herself into a less virtuous person, and so will not choose
to try to change so as to be able to feel the attractions of immorality.[7]

Silencing, then, is to some degree a phenomenon that is forced on us
(by the plurality of values and the finitude of human capacities for value
appreciation), but at the same time it is also, to a significant degree, something we choose and endorse. Where the proper appreciation of a given
value calls for loyalty or fidelity of some sort, an agent who genuinely
appreciates it not only will not be but will not want to be strongly aware
of (i.e., tempted by) other, competing values. Certain values—those that
call for responses involving reverence, awe, and wonder—tend to fill the
mind to the exclusion of other attractors of attention and so to manifest
themselves to us in ways that involve the silencing of competing values.
But it is unusual for an agent to be *completely* captivated by any such
value without having chosen, at some level, to be so captivated. Human
agents are imperfect, their attention can easily wander, and where there
is no willed commitment to a value of that sort, silencing cannot be expected to be complete or entirely unwavering.

This chapter builds on the previous one in continuing to explore the
ways in which human agents respond to values. Here the focus is on the
nature of the experience of value and in particular on the kind of "spontaneous" motivation that arises from the direct perception and experience of a value. One thing we might wonder about is how agents deal

with fluctuations or lapses in such motivation with respect to the values they care about or are committed to. I have suggested that love is best regarded not purely as a response to the beloved or solely as a commitment to him, but rather as a response—one that involves the bestowing of appreciative and generous attention—combined with a commitment to having that sort of response. The overall aim of this chapter is to come to understand the distinction between valuing and judging to be valuable. This distinction, as I have already suggested, is necessary if we are to understand the way in which love for persons, despite its apparently irrational elements, constitutes a type of reason-guided response to value.

Value, Reasons, and Actions

Support for the antirationalist position typically originates in a certain story about the way in which valuable features generate reasons. I proceed by returning to the simplest version of that story, in the hope that seeing why it is *too* simple will lead us to a more adequate view. This story, in its simplest version, holds that every value gives rise to a reason for action whose strength corresponds to the degree of the value itself, and that rational agents simply act in direct response to whatever values there are in the world, acting in cases of conflict on more significant values in preference to less significant ones.

Surely this story gets something right. At the very least, we would be crippled in our attempts to understand human behavior if we were not permitted to interpret human agents, in a very large number of cases, as being engaged in the attempt to respond to values in appropriate ways. Knowing what a person is trying to do in bringing about a certain situation is nearly always a matter, at least in large part, of knowing what she takes to be good about the situation she is trying to bring about (or, what amounts to the same thing, knowing what is bad about whatever situation she is trying to avoid). The appeal to values is no shallow feature of our attempts to explain and understand in this area. Rather, it lies at the core of such attempts.

Nonetheless, the simple story must be rejected as too simple. First, it might be pointed out that people do not act on what values there *are*, but rather on what values they *think* there are. Since people sometimes make mistakes about values, they do not always have the reasons they think they have, and in fact they sometimes act without any good reason at all.

It will not, perhaps, be excessively difficult to revise the simple story so as to acknowledge this. But there are other complications that are potentially more troublesome, for people often knowingly fail to act on certain values they are aware of, accept as legitimate, and think they ought to act on. Human beings are variable and inconsistent in their susceptibility to value. They are subject to boredom or depression; they are easily distracted; they are moody; worst of all, they are sometimes perverse. Values that on certain occasions strike one with force and give rise to spontaneous motivation without any conscious effort at all can on other occasions have little if any effect on the very same person. In his biography of the poet John Clare, Frederick Martin writes:

> His intense admiration and worship of nature could not brook confinement of any sort, even such as suffered within the vast domain of Burghley Park. While gardener at the latter place, his poetical vein lay entirely dormant; he was never for a moment in the mood of writing nor even of reading verses. Perhaps the habits of dissipation into which he had fallen had something to do with this; yet it was owing still more to the position in which he was placed. The same scenery which had inspired him to his first poetical composition, when viewed in the glowing light of a beautiful morning in spring, left him cold and uninspired ever after. He often complained to his fellow-laborers, that he could not "see far enough": it was as if he felt the rattling of the chain, which bound him to the spot. A yearning after absolute freedom, mental as well as physical, was one of his strongest instincts through life, and not possessing this, he appeared to value little else.[8]

Clare seems to have been suffering from what philosophers frequently call *accidie*. It is one of a family of phenomena—others include *akrasia* and weakness of will—that affect the functioning of a practical agent and prevent agents from being fully practically rational. Consider the agent who says, "I know I should quit smoking for the sake of my health, and I want to, but I just can't"; the depressed agent who knows that she ought to seek professional help but cannot motivate herself to leave the house; or the neurotic who repeatedly sabotages his career or his relationships, knowing full well that doing so will only cause him further distress. Such agents are not acting on the values that they take to be in the world, however much they might wish they were able to do so. Whether or not we convict the agent in any particular case of full-fledged irrationality, all such cases seem to involve some sort of deep failure of practical reason and open a gulf between an agent's motivations and the values and reasons she knows to be present but just cannot bring herself to be moved by.

There are also situations that show a discernible gap between the values and reasons themselves. And in many of these cases—unlike cases of akrasia, accidie, weakness of will, and so forth—an agent need not be at all irrational, or less than perfectly rational, in failing to act on values she recognizes as real and as perfectly legitimate. Some writers or artists find it necessary to become obsessed with their current project, to the point where potential distractions, including a great many things they might ordinarily find pleasurable, satisfying, or otherwise worthwhile, simply fail to engage them. Addicts and dieters might acknowledge that it would be pleasant to shoot up or eat the chocolate cake—and thus acknowledge that there is at least some reason that speaks in favor of these actions—while nevertheless striving (or at least wishing) not to be moved by those reasons. Similarly, whether the potentially tempted husband who is offered an opportunity for infidelity is *actually* tempted depends not on whether he recognizes that cheating would be enjoyable—of course he knows that it would be—but on whether he allows the prospect of this pleasure to engage his motivations. The ability to be moved by one's perceptions of value is necessary to being an agent, but the ability to *resist* being moved by at least some of those perceptions is also a requirement of agency in its fullest sense.

The choice to engage with some values while disengaging from others helps shape and form one's life as a whole. In committing to a certain cause, for instance, an agent will tend to detach herself from other potential causes and pursuits. This is simply part of what commitment is. (One can, of course, be committed to more than one cause, though perhaps with some risk of conflict; what one cannot do is commit oneself to *every* legitimate cause.) The result is that many other causes, projects, and goals, which may be acknowledged to express or involve perfectly legitimate values—values that are fully capable of providing real and substantial reasons for action to *other* agents, who have chosen to adopt those causes, projects, and goals as their own—will nonetheless not be treated by the agent in question as giving rise to such reasons for *her*.

Similarly, in the case of a love relationship, we might think it perfectly reasonable for Sam (in chapter 2's Drowning Wife case) to acknowledge the value of Daniel's life—and, indeed, to acknowledge that that value is no less real or significant than the value of Andrea's life—while still regarding the threat to Andrea's life as giving rise to what are, for Sam, particularly urgent and compelling reasons for action of a sort that are not generated by Daniel's predicament. This is not to say that the danger to Daniel fails to give rise to *any* sort of reason for saving him, but only that the reasons generated by the threat to Andrea, given her relationship with Sam and his feelings for her, are of a different order and seriousness. Sam judges Daniel's life to be valuable, even as valuable as Andrea's, objectively speaking. But he himself does not value Daniel's life in the same way, with the result that in this case Sam's reasons for saving Daniel are, in a real sense, silenced by his reasons for saving Andrea.[9]

The distinction between judging something to be valuable and actually valuing it is not one that turns on a single dimension. Rather, a number of features of a response contribute to its being a case of full-fledged valuing, rather than simply a case of judging to be valuable. We can make some headway, I suggest, by considering *paradigmatic* experiences of value—cases that involve not just the judgment that something is valuable but the experience of that thing *as* valuable. By distinguishing the elements of such a response, and then considering what happens when we take certain elements away or isolate them from one another, we can reach a better understanding of the distinction between judging x to be valuable and actually valuing x. And this, in turn, will put us in a position fully to answer the various puzzles about love that are sometimes alleged to make trouble for the vision view.

Responding to Value: Acknowledging versus Appreciating

As I suggested earlier, one way to understand the range of possible responses to a given value is to begin by describing what we might consider a "full" or "complete" response (that is, the direct, unimpeded experience of some value perceived as real and compelling), attempting to isolate the various elements present in such a response, and then considering what happens when some of these elements, but not others, are present. This, at any rate, is the procedure I will follow.

Consider, then, an agent caught in the act, so to speak, of responding to a given value, as instantiated in some object or other, in the manner suggested earlier. (For convenience, I will refer to such cases as instances of *paradigmatic valuing*.) This might be a person in love gazing at her beloved or a music lover listening to a favorite recording. It might be someone reveling in the sight of the starry heavens above, contemplating the moral law within, or, for that matter, any number of less high-minded examples—a person enjoying a slice of chocolate cake, for instance. Again, we are to imagine an agent whose attention is undivided and whose response to the value in question is wholehearted and uninhibited. (I will concentrate on examples of positive value, but we could make the same points with respect to cases of negative value. An agent who is overcome by severe physical pain, for example, is also undergoing what can be considered a kind of paradigmatic valuing.)

What is taking place in the minds of such persons? Obviously there are a great many things that might be going on: memories, images, speculations, hopes and fears for the future, and so forth. The phenomenology can be expected to be complex and to vary from one individual to another and from one occasion to another. I suggest, though, that at least four elements are necessary if the value response in question is to constitute what I call a *full* response.

First, as I suggested earlier, there must be a *judgment* that the value in question is a real, that is to say legitimate, value (and, as well, that the object in question really does possess it). Along with this, the agent must also determine, in effect, that the value in question, in its particular instantiation here, is *relevant* to her situation. Third, there must be a kind of affective response: the agent will see the object in a positive light, will at least typically take pleasure in the experience, and so forth. And fourth, there must also be a motivational response: the agent must to some degree be moved, *at least hypothetically*, to behave in appropriate ways toward the valued object (for instance, to protect it from harm, to encourage it to flourish, to refrain from denigrating it; also, to prolong one's experience of it or increase future opportunities for additional experiences of it, and so forth.)

There is more to say about all of these responses. Let us first pause, however, to note the importance of the fact that the analysis of "*A* values *x*" that I propose does not attempt to analyze valuing in terms of any *single* attitude or mental act. Indeed, because full-fledged instances of paradigmatic valuing involve separate elements of quite different sorts, attempts to analyze "valuing *x*" in terms of a single type of mental entity are doomed to failure. Philosophers have observed for some time that valuing cannot be straightforwardly analyzed in terms of desire, despite the fact that valuing frequently involves a desire for the valued thing.[10] The analysis I suggest here recognizes the importance of desiring to valuing without committing itself to the implausible view that desiring *x* can *in itself* amount to valuing *x*. And by holding the various elements to be at least somewhat independent of one another, the account helps explain why it has turned out to be so difficult to draw a hard line between cases in which an agent really does value some object of her attention and cases in which she does not.

However, in suggesting that these can be distinguished as separate elements of paradigmatic valuing, I do not claim that they will be experienced as separate by the evaluator. As I have said before, perception tends to be holistic, and the direct perception of values is no exception. The separation between the elements is conceptual, not psychological. Indeed, where the response in question is genuinely paradigmatic, the judgments about value and the affective and motivational responses will tend to present themselves as a single experience; in such cases of wholehearted, uninhibited valuing, the evaluator is *all at once* moved by the object (the judgments and the affective response, presented as a single "way of seeing") to behave in certain ways (the motivational response). Theoretically speaking, we may distinguish between judgments and motivations. And indeed, as we have already noted, in some instances of agents responding to value, particularly those that fall short in some way of what we consider a fully rational response, these elements will come apart; an agent may, for instance, have the judgment that *x* is valuable and relevant but not have the affective or motivational response, and vice versa. But these are not instances of the sort of wholehearted, unreserved response to value I am taking as paradigmatic. I return to this point below.

Keeping these points in mind, let us consider the four elements of the experience of *paradigmatically valuing x*. The first element is the simple judgment that *x* is valuable, in some manner or other. We are speaking here of *final* value, not *instrumental* value; cases of instrumental value, in which *x* is good only as a means for obtaining or bringing about some other good thing, are not cases in which *x* can be valued *fully*, in the sense that I intend. However, we need not be speaking here of moral value or of any particular species of value; the point is simply that a person enjoying, and hence valuing, a recording of a musical performance, a slice of chocolate cake, or any other item must regard the thing she is enjoying as *in some way* good, for if she did not so regard it, her experience could not be said to be one of valuing. (Note that I am *not* asserting the converse, that judging *x* to be good must involve *seeing it as* good. Indeed, we will need to keep these apart in order to make room for the various distinctions and phenomena we are trying to understand.)

The second element is the agent's determination that the value of *x* is not only real but also *relevant* to herself—that is, to her own situation and decision making. (I refer to this as a *determination* rather than a judgment for reasons that will be made clear later in the chapter.) As we have already noted, there are plenty of values in the world that are perfectly real and yet do not play a significant role in a given agent's practical deliberations, simply because they are not relevant; they are not part of the set of her projects, her commitments, her concerns.[11] These values are relational or agent-relative in some important manner; they apply to some people but not others. For example, the Basque Nationalist cause plays a significant role in the practical deliberations of Basque Nationalists and in those of their opponents, but not in my deliberations. Since I am neither a proponent nor an opponent of Basque Nationalism, that value is not relevant to me. It should be clear, though, that I can deny its relevance to myself without denying that it does constitute a perfectly legitimate value that is quite relevant to the situations and decision making of others. A person who denies the relevance of Basque Nationalism to her own deliberations need not see the actions of Basque Nationalists as perplexing or unintelligible, as one presumably would who took their cause not to possess any sort of value at all or to be irrelevant not just to herself but to everyone.

There is a close relation between relevance and silencing. Consider the faithful wife in chapter 2's infidelity example, who is not even a little tempted by the charms of the attractive stranger. To say that his attractive features have, for her, been silenced by her love for her husband comes close to saying that she has, in some significant way, determined those values to be irrelevant. She need not deny that the stranger *is* genuinely attractive, perhaps even as attractive as her husband; it is simply that for her, the question of how attractive he is is beside the point. She does not occupy the comparative perspective demanded by pure self-interest, the sort of perspective from which her husband's attractions, and the benefits of being faithful to him, would have to be evaluated neutrally against the attractions and possible benefits of other potential partners. Rather, she occupies a loving perspective, from which the focus of her attention will be on her husband and their relationship.

The fact that silencing is involved in this way should make it clear that a determination of relevance need not be, and frequently will not be, an explicit matter; the thought "This value is relevant to me" need not pass through the agent's mind, not even momentarily. The fact that a given value engages her, and that no judgment or hesitation arises during the process of her responding that prevents it from engaging her, is enough to show that she is treating the value in question as relevant. Of course, there will be occasions on which the agent does pose the matter explicitly to herself: those, particularly, in which an agent notices that she has a tendency automatically to treat certain values as relevant and begins to wonder whether it is appropriate that she do so or those, too, in which there are greater than usual costs attached to treating a certain value as relevant.

The third element of paradigmatic valuing is some sort of affective response to the thing valued. One sees it in a positive light; one's pulse quickens; maybe one catches one's breath at its beauty; perhaps one is so struck by it that one feels humbled or awestruck or is stopped in one's tracks. Particularly where the value bearer is a person, one might feel emotionally vulnerable to that person's moods, feelings, and perceptions (especially her perceptions of oneself). And of course, positive experiences of value tend to make people happy. In less extreme cases, like the chocolate cake, one simply experiences pleasure or enjoyment of some sort. Where the value bearer is not already possessed or is far away, one may contemplate with pleasure the thought of possessing it, of spending time in its vicinity, or of being united or reunited with it.[12]

Similarly, with respect to the fourth element, valuing x wholeheartedly and uninhibitedly must involve being motivated, at least to some degree, to act in certain ways toward x. Exactly how one is motivated to act depends on the nature of the thing being valued and on one's beliefs regarding how such things ought to be valued, as well as on the particular circumstances of the encounter; it is not always necessary that one be moved to action, only that one be pulled in the direction of being prepared to act should action be necessary and appropriate. Sometimes the pull is toward coming to possess x or toward changing one's life in other ways that will increase one's chances to experience and enjoy x. At other times the motivation is not so much to perform some action that is for one's own benefit as to do something for x's benefit, as when x is vulnerable and stands in need of protection or assistance. In urgent cases, the motivation must be strong enough to lead to direct action. In Drowning Wife Sam's valuing of Andrea will manifest itself primarily as a very strong urge to jump into the water or do whatever else is necessary to save her from drowning. Under more ordinary circumstances, his valuing her will lead him to engage in many types of complex behavior: seeking out her company; being physically and verbally affectionate; attempting to initiate joint projects with her; being sensitive to her moods and emotional needs; providing a sympathetic ear when needed; revealing things to her that he would not share with others; and so forth. A full list, if there could even be such a thing, would be very long indeed.

In cases of paradigmatic valuing, all four of the elements we have identified occur together, forming a unified whole. Indeed, they often appear quite inseparable to the agent who experiences them. I do not claim, again, that the elements cannot come apart; obviously they can. I only claim that cases in which they come apart are not paradigmatic; they are not cases of wholehearted, unimpeded, and uninhibited valuing. Many types of cases in which the four elements come apart are quite familiar to us and have received considerable philosophical attention.

Consider, for example, a variant of Drowning Wife in which Sam is suffering from accidie rooted in depression. He is so radically depressed that when he sees Andrea floundering in the water, he feels nothing. He knows that he ought to be horrified and be motivated to jump into the water, but the ordinary affective and motivational resources simply are not there. Despite his failure to have the appropriate affective response, Sam might be able, depending on how seriously depressed he is, to summon the motivation to jump in the water. After all, he still judges Andrea's life to be valuable and takes that value as relevant to himself. Moreover, he may be sufficiently self-aware to understand *why* he feels no spontaneous urge to save her and to realize that this lack of motivation should not be taken as evidence that there is no reason for him to save her. In fact, there are two strong reasons. First, there is a reason that anyone would have: Andrea is an innocent person and does not want to die. And second, there is an especially strong reason: she is his wife, and he loves her. The fact that Sam is for the moment incapable of feeling moved by the force of either of these reasons does not suggest that they have somehow evaporated or lost their normative force. So long as Sam is rational enough to recognize this, he ought to be able to find what we might call an external or nonspontaneous motivation to function in the place of the internal motivation that would, were he in a healthier psychological state, arise spontaneously from his perception of the situation.

We can distinguish, then, between two ways of recognizing that one has a reason for action. An agent *appreciates* her reason when she feels the full force of it: she is in its grip, as a result of either direct experience (beholding the painting, hearing her beloved's laugh, eating the cake) or vivid imagining of such experience. By contrast, an agent merely *acknowledges* a reason when she makes an intellectual judgment that she does have that reason without feeling its force in this way. There are many ways in which an agent might justify such an acknowledgment. She might, as in the case of the depressed Sam, recognize that x has a certain value that is relevant to her and thus generates reasons for her on the basis of her having directly experienced that value in the past, even though she is unable to do so at the moment. Thus I know that I have reason to listen to the Rolling Stones' *Let It Bleed* because I remember having enjoyed it greatly in the past, even though I am not currently listening to it or even imagining doing so. Alternatively, she might recognize some values and reasons on the basis of other people's testimony regarding *their* experiences of them. Someone who is unable to see what is so special about Mark Rothko's paintings might nonetheless accept the word of his trusted art instructor that they are great works of art and thus be moved to seek them out, keep looking at them, and try to learn more about them, in the hope of eventually coming to that full understanding. Moreover, a version of the same situation might be repeated much later: even after one has learned to see Rothko's works with an appreciating eye, one's intellectual knowledge that they are great paintings will persist, and be available as knowledge, even when one is not looking at or vividly imagining looking at the works and is thus in a certain sense alienated, albeit contingently and temporarily, from their value. The ability to see with understanding and appreciation is necessary to a full experience of value, but the presence of the thing—in imagination, if not in reality—is also necessary.[13]

The distinction between merely acknowledging one's reasons and appreciating them in the fullest sense thus reflects both the fact that we are not always in direct contact with the value-bearing objects relevant to our decisions and the fact that even when we are in contact with them, we do not always manage to respond to them fully. We might think of the first two elements identified above—the judgment as to value and the determination of relevance—as being connected to *endorsement*, and the second two—the affective and motivational responses—as being connected to *engagement*. That is, an agent endorses a given bearer of value by judging it to be valuable and by taking its value to be directly relevant to her own decision making. (By going this far, she has already, in essence, acknowledged that it gives her certain reasons for action.) She engages with a bearer of value by having the appropriate affective response to it and by being spontaneously motivated—that is, motivated by her perception of its value—to act toward it in appropriate ways. In so engaging with it, she makes it a part of her life that has some significance for her.[14] In cases that fall short of full paradigmatic valuing—cases of accidie or simply of absentmindedness—an agent endorses a value without being able to properly engage with it; she knows, on an intellectual level, that the object of her attention is valuable and that its value is relevant to her, but the affective and motivational responses that ought naturally to accompany this recognition do not occur. This alienation of experience is beautifully captured in a passage from E. M. Forster's *A Passage to India*:

> It was the last moment of the light, and as he gazed at the Marabar Hills they seemed to move graciously towards him like a queen, and their charm became the sky's. At the moment they vanished they were everywhere, the cool benediction of the night descended, the stars sparkled, and the whole universe was a hill. Lovely, exquisite moment—but passing the Englishman with averted face and on swift wings. He experienced nothing himself; it was as if someone had told him there was such a moment, and he was obliged to believe.[15]

Similarly, an agent might find herself being engaged by a value she does not fully endorse. Consider an agent who finds herself attracted, unwillingly, to a man other than her husband. The attractive stranger is, of course, a bearer of genuine value—he really is, let us suppose, handsome, witty, and sympathetic—and a romantic relationship with him would also bear certain sorts of real value; but these are values the agent thinks she ought to regard, and indeed wishes to regard, as irrelevant to her situation. She would like the stranger's attractions to be silenced for her. If she possessed voluntary control over her affective and motivational responses, this is how she would choose to feel, or rather choose not to feel. But try as she might, she may well find herself unable to end the conflict between the unruly elements of her responsive nature through force of will alone.

There are a great many ways in which a response to value can fall short of ideal response recognized by and instantiated in the paradigm of full responsiveness I have sketched. The fact that our responses are rarely fully ideal has important implications for human agents and for the nature of the role that commitment, in particular, plays in practical reasoning and action—implications that shed considerable light on personal relationships.

Backgrounds and Frameworks

Accidie and absentmindedness are fairly common phenomena in our practical lives. Just as frequently, perhaps, agents are assailed by temptations, moved by values they know they ought not to be moved by. What, then, is the imperfectly rational agent, afflicted with accidie or plagued by temptation, to do?

One might imagine an agent for whom this question is not really a question. I am thinking of the sort of agent who places a great deal of credence in his immediate value experiences, who takes these experiences as an infallible guide to action. When this agent experiences an overwhelming attraction to some value bearer or other, he does not stop to consider whether acting on this urge coheres well with his long-term plans and more settled desires; nor does he ask himself how long this urge is likely to continue, what its source might be, how it might feel to act on it or fulfill it or, alternatively, to resist it, or any other question that might speak to the issue of how reliable, as a guide to action, this urge might be. He simply goes for it.[16] (Or, if at this particular moment he fails to feel a strong urge to do something—even something a rational agent would see that there is good reason to do—he does not go for it.)

Such an agent is naive; he places too much credence in his immediate value experiences. He falsely believes, or acts as if he believes, that the fact that he is experiencing a given object as overwhelmingly attractive or desirable must mean that it is a worthy object of his attention, pursuit, and, if possible, possession and that he necessarily has reason to respond in these ways. And he also seems to believe that the fact that he *does not*, at this moment, experience a given value bearer as valuable must indicate that it has, at the present time, no value that is relevant to his decisions and actions.

Fortunately, most agents know better. They have learned, frequently through hard experience, that human beings are imperfect and sometimes conceive powerful desires for things that are not good for them and that in some sense they do not even really want, or that they fail to be moved by things that they value very much. Akrasia, accidie, weakness of will—all these phenomena occur when an agent's immediate inclinations and value experiences fail to match her well-grounded judgments about which values are real and relevant to her situation. Although experiences of value function as important indicators of value and relevance, then, they are not and ought not to be taken as automatically authoritative or decisive.

In the reasoning of ordinary agents, there is a further level of judgment that happens *after* the initial response to value, during which the agent assesses this response and then reaches a verdict both with respect to what her reasons are and (what is closely related but not quite the same thing) with respect to how she will act. We might compare this with the perceptual case. Here, too, a reasonable agent will be capable of examining her immediate (perceptual) experiences of her environment and interrogating them as to how reliable they really are, how much credence she ought to place in them, before allowing herself to come to a final verdict regarding whether to accept or reject the judgments of her environment toward which her immediate experiences incline her. (The stick that is partly in water looks bent, but that does not mean that it is *really* bent; the sun looks to be about the size of a small coin, but she knows it is much larger; etc.)

It is the existence of this further stage of self-interrogation prior to arriving at a verdict about how one ought to act that will make it possible for an agent like the depressed Sam, whose natural and spontaneous motivation has been erased by his accidie, to nonetheless decide to act on his judgment, form what I have referred to as an external motivation, and jump into the water to save his wife. Moreover, the formation of external motivations at this stage of the deliberative process does not appear only in dramatic situations involving drowning spouses or opportunities for infidelity. It is, rather, an exceedingly common event in the daily goings-on of ordinary humans.

Thus, in describing the situations of agents whose responses to value are "unruly" in the sense of failing to be unified and to some extent being in conflict with themselves, I do not take myself to be describing situations that are extreme or unusual. Quite the contrary, a lack of total integration among the various elements of the value response that I have identified is a very common predicament for human beings. No human being is capable of *always* fully perceiving and appreciating the values that give rise to her reasons for action. All of us, at least much of the time, need to summon external motivations for performing actions that we judge to be supported by reasons that are not, at the moment, functioning as full-fledged sources of spontaneous motivation. This applies to trivial actions as well. If I stop on the way home from work to buy a slice of chocolate cake for later, I might not be imagining how good the cake will taste, even though the anticipated pleasure of that experience gave me the reason to buy it. I simply know that I will enjoy eating it later, without having to dwell on or imagine the experience.[17]

Much of the time, then, particularly in the case of actions that are habitual or not too costly to perform, one simply does not need to fully appreciate one's reasons for acting in order to bring oneself to act on them. It is enough, if an agent is sufficiently rational, for her simply to acknowledge these reasons. Of course, agents are not always sufficiently rational. Failures of appreciation can lead to failures of acknowledgment or a failure to remember what one has acknowledged; it is possible for certain reasons and values simply to slip one's mind if they are too infrequently appreciated or dwelled on. The self-help literature is full of exhortations to do things that we ought to do without needing to be told. "Make some time for yourself!" "Do something fun!" "Don't forget to tell your family that you love them!" And so on. There is also a further difficulty caused by the fact that one's motivation is sometimes relevant not only to the question of *whether* one performs a certain task but also to *how well* one performs it. This is the point the journalist Alistair Cooke was getting at when he famously said that "a professional is someone who can do his best work when he doesn't particularly feel like it."[18]

In such cases—where a motivation must not only exist but must be sufficiently robust to provide the impetus or inspiration for performing well or to overpower competing considerations that speak in favor of choosing some other superficially attractive but ultimately less justifiable course of action—mere acknowledgment will often not be enough;[19] what is required is precisely some degree of appreciation of the reasons and values that support that particular course of action. The rewards of being faithful to one's spouse or of sticking to one's diet may seem somewhat distant, abstract, or wan compared with the immediate pleasures of going to bed with the attractive stranger or eating the chocolate cake. Still, agents do manage to act as they judge they ought to act much of the time—even when their immediate value experiences are inclining them to act in some other way. After all, although I began this chapter by considering value responsiveness as a fundamentally *episodic* matter—as manifested in particular, relatively isolated episodes in which some value or other was directly perceived and experienced—we must not forget that an agent's value relations are not only, or even primarily, composed of relatively discrete individual episodes of directly experienced value. Rather, human agents tend to display relatively consistent patterns of behavior toward certain values over extended periods of time. In particular, they tend to display fairly consistent patterns of response to certain values—patterns of response that consist partly in judgment and partly in feeling and action. These patterns of response, which in large part constitute the particular commitments of a given agent, tend to be maintained and to continue to function even when not being bolstered or confirmed by particular experiences of value.

Let us return, for a moment, to the agent we were considering earlier—an agent who put so much credence in each ephemeral value experience that he never bothered to inquire as to which of them he ought, and which he ought not, to act on. Such an agent would not bother to form "external" motivations, since he would deem his spontaneous motivations to be sufficient. This agent's relations to value would be profoundly and pervasively episodic and might vary considerably from one episode of engagement to the next. It is hard to see how such an agent could form commitments to any values or value bearers, or for that matter how he could have lasting relationships with other individuals. Indeed, the existence that such an agent pursued would probably not be recognizable as

anything resembling what we normally think of as a human life. Whatever else we might mean by that phrase, we tend to think of such a life as
having a certain integrity—something that is structured, at least to a considerable degree, by commitments and patterns of consistent behavior.
An agent who endorsed and acted on his current whims and desires at a
particular moment would surely *not* display anything resembling consistent behavior over time, for the whims and desires in question would be
constantly changing and would, taken together, form a multifarious and
fairly incoherent set.

Why is this so? A pessimist might conclude that whatever apparatus
is responsible for arriving at value judgments must be deeply flawed, resulting in a deep disconnect between values and human experiences of
value. But the evidence does not justify this conclusion. After all, on a
case-by-case basis, an ordinary agent's experiences of value seem to be, in
very large part, experiences of actual and not imagined values, no matter
how chaotic and discordant the full set of such experiences might be. The
better explanation, as suggested by the discussion in chapter 4, is that
values themselves are, in a sense, incoherent, or at any rate pluralistic;
not all value bearers, and indeed not all values, can be fully recognized
or incorporated into a single life. Because many values compete with
each other for our attention, an agent who merely lets himself be guided
by "whatever values there are," and thus responds to each one in turn
as it is perceived and appreciated, risks incoherence and perhaps even
unintelligibility.

Admittedly, such behavior exhibits a degree of intelligibility; after all,
the agent is allowing his actions to be guided by *value*. Still, unless we
are somehow in a position to predict which values are likely to strike
him as compelling, we will be highly unlikely to predict his behavior.
(Worse still, he will be in the same situation with respect to himself.) And
although each individual action may be intelligible—in terms of whatever
value it is aimed at honoring, promoting, attaining, or recognizing—it is
not likely that these individual actions will very often add up to constitute a meaningful pattern of behavior over time, a pattern that might,
among other things, help us answer the fundamental question regarding
the agent's identity: just who, exactly, *is* this person? Indeed, beyond the
bare description "a pursuer of values," it is not clear that there will be a
definite or substantial answer to that question.

Agents avoid such unintelligibility and forge identities for themselves
by committing to particular values that thereby become important to
them. Indeed, the decision to commit oneself to a given value is, in essence, the decision to treat it as important. Committing oneself to a particular person, for instance—this is far from the only type of commitment
one could discuss but is most relevant for us here—involves taking that

person's happiness, well-being, interests, and so forth, to generate compelling reasons for action in a way that similar considerations attached
to other agents do not. A friendship or a romantic love relationship is
largely constituted by the partners' commitment to each other in this
sense, where the commitment involves not only the intellectual judgment
that the beloved's interests and flourishing are worth promoting, nor only
the volitional decision to treat these things as matters of great significance, but also the appropriate attendant emotions and perceptions: one
must see them as important, one must feel their importance, and one
must thus be spontaneously motivated to treat one's beloved in a caring
and loving matter. At least, this must be true much of the time; we can acknowledge, again, that all of us are at least sometimes victims of accidie,
akrasia, and so on. After all, nobody's perfect.

Commitments of this sort help shape an agent's life. They also shape
an agent's perceptions, by helping to determine which elements of an
agent's situation will present themselves with special salience and which
others will retreat quietly into the background. Thus the commitment of
the will that is involved shapes one's perceptions of the considerations
that are relevant to one's practical reasoning in a way that is connected
with the phenomenon I have been referring to as silencing. To an extent,
an agent, once committed to certain values and value bearers, will not
even notice the potential reason-giving force of considerations that are
unrelated to, or in competition with, her own commitments—considerations that will generate perfectly legitimate and compelling reasons for
other agents and that might have done so for her had she committed
herself differently.

To say that an agent will tend not to notice considerations that are
irrelevant to her own commitments, and to the rest of her situation, is
certainly not to say that she will notice every consideration that is relevant to her situation. After all, different considerations operate in different ways. Some operate in the most straightforward manner, simply
by generating reasons in favor of a certain action or response. Following
Jonathan Dancy, we might refer to these as "favorers." But others operate
in other ways. An enabler, for instance, is a condition that does not generate a reason for an agent to act but whose presence allows some other
condition to serve as a favorer. To borrow an example from Dancy: it
seems plausible to think that one ought to keep one's promises, but only
if what one has promised is just; a case in which one has promised to do
something unjust is a case in which one ought not to keep one's promise.[20] It would be a mistake, though, to think that in the ordinary case of
having promised to do x, the fact that x is just is a reason for keeping the
promise. The reason, rather, is simply that one has promised to do x. "X
is just" is not a reason or the source of a reason, even though its truth is

necessary in order for the fact that one promised to x to give one a reason for doing x. "X is just," then, is not a reason or a source of a reason but an enabler, a kind of background condition that allows some other consideration to generate a reason. Similarly, an intensifier is a background condition that makes a favoring reason stronger than it would otherwise be. The favoring reason here does not need the background condition in order to exist—it would still be present even if that condition did not obtain—but it does need it to obtain in order to be as strong as it is.[21]

It is often quite plausible to see personal relationships as enablers—or, in many cases, intensifiers—rather than as generators of reasons. Enablers and intensifiers form the background against which other considerations can count, for a given agent, as reasons of a particular strength. And this is just what relationships seem to do. As we have already noted with respect to Drowning Wife, it is at least somewhat odd for Sam to be too conscious of the fact that *it is his wife* who is drowning; not (again) that he should somehow *fail* to be conscious of this fact—it is simply part of his conception of the situation—but there would be something unusual and inappropriate about his dwelling at length on the nature of their relationship at this particular time. The hypothesis that a relationship functions as an enabler or intensifier rather than as a favoring reason seems to capture this intuition. On this view, Sam's reason for acting matches the content of the thought most people think he ought to have: "Andrea is drowning!" That the fact that Andrea is drowning is especially significant for him, and so gives rise to a particularly strong and compelling reason for him to act, is explained by various other facts: she is his wife, he loves her, they have a certain history, and so forth. But all these are background facts, relevant to the situation and to his action but not reasons themselves or facts that ought to pass explicitly through his mind. (As Frankfurt writes, "I cannot help wondering why the man should have even the one thought that it's his wife. Are we supposed to imagine that at first he didn't recognize her?")

Another way of describing the situation would be to adapt Michael Bratman's suggestion that certain considerations (Bratman's particular concern is intentions) may be seen as generating reasons, but not reasons of the ordinary sort; rather, they generate *framework reasons*.

> So, do intentions provide reasons for action or not? On the one hand, intentions do provide—by way of demands for coherence and consistency—considerations that are directly relevant in deliberation to the rationality of the ensuing intention and action. On the other hand, intentions do not provide reasons that are to be weighed along with desire-belief reasons in favor of one considered alternative over another. The best thing to say is that intentions provide special kinds of reasons—*framework reasons*—

whose role is to help determine the relevance and admissibility of options. These reasons do not compete with desire-belief reasons, but rather structure the process of weighing such reasons.[22]

Again, one might well see relationships, or commitments to relationships, as operating in much the same way.[23] It seems exactly right that one of the major roles of a personal relationship, like that of an intention, is to "determine the relevance and admissibility" not only of options but also of potentially reason-generating considerations that will affect our choices from among these options. It is, again, his love for Andrea that makes her peril relevant to Sam's situation in a way that Daniel's is not. And it is certainly *possible* to say that intentions and commitments work by providing reasons—so long as we keep in mind that these are not reasons for choosing one action over another, but rather reasons for regarding certain considerations as opposed to others as generating a further level of reasons, those that speak in favor of or against certain actions.

I do not think that it makes much difference whether we deny that personal relationships generate *any* sort of reason and view them instead as enablers or intensifiers, or whether we allow that they generate reasons but insist that they are framework reasons rather than ordinary favoring reasons. Both pictures allow us to capture the important insight here, which is that the main practical role of personal relationships is not to generate reasons for action of the most straightforward sort: reasons for action that directly favor or disfavor actions and are to be balanced against whatever other, competing reasons for action arise in any given situation, in order to see which outweighs which. (A picture that regarded personal relationships primarily as generators of this sort of reason would, among other difficulties, have trouble accounting for silencing, since silenced reasons are not simply outweighed but are thrown out of court altogether, so to speak.) Personal relationships, rather, form part of the background against which practical reasoning, including the perception of one's reasons, takes place; what counts as a reason is determined largely by the relationships and value commitments one brings to the situation.

Personal relationships are not, of course, the only types of enabling conditions that operate in this area. Indeed, once we have the idea of enablers on the table, we find ourselves in a position to more clearly articulate what the defender of the vision view will want to say about Green's argument that the fact that "Antony knows many beautiful women in Egypt and Rome, and he doesn't pursue them all," shows that Antony's thinking that Cleopatra is beautiful cannot be his reason for pursuing her. The proper response to this is that Cleopatra's beauty *can* be a reason for Antony to love her, so long as its reason-generating capacity is enabled by some sort of background condition—one that does not simultaneously enable the beauty of other women to generate reasons in the same way. There are many possibilities for what this enabler might be, but the most obvious candidate might be Antony's receptiveness to certain sorts of beauty or the fact that he saw Cleopatra at a time when he happened to be particularly susceptible to beauty. (Later in the relationship, his love for her will serve as an enabler, if I am right that love is, in large part, a commitment to seeing someone in a certain way.) Antony's finding Cleopatra more beautiful than any other woman is not a matter of her being, objectively speaking, the most beautiful. It is a matter of how he sees her. But it does not follow from this that his perception of her beauty is illusory or a mere projection. Nor does it follow that her beauty cannot serve as one of his reasons for loving her.

Commitments and Importance

> Goodness all by itself is not enough: we must bring the object into relation with our own urgent strivings in order for its goodness to be something for us, to excite our emotions.
>
> —Spinoza

Forming a commitment is, at least sometimes, something one chooses to do. Presented with an array of values, an agent may decide to commit herself to some values and not to others. Still, the matter is not always entirely under the agent's control. Sometimes an agent is so strongly attracted to some value bearer or other that she cannot help but commit herself to it. There is also the converse case, of choosing to commit oneself to a given value bearer and then finding that one does *not* experience the expected or desired emotional-motivational response. Where the disparity is minor, an agent might be able to get by in the manner suggested above, by giving herself artificial, external motivations for performing the actions necessary to maintaining her commitments—actions that she would be spontaneously motivated to perform if only her perceptions of value were in line with her commitments and her practical agency was otherwise in good shape. How much effort an agent is willing to put into this will depend both on her intellectual judgments regarding the importance, to her, of the commitment in question and on her perceptions of value and the motivations these generate or fail to generate. In the long run, maintaining a commitment when one has no naturally occurring motivation for doing so is a difficult, perhaps even impossible task.

Earlier, when I listed the four elements of what I referred to as a paradigmatic response to value, I wrote that the second element—the agent's determination that the value in question was relevant to himself—was better thought of as a determination than as a judgment. We are now in a position to see why this is so.

Consider an agent who already has preexisting commitments (as all agents do) and who is faced with a decision of apparent significance whose resolution is not immediately obvious to her: an agent, let us say, who is deciding whether to leave her husband. Part of what is being determined is what the agent has reason to do, in light of her prior commitments; and this is indeed a matter of judgment. But there is also something else in question, which is in a sense prior to this judgment, and that is precisely whether the agent is to continue upholding and maintaining those prior commitments—whether she is to *continue* being committed in this way and whether future determinations of that agent's reasons are to be made in that light. After all, except in somewhat unusual cases (cases of what Frankfurt terms "volitional necessities"), temporarily suspending or even permanently abandoning one's commitments is always, at least in principle, an option; one is not *forced* by one's commitments, or by anything else, to continue to honor those commitments, even if doing so is, for the most part, the natural thing to do.

This more fundamental part of the determination will involve various judgments: judgments as to one's obligations in light of implied promises, predictions regarding the likely consequences of maintaining versus abandoning one's commitments, and so on. But although there are judgments involved, this part of the determination is not entirely composed of mental acts that can usefully be thought of as judgments. In the process of deciding whether a given commitment or value is important to her, an agent is not simply searching out some preexisting matter of fact that is already written in the stars or etched into the fabric of the universe. Nor is such an agent simply trying to discern a matter of fact that is already established in her own psychological outlook. For no matter what she finds out about herself—what she finds she has tended to do in the past, for example, or even what she finds she is most disposed to do on the present occasion—it will be an option for her to go against these psychological data and choose something quite other than what those data would predict.

To a considerable extent an agent, presented with a vast array of pluralistic values, makes certain values rather than others important to her precisely by committing to treating them *as* important. This is not purely an act of judgment or of will; rather, it is a combination of the two. By the same token, both will and judgment are involved when an agent chooses to continue to honor an existing commitment. Of course, such choices are supported by a certain momentum: having come this far in one's commitment to a value, why stop now? But sometimes there are reasons to stop. (A depressed agent might well think, "Having come this far, why go on?" And an agent who finds herself somewhat bored and ready for something new might think, "I've come this far—isn't that enough?")

Determinations of relevance, then, have a special status. Insofar as such a determination represents the agent's appraisal of the extent to which a certain consideration generates reasons against a background of commitments that are to be held constant, it is essentially a judgment. But insofar as those commitments are considered as being in question—an element of the agent's practical stance that might be affirmed or rejected by what she chooses to do—or insofar as there is a possibility of creating a *new* commitment (one that might or might not conflict with those that exist), the determination is no mere judgment but an act by which the agent makes something important. Such an act will feel less like a judgment *that* and more like a decision *to*.

It is no wonder, then, that love is often felt to involve a kind of volitional activity that goes well beyond judgment. In loving a person, one determines that considerations having to do with him—the valuable and attractive properties to which one responds with appreciative and generous attention, and the needs, interests, and desires that one takes to be central to one's own practical living and decision making—will be relevant to oneself in a way that almost all other such considerations are not. And no judgment, or other purely intellectual act, can tell an agent to do this or decide for her which person's attractions and interests will serve this role for her. It would be a mistake, however, to let this commit us to the sort of antirationalistic account of love that denies that a lover is responding to facts about the beloved in loving him, or that her love for him is a rational phenomenon in the sense of being supported by reasons. One may not have *conclusive* reasons for choosing him rather than someone else—at any rate, one will not be rationally obligated to do so, regardless of what considerations are potentially at play. But as we have seen, the fact that the choice of the particular individual whom one loves transcends rationality and judgment does not extend beyond this to the further conclusion that loving a person is not a response to her nature and properties. Only an unrealistic picture of what reason must involve would require us to deny that love is in this sense a phenomenon of reason.

Conclusion: Commitments, Importance, and Reciprocation

A practical agent's relationships, like her other serious commitments, play a crucial role in making her the person she is. But she is also partly defined by the way she treats her commitments, intentions, and relationships; how much it takes, for instance, to make her reconsider them when they lead to unexpected consequences or costs or when she finds that the spontaneous motivation to meet their demands is not forthcoming. As

Bratman points out, there is a range of stances an agent might adopt with respect to this matter.

> On one extreme is the person who always seriously reconsiders his prior plans in the face of any new information, no matter how trivial. Such a person would constantly be starting from scratch and would be unlikely to achieve many of the benefits of planning. On the other extreme is the overly rigid planner—one who almost never reconsiders, even in the face of important new information. . . . An instrumentally rational planner will have mechanisms and strategies of reconsideration that sometimes block reconsideration of a prior intention in the face of merely temporary preference change.[24]

Where on the continuum that runs between pure rigidity and complete flexibility do we find the lover? It seems plausible to think that he will be found closer to the pole occupied by the "overly rigid planner" than that occupied by the person who "always seriously reconsiders his prior plans." This is not to say that a lover should *never* be reflective about his commitments—the idea that a commitment to love, once made, can never be unmade or meaningfully reconsidered is obviously false. But love is unlikely to survive if one too frequently engages in serious questionings of this sort. (Anyone who has been engaged in a long-term love relationship will know that serious reconsiderations of one's commitment, particularly if they are brought out into the open and shared with one's partner, tend to be disturbing if not traumatic.) Since the lover's *initial* choice of the beloved is not made from a neutral or impersonal standpoint, she is at no time obligated to attempt to occupy such a standpoint in order to reaffirm her commitment. Nor—unlike the "instrumentally rational planner" who is Bratman's main concern—does she regard love as a means to maximizing some further value (even one defined relative to herself—her own happiness, for example) or satisfying some independently specified end. Rather, her relationship with her beloved is *itself* one of her most important ends; rather than simply functioning as an input to her practical deliberations, loving, as it were, sets the shape of such reasoning, determining both what counts as an admissible input and what constitutes a successful outcome.

As Frankfurt has observed, one treats the persons one loves as final ends, and it is important that one treat them in this way precisely because it is important to people to have final ends.[25] What the having of final ends does, he argues, is to allow some things to be important to an agent; and it is important that something in one's life be important, because a life in which nothing bears any importance would be sorely lacking. An agent with such a life would be depressed, or terminally bored, and might fail to be a genuine agent at all, since nothing would count, for her, as a reason. Such a life, in which a person saw no reason to do anything, would be sad indeed.

We see the same idea—that love, by causing things to be important for an agent, gives her life a practical background structure against which things can count as reasons—in another of Alice Munro's short stories, "Runaway."

> The strange and terrible thing coming clear to her about that world of the future, as she now pictured it, was that she would not exist there. She would only walk around, and open her mouth and speak, and do this and do that. She would not really be there. And what was strange about it was that she was doing all this, she was riding on this bus in the hope of recovering herself. As Mrs. Jamieson might say—and as she herself might with satisfaction have said—*taking charge of her own life*. With nobody glowering over her, nobody's mood infecting her with misery.
>
> But what would she care about? How would she know that she was alive?
>
> While she was running away from him—now—Clark still kept his place in her life. But when she was finished running away, when she just went on, what would she put in his place? What else—who else—could ever be so vivid a challenge? . . .
>
> She would be lost. What would be the point of getting into a taxi and giving the new address, of getting up in the morning and brushing her teeth and going into the world? Why should she get a job, put food in her mouth, be carried by public transportation from place to place?[26]

One might wonder, though, why it is so common to choose *persons*, and the flourishing of individual persons and of our relationships with them, as final ends. Indeed, on Frankfurt's view it is not particularly important that our love be directed at persons; rather, any object that can stimulate the appropriate sort of caring will do. But I suggest two reasons for thinking that persons are particularly appropriate and significant objects of love, both of which will serve to set my picture apart from Frankfurt's to some degree. The first reason is simply that agents' judgments of value do tend, in various ways, to be responsive to objective values, and, as I have already suggested, persons are *especially* objectively valuable; indeed, a person is a type of thing that possesses values found nowhere else in the known universe. Given this, and given Frankfurt's observations regarding the importance of importance, it is not surprising that agents should often choose from among the most valuable of objects available to them as foci of their attention.

Frankfurt would be hesitant to endorse this position, given his resistance to the idea of objective value—attempts to make sense of which, as he writes, "tend to turn out badly."[27] Such skepticism leads Frankfurt to the view that the reason loving matters is that the subjective value bestowed by love is the only sort of value that can exist; if things matter at all, they must matter subjectively, that is, by being loved or cared about by someone. The question of objective value is, obviously, too large and difficult to settle here; what is essential is to emphasize that the type of antirationalism Frankfurt prefers cannot be established simply by the fact that the agent's will has a significant role in determining what is valuable (and hence important) to her. As should by now be clear, there is another possible diagnosis of the necessity of volitional commitments in the life of a practical agent, and this is that rather than there being a *shortage* of values in the world (so that we must create our own), there are *too many*—the universe is in fact full of values and value bearers, far too many for a person to be able to respond adequately to them all. The result is that each agent must choose which of those potential objects of her concern and devotion she will concern herself with and devote herself to.

On this sort of view, it is not that I literally make someone important by loving her but rather that loving someone is a matter of making her important *to me*. And yet, as we saw in chapter 4, ordinarily it is important to the beloved that she be important to someone, not because she would not matter at all if she did not matter to anyone in particular—if this were true, how could it matter whether or not she mattered to anyone?—but because there *is* a sense in which mere objective mattering is not enough. To attribute objective value to something is in one sense a kind of counterfactual judgment; it is to say that *if* someone valued it in certain ways, their valuing would be justified and appropriate. But there is, then, a sense in which a thing that has objective value but is not valued by anyone—whose value is unrecognized or even intellectually acknowledged but not fully appreciated—has a value that is not fully instantiated in the world.

This may well be a cause of regret—particularly when the valuable thing is an individual person, who can be aware that she is not being fully valued, that she is not at the center of anyone's world, that she is not, in anyone's eyes, especially important. (Recall again the character in Munro's "Floating Bridge," who worried that once she left her husband, "Her feelings might become of no importance to anybody but herself, and yet they would be bulging up inside her, squeezing her heart and breath.")

It is not at all surprising, then, that we want to be loved or that we want to be loved especially by those whom we love. And to say this is to reveal the second reason why persons are so frequently chosen as final ends. There are many things the world offers us to care about. Jim Dine's *The Heart, South of Naples* is, for instance, a wonderful painting, and I value it and care about it. But *The Heart, South of Naples* does not care whether I care, and it never will. The special opportunity that love for persons affords us is the opportunity to care about something that can care about us. It is because our loved ones care whether or not we care that our caring about them matters in the fullest possible sense.

six

Valuing Persons

Rationality without Promiscuity: The Vision View Defended

In chapter 1 I suggested that we should see love as "something in be-tween"—between the purely arational phenomenon the antirationalists believe it to be and the hyper-rationalistic phenomenon they assume it would have to be were it a matter of reason. Love is in fact a matter of reason, I have been arguing; but this must be understood in a way that avoids the unacceptable implications of hyper-rationalism and preserves the main antirationalist insights. The account of love I have been devel-oping—the vision view—is centered on the idea that loving someone is a way of opening one's eyes to her (and of being committed to this way of seeing) in a way that involves both appreciating the properties she bears as an *object* and identifying with her as a *subject*.

I hope that by now it is clear that the problems for rationalistic ac-counts of love—what I called the universality, promiscuity, and trading-up problems—do not, in fact, pose insurmountable difficulties for the vision view, properly understood.[1] The vision view, after all, claims only that Alighieri's love for Beatrice is, fundamentally, a reason-conditioned response to Beatrice's properties. That claim becomes problematic only if it is extended to the further, considerably more demanding claim that in responding to Beatrice's properties, Alighieri must act as a comprehensive comparative surveyor in comparing her desirable features with those of others in as impartial a manner as possible. As we have seen, though, this is precisely what love does *not* require.

Indeed, in chapters 2 and 3 I argued that love involves a form of blind-ing that *prevents* a lover from engaging in an unbiased comparison of his beloved's virtues with those of others. And in chapters 4 and 5 I ar-gued that the refusal to compare, at least in the proper context, does not render one's evaluative thought irrational or deficient in any way. Some value-bearing properties are correctly perceived and evaluated from a standpoint that is committed, involved, and engaged, a standpoint that is anything but detached, impartial, and objective. Indeed, an agent who could respond to values *only* from a detached perspective of this sort would be quite hampered in her relationships with various values, particularly those connected with personal, intimate relationships. (She might be able to make a large number of correct value *judgments*—though even this will be problematic in some cases—but as I argue in chapter 5, there is a significant distinction between judging something to be valuable and actually valuing it.)

There need be no implication, then, that in loving Beatrice for her beauty, Alighieri thus commits himself to loving any beautiful woman or to abandoning the woman he currently loves for a slightly more beautiful woman who comes along. If he is truly in love with Beatrice, he will be unlikely to see anyone as more beautiful than her anyway; he might, of course, judge someone to be beautiful objectively speaking, and this might move him to a degree, but not in the special way in which he is moved by the beauty of his beloved. Nor is there any implication that in accepting Alighieri's account of his reasons for loving Beatrice as reasonable and intelligible, I must come to love her myself; the judgment that an individual is *worthy* of love does not include the requirement that one be moved to love her.

The standpoint of love is thus not a standpoint from which all persons are seen equally; some receive more attention, and more generous and charitable attention, than others. As I have emphasized, however, it does not follow from this that the person occupying the standpoint of love does not *know* that all persons are, in a highly significant sense, equal. She does know it, in very much the way that I know that the sun is extremely large even though, from where I am situated, it looks much smaller than my fist. A reasonable lover *knows* that other people are, in a fundamental moral sense, as significant as her beloved, just as she knows that there are other people in the world who are as beautiful as the person whose beauty moves her or as intelligent, as charming, as witty, as creative, as admirable, and so forth. She knows these things, and she acknowledges that other persons have values similar in many respects to those of her beloved. But in the case of her beloved, she does more than simply acknowledge his valuable characteristics: she *appreciates* them.

The lover takes the features of her beloved to which she is responding to be real and genuinely valuable, independent of her own attitudes; she does not create these values but notices and appreciates them. Contra the typical antirationalist position, it is not value but generous attention that is bestowed upon the beloved. In this sense, then, she recognizes the possibility of providing a justification for her love—a demonstration that her love is a response to real and genuinely valuable features.[2] Of course, some of these features are less available than others to observers who stand outside the perspective of love; nearly everyone might be able to see and appreciate the beauty of a physically beautiful beloved, but only her lover is likely to view the way she dribbles in her sleep as charming. Still, the majority of relevant properties will be conceived as real and universalizable: they are there for anyone to see and appreciate, so long as one looks in the right way.

But to say that the lover recognizes the possibility of providing a justification in this sense[3] is not to say that she thinks it important to provide or possess a justification, from an impersonal or otherwise neutral point of view, for her decision to commit herself to the values instantiated by this particular individual as opposed to some other. For while she thinks that the attractive properties of her beloved are there to be seen by anyone who looks in the right way, she knows that not everyone will see the beloved in that way—indeed, few will. Moreover, she did not reach her own perspective by deliberating from the standpoint of an impersonal point of view. She most likely did not reach this commitment by *deliberating* at all. She has, let us suppose, committed herself to a certain individual who is, in her eyes, intelligent, compassionate, witty, and good-looking; but she has done so while remaining perfectly aware that he is far from the only person in the world to possess these attributes, and that almost surely there are persons who possess some or even all of these attributes to an even greater degree.

The lover's justification for her commitment to her beloved, and for the actions and way of life that follow from that commitment, adverts to the beloved's properties. This is as far as the justification goes, and it is as far as it needs to go. The most fundamental of these properties is the basic fact that the beloved is the appropriate sort of target of such love—that is, that she exists as a subject and so is the sort of thing with a perspective on the world, the sort of thing for whom a world exists. This property, of course, is not what the typical lover has in mind or is likely to say when thinking or talking about his lover or his reasons for loving her; rather, this fact is simply so basic that it will be taken for granted. Nonetheless, it is crucial that the justification he possesses for loving her is, once again, an *enabler* rather than a *favorer*. The favorers will be the more particular personal qualities that make his beloved stand out from the crowd *in his way of seeing*. But although these will play a much more substantial and detailed role in explaining his love, they still will not go so far as to show that he *must* love her. They will not, that is, turn his case for loving, no matter how urgent and compelling it may feel to him, into a matter of rational obligation.

Justifying love is a matter of showing that one's reasons are strong enough—that is, that the values to which the lover is responding are real, relevant, and sufficiently present. She need not show that her way of recognizing those values—a response that involves the special directed attention and focus of the way of seeing that constitutes love—is mandatory for everyone. A true lover will not and need not think that this is so. Nor, for that matter, would she want it to be so.

Love for Properties or Love for Persons?

"Look," Robert Towne reminded me when I asked him whether he thought Roman [Polanski] at all exploitative of the women he courted, "in those days, all of us—men and women—were treating each other as objects, and at the time nobody felt anybody was being exploited. Or anyway, that was the most *willing* group of victims you'll ever see."

—Lawrence Weschler, *Vermeer in Bosnia*

The vision view holds that love is constituted, in large part, by a positive, appreciative response to a person in virtue of his valuable or attractive qualities. It is a way of seeing those qualities and their bearer as worthy of special attention on account, in part, of his possession of them. Love is largely a matter of valuing and appreciating those qualities and, at the same time, a way of valuing and appreciating the person. But many writers on love have been troubled by the nagging worry that we cannot combine these various attitudes. One might claim, for instance, that one cannot *both* value a person's qualities *and* value the person herself; valuing one of these prevents one from valuing the other.

The most common version of the worry goes something like this: to value a person's properties is to value her as a mere object, and objectifying her in this way is simply incompatible with valuing her as a subject or a person. If, as seems plausible, valuing a person's qualities is part of valuing a person *in virtue of* her qualities, then this claim would seem to imply that valuing a person in virtue of her qualities is impossible (since one would have to value her qualities to do that, but valuing a person's qualities, by the claim just considered, *prevents* one from valuing the person). At any rate, at least some writers—McTaggart, for instance—have indeed denied both that love involves valuing the beloved's qualities and that it involves valuing the beloved in virtue of her qualities. "Love is for the person, and not for his qualities, nor is it for him in respect of his qualities," McTaggart writes. "It is for him."[4]

Why should we think, though, that there must be deep tension between valuing a person and valuing her qualities? To be clear, the question is whether valuing a person's qualities *must be* in conflict with valuing the person herself, not whether it *can* be; it cannot plausibly be denied that in some cases the two do come apart. As we noted in chapter 1, a person might be valued for the wrong qualities; where the qualities are distant enough from the ones that are essential or fundamental to the person's identity, love might seem to miss its mark and focus on something other than the person. A quite reliable sign that love has gone awry in more or less this way is that the lover would be too willing to accept a substitute or replacement who, so long as she has the right set of qualities, would be considered by him to be equally good, to "do as well" for the purposes he has in mind. Thus, Jane Austen's Mr. Collins seems to value Elizabeth Bennet, but only for a few qualities that do not touch, let alone exhaust, who she really is and what is particularly special and significant about her; indeed, in Mr. Collins's eyes any of Elizabeth's sisters would do more or less as well. Christopher Grau offers, as a more recent real-world example, the owners of the dog Missy, who, after her death, spent a considerable sum of money in attempting to clone their beloved pet. Missy herself, Grau suggests, might well be offended by the effort; he imagines her complaining as follows:

> Part of what bothers me is that it raises the suspicion that you haven't really loved *me* all these years after all. Sure, you loved my shiny coat, my playful disposition, and even my stubborn refusal to come when called, but loving all these characteristics of mine isn't the same as truly loving me. If your love could so easily be transferred to another dog with the same characteristics, I can't help but feel that there is a way in which I am not being appreciated as an individual. . . . I may not deserve all the consideration due to a full human being, but I also don't deserve to be treated like a toaster oven: i.e., something that can simply be replaced with a functional equivalent when it ceases to operate.[5]

Grau's point is not that the fact that Missy's owners valued her shiny coat showed that they did not value *her*. Rather, it is the fact that they valued *only* the coat and other replaceable characteristics that shows that those characteristics, and not Missy herself, were the objects of their valuing. At any rate, assuming that it is true that they would have viewed a qualitative duplicate of Missy as, for their purposes, as good as the original, they certainly cannot be said genuinely to have loved Missy, for love attaches itself to the beloved in a way that does not allow for a replacement of this sort. Nothing in this attachment, though, prevents it from being the case that a large part of a genuine lover's response to Missy might well be composed of his appreciation of her valuable and attractive qualities.

There are, undoubtedly, different ways of valuing persons, and some are more objectifying than others. What makes a certain mode of valuing into an objectionable form of objectification, though, must be something more than the mere fact that it involves noticing and appreciating the qualities of the valued person; rather, there must be some further fact about it—the type of property that is valued, the fact that the qualities are valued only instrumentally, or the fact that the lover would be too willing to accept a replacement—that renders the valuing objectifying in an objectionable manner.[6]

This point is frequently obscured by philosophers who assume an overly simplistic model of motivation according to which a person's taking pleasure or having any other sort of interest in something is automatically reduced to the crudest form of self-interest. Kant, for instance, believed that sexual desire made a person a mere "thing, whereby the other's appetite is sated. . . . Since the sexual impulse is not an inclination that one human has for another, qua human, but an inclination for their sex, it is therefore a principle of the debasement of humanity."[7] As before, this is true in some cases, but why assume that it must be so in every case? A desire for sex with someone that is combined with a genuine interest in the desired person *as a person*—as indicated, in part, by the fact that what is desired is sexual activity (and, presumably, other sorts of activity) with *her* and not just with *any* partner bearing the appropriate anatomy—seems less objectionably objectifying than, say, the desire of Missy's owners to enjoy the sight of Missy's shiny coat, or the sight of any equally attractive coat, including the one that will presumably belong to Missy's genetic duplicate.

Let us, for simplicity's sake, think of modes of valuing as lying along a continuum, with one pole of the continuum occupied by the mode of valuing that is appropriate in the case of "pure" or "mere" objects—that is, objects that are not also subjects, such as ballpoint pens, baseballs, blueberry pies, and so forth—and the other pole occupied by whatever mode of valuing is appropriately directed toward subjects, and in particular persons. Now, what can we say about these poles? It seems natural to begin by saying that the mode of valuing appropriately directed toward mere objects tends to be less, rather than more, disinterested; indeed, one tends to value mere objects, for the most part, in instrumental terms, and appreciation of them tends to involve an appraisal of their value relative to one's own needs and interests. Thus we tend not to be much interested in specific objects; one omelet or ballpoint pen is, ordinarily, as good as another, and the refusal to accept a (functionally equivalent) replacement strikes us as a kind of fetishism or bizarre sentimentality, unless there is some sort of story to tell (the pen used to belong to my grandfather and is the last of his remaining possessions, for instance). There is a sense, then, in which valuing of this sort tends to focus on the qualities possessed by the object, rather than on the object itself. Such valuing, moreover, tends to be conditional and to be subject to revocation: if I decide that my appraisal of an object was inflated or it loses the valuable characteristics it once possessed, my sense of its value will be diminished and I will be more likely to give it up.

Things are different, however, when we think of the sort of valuing that is properly directed at persons. Responding in the fullest sense to the special value an individual possesses is less a matter of appraising her value than of identifying with her. The Kantian insight that persons must be treated not as mere objects but as ends in themselves is a way of getting at this: a person who is in my vicinity ought to be treated as having needs, desires, and interests that matter in much the same way that my own needs, desires, and interests matter. The point is not that I am not permitted to favor my own needs, but that other people's needs count as potential generators of reasons and claims in a way that does not apply even to those mere objects that can be *metaphorically* said to have needs and interests of their own. (My car needs regular oil changes to keep running, but although it matters to me that it keep running, it really does not matter to it: it is all the same to the car whether it runs well, poorly, or not at all.)

Recognizing and valuing a person as an autonomous subject is not sufficient for love, but it is certainly a necessary element of it. Such valuing is, as should be clear, profoundly noninstrumental in nature; and it is partly for this reason that love for persons, at least in its ideal forms, is often said to be disinterested. This might or might not be correct, but I suspect that this particular word leads people astray more often than it leads them to enlightenment. At the very least we can surely say that it is highly doubtful that any real instance of love is such that no interests of any sort come into play. There is no such thing as a purely disinterested love; but again, the mere presence of interests in an instance of love gives us little if any reason to conclude that the love must not be genuine.

The fact that Alighieri takes pleasure in Beatrice's charm or beauty, for instance, is surely no objection to the claim that he truly loves her; nor is it a sign that the love is in some way deficient. Of course, if we found that he was interested in only these qualities of hers, so that he was committed to abandoning her if she lost these qualities or if someone possessing them in greater abundance should happen to come along and offer herself, we would then be in a position to deny Alighieri's claim to be a genuine lover. Worse still, we might find out that he does not appreciate these qualities for their own sake but that he values them only because other people value them, and he enjoys their envy. But the mere fact that a putative lover's love is interested—the fact that he takes pleasure in various aspects of his beloved and of the relationship, that he wants the relationship to continue and the beloved to flourish in part because its continuing and her flourishing enhance his life and well-being—has, in itself, no interesting implications as to whether or not his love is genuine.

To show, then, that there is a deep tension between valuing a person and valuing her qualities, it is not enough to show that valuing can take different forms, some more appropriate to subjects and others to mere objects. That valuing can take different forms is no doubt true. But this fact is a problem only for accounts of love that take loving to be a form of valuing—one that involves the valuing of both the person and her qualities—if it can be combined with some sort of argument to establish that these different forms of valuing somehow compete with or impede one another. And this is, at any rate, not obviously true, any more than it is obviously true that one's being valued as a singer must somehow compete with or impede one's being valued as a dancer. There is no clear reason why one cannot be appreciated for both. The same, I suggest, is true with respect to a person's being valued (that is, identified with) as a subject and a person's being valued (that is, favorably judged or appraised) as an object. There is simply no reason why these need to be in any tension at all.

Accidents and Quirks

McTaggart writes the following:

> To love one person above all the world for all one's life because her eyes are beautiful when she is young, is to be determined to a very great thing by a very small cause. But if what is caused is really love—and this is sometimes the case—it is not condemned on that ground. It is there, and that is enough. This would seem to indicate that the emotion is directed to the person, independently of his qualities, and that the determining qualities are not the justification of that emotion, but only the means by which it arises.[8]

McTaggart is right that genuine love is directed to the person but wrong to assume that this is incompatible with its being directed to the person's qualities. According to the vision view, true lovers value their beloveds both as subjects and as objects, and there is no necessary conflict between these two ways of seeing. After all, it is often possible to appreciate one's own good properties from one's own point of view, and doing so does not seem to imply that one is somehow alienated from oneself or objectifying oneself in an objectionable way!

The lover's response to the beloved as subject—a valuing that takes the form of her identifying with the beloved and thus seeing the world from his point of view—sits alongside her valuing of the beloved's attractive properties: his being intelligent, charming, witty, physically beautiful, and so on. Indeed, the two forms of valuing encourage each other. The more attractive we find our beloved's various features, the more inclined we will be to identify with him; and the more we do that, the more likely we will be to regard the beloved's observable qualities with the sort of attention, insight, and understanding that is more easily achieved from the first-person standpoint than other standpoints, and hence to regard him generously and appreciatively.[9] It does not follow, either from the fact that someone is loved *in virtue of* her properties or from the fact that her properties themselves are objects of her lover's valuing, that it must be the properties, and not the person, that are really being loved.

Do these observations dispose entirely of the worry that valuing properties gets in the way of our valuing persons? Perhaps there is still the residual suspicion that there is something illicit about valuing properties—that the sort of properties by which people tend to attract attention and incite desire, at any rate, are too shallow to ground or sustain genuine love. The fundamental worry, once again, is that one cannot make identification with the beloved as subject a fundamental element of one's view of what love is, while at the same time holding love to involve, in an important way, the lover's appreciation of the attractive properties that attach to the beloved as an *object*. Frankfurt may have something like this thought in mind when he writes that "the focus of a person's love is not those general and hence repeatable characteristics that make his beloved *describable*. Rather, it is the specific particularity that makes his beloved *nameable*—something that is more mysterious than describability, and that is in any case manifestly impossible to define."[10]

This is a provocative but somewhat obscure passage, and it is difficult for me to tell just how much disagreement there is here between Frankfurt's position and my own. At any rate, I am perfectly willing to accept that the primary focus of love is precisely the *particular individual person*, and not that individual's properties. At least, I will insist on this if we make the assumption that the latter view would rationally oblige the lover to respond to those properties in the same way when they are manifested in others, and thus to transfer his love to someone else who possessed the same properties in greater amounts, and so forth. But to say that in *this* sense the lover's focus is the beloved, and not the beloved's properties, certainly should not be taken to imply that the beloved's properties somehow escape the lover's notice or that his appreciation of them can play no role in his love for her. To think otherwise is to fall victim to a false dilemma. Why think that the lover's attention must be focused on what makes the beloved nameable—that is, her identity as a particular individual—*as opposed to* what renders her describable? Is it not more reasonable, in fact, to think that his attention will be directed toward both?

Those who want to answer this question in the negative might find themselves turning to Pascal's famous passage from the *Pensées* (number 688):

A man goes to the window to see the people passing by; if I pass by, can I say he went there to see me? No, for he is not thinking of me in particular. But what about a person who loves someone for the sake of her beauty; does he love *her*? No, for smallpox, which will destroy beauty without destroying the person, will put an end to his love for her.

And if someone loves me for my judgment or my memory, do they love me? *me*, myself? No, for I could lose these qualities without losing my self. Where then is this self, if it is neither in the body nor the soul? And how can one love the body or the soul except for the sake of such qualities, which are not what make up the self, since they are perishable? Would we love the substance of the person's soul, in the abstract, whatever qualities might be in it? That is not possible, and it would be wrong. Therefore we never love anyone, but only qualities.[11]

Some people worry that love for properties is unstable, since we may lose our properties. Pascal endorses the latter claim but does not argue that true love is therefore for persons *rather than* properties. Instead he accepts the pessimistic conclusion that love for persons is impossible; the *only* sort of love available to us is love for properties. The instability of properties, in Pascal's view, matters not because we ought therefore to reject them as possible objects or grounds of love, but rather because it shows that the properties are not identical with the person (since the person can survive the loss of her properties), and thus that when properties are loved (which is in every case, since properties are the only things we can love) what is loved is something that is not identical with the person. Persons, in Pascal's view, are simply never loved at all.

Considered as a straightforward logical inference, Pascal's argument fails. The fact that Beatrice could survive the loss of her beauty does not show that she is not beautiful or that the property of beauty is not one of the properties that make her who she is. What it shows is just that she is not *necessarily* or *essentially* beautiful. But that is presumably the basis of the point Pascal wants to make: really to be loved as a person, and not as a mere object, is surely to be loved for what one *essentially* is, and not merely for accidents. Of course, it does not follow from this that one cannot value a person as a mere object *and*, at the same time, identify with her as a subject. However, Pascal's claim does seem strongly to suggest that these two valuings have very little to do with each other; one is a valuing of the properties, the other is a valuing of the person, and the two are not only logically independent, but it has perhaps become somewhat hard to see how one could even lead to, or encourage, the other. The thought, then, is that Beatrice's beauty, her wit, her charm, and other such properties are not *really* hers; they are not, let us say, part of her essential nature. Rather, they are mere accidents; she might, after all, have come to possess very different qualities and yet still have been the same person. And so, to the extent that she is loved for these, it is not really *Beatrice* who is loved at all.

But this inference too seems questionable. After all, my properties are still my properties, whether I possess them necessarily or only contingently. Discovering that one's beloved is not actually P, Q, and R when P, Q, and R are the main features in virtue of which one loves her, would of course threaten one's love. But the discovery that one's beloved, while she does indeed possess P, Q, and R, does not possess them *essentially* is not clearly relevant at all. (Can we imagine someone saying, "I could no longer love my beautiful, charming, and witty girlfriend once I realized that, had her early life gone differently, she might not have turned out to be beautiful, charming, or witty at all"?)

It is simply not clear why the fact that a property is not essential in this sense should imply that it cannot serve as a proper object of loving appreciation, or why such appreciation must be somehow incompatible with loving the *person*. Indeed, people are very frequently appraised in terms of qualities that are not essential to them, including, it is reasonable to suppose, their moral qualities. As Aristotle was well aware, it takes a certain sort of upbringing to make a person virtuous; a person who turns out to be virtuous, then, is that way largely as a result of luck and contingent circumstance. But this hardly seems to disqualify one's positive moral qualities as qualities that may be admired. Nor does it suggest that a person cannot be admired *for* such properties.

The position defended by Velleman in "Love as a Moral Emotion" seems to be largely motivated by the thought that love should not be directed toward or grounded in accidental properties. Velleman argues that in loving a person, we do not value the distinctive features that make her the particular person she is; rather, we value her rational personhood, as understood in a Kantian sense, namely her "capacity to be actuated by reasons[, which] is a capacity for appreciating the value of ends, including self-existent ends such as persons."[12] Part of this, I think, is on the mark; surely a person's capacity for appreciating value is *one* of the things we value about her, for without that she would not be a person at all. To occupy a given subjective standpoint on the world is, in part, to value certain things as against others. Velleman nicely suggests the importance of this element of love's ground by suggesting that his claim amounts to the claim that "what we respond to, in loving people, is their capacity to feel love: it's just another way of saying that what our hearts respond to is another heart."[13] But none of this requires us to hold that it is *only* the capacity to value, love, and respond to reasons that we value in loving a person, and there is no apparent reason why we should agree with Velleman that the desire to be loved

> is not a desire to be valued on the basis of one's distinctive features. It is rather a desire that one's own rendition of humanity, however distinctive, should succeed in communicating a value that is perfectly universal. (In this respect, it's like the desire to be found beautiful.) One doesn't want one's value as a person to be eclipsed by the intrinsic value of one's appearance or behavior; one wants them to elicit a valuation that looks through them, to the value of one's inner self.[14]

This seems like the same old false dilemma: why would a person not want to be appreciated *both* for what is distinctive about her as a person *and* for what is universal? Of course, if appreciation of the former must, for some reason, "eclipse" appreciation of the latter, then one would have to choose; but again, where is the argument that such eclipsing must take place? Perhaps what Velleman is really worried about is not the desire "to be valued on the basis of one's distinctive features," but rather the desire to be valued *only* on the basis of such features. This, I have already acknowledged, is a legitimate worry.

But most of Velleman's language in this passage and elsewhere suggests a strong "either-or"' position: one must *either* be valued for shallow and accidental properties like "one's appearance or behavior" *or* be valued for "one's inner self"; one simply cannot have both. The clear implication is that since our distinctive properties—those which set us apart from others—are not part of our true selves, we should not want to be loved for them: "Once you realize that someone's love can single you out without basing itself on your distinguishing characteristics, you are in a position to realize, further, that the latter sort of love would in fact be undesirable. Someone who loved you for your quirks would have to be a quirk-lover, on the way to being a fetishist."[15]

I think it is a mistake—though one we can perhaps understand, given the Kantian assumptions that underlie Velleman's approach—to classify all distinctive qualities as "quirks." A distinctive feature might well be treated as a quirk by some appreciator or other, but not every such feature must be treated in this way, and indeed, some distinctive features seem to demand *not* to be so treated. It is very peculiar, for instance, to think of intelligence as a "quirk" or something that only a "fetishist" could appreciate. Yet intelligence is always a highly distinctive characteristic of individual persons, not only because different individuals have different levels of intelligence, but because each person's intelligence is of a different sort and has its own distinct character.

The force of this point will be particularly apparent when we remind ourselves that among a person's distinctive features are the characteristics that make her *the particular person she is*, even insofar as she is considered as an instance of Kantian rationality. Just as every face is a particular face—there is no such thing as a genuinely generic or "universal" human face—so every person is a particular person; to be a person is to occupy a perspective on the world, and this involves valuing certain things more than, or as opposed to, others. It is thus more correct to say that we love persons (who possess the abstract property of Kantian rational personhood by virtue of the more particular features they possess) than to say that we love *bare personhood* (which cannot, *in itself,* exist at all).

Far from there being a conflict, then, between a person's distinctive features and her essential inner personhood, we should expect a large degree of overlap between them. Given Velleman's claim that it is mostly by means of one's distinctive qualities that one's personhood and existence as a rational being are expressed, it is odd that he should insist that the one but not the other may properly be valued by one's lover. The fact is that a great many of the qualities that are most likely to be named by lovers as reasons for loving their beloveds—intelligence, charm, wit, humor, insight, courage, passion, and so on—are qualities that we expect to play a role not only in the lover's account of how she regards and construes the beloved (and thus in her explanation of why she loves him), but also in the *beloved's* account of how he regards and construes *himself*. Such qualities are discernible both by those who possess them and by others, and they tend to be acknowledged as valuable on all hands.

History and Constancy

> *Audience member*: What I can't see, on your account, is how there is any assurance that my wife will continue to love me.
> *Harry Frankfurt*: I'm sorry, sir, I'm afraid I can't help you with that.

There is another reason, though, why the idea that love is largely a response to accidental properties sometimes strikes people as implausible or threatening. This is the fact that many accidental properties, including, it might appear, a great many of the qualities that will play significant roles in grounding love if the vision view is right, are not only properties that their bearers do not possess *essentially*, but properties that their bearers can *lose*. Many of us are inclined to agree with Shakespeare's claim that "love is not love that alters / when it alteration finds" (Sonnet 116)—but if love is largely a response to alterable properties, then, it might be claimed, it is hard to see why love would not change when those properties were altered. Indeed, the vision view might seem to imply that there would be a rational *obligation* for the lover to retract her love, once the properties on which the love was formerly grounded were lost.

This, of course, is the basis of the inconstancy problem, the fourth objection to the vision view, which I introduced in chapter 1:

The inconstancy problem: If Alighieri loves Beatrice for her valuable properties, then rationally he ought to stop loving Beatrice when she loses those properties.

What can the vision theorist say about the inconstancy objection? It is important to start by distinguishing between two separate but easily conflated issues. First, can the vision view ground a rational requirement that a lover *continue* loving her beloved even when he loses his attractive properties? Second, does the vision view require a lover to *stop* loving her beloved under these conditions?

The first issue is complex. After all, it is simply not clear that there *is* a rational requirement to continue loving one's beloved even when her qualities change. Indeed, although antirationalists sometimes complain that the vision view and other rationalist accounts of love make love unacceptably unstable by tying it to contingently possessed properties, they themselves, in taking love to be a fundamentally arational phenomenon, implicitly deny the existence of any such rational requirement.[16] Even if the specter raised by rationalist accounts of love—that love might fade if the beloved loses her lovable qualities—is genuine, it does not seem quite as threatening as that raised by the antirationalist view that love is *not* a response to one's qualities, which suggests that love might well fade whether one keeps one's qualities or not. It is thus understandable why Harry Frankfurt, or for that matter any other antirationalist, would respond to a questioner who desires a guarantee that his wife will continue to love him by admitting, "I'm afraid I can't help you with that." A proponent of the vision view who chooses to deny the existence of such a rational requirement will not, then, be alone in doing so; on this issue, at least, she will find herself in agreement with the antirationalists.

The incompleteness thesis, too, may seem strongly to suggest that there can be no rational requirement for one person to love another under any circumstances. It is worth remembering, though, that the incompleteness thesis does not, strictly speaking, entail this; rather, that thesis restricts itself to the lover's *qualities* and thus leaves it open, at least in principle, that Beatrice's valuable qualities *plus* some other fact—the fact, perhaps, that Alighieri already loves her—might be able to combine to generate a rational obligation for him to continue to love her. And the fact that we sometimes say things like "What do you mean, you don't love her anymore? You're crazy!" does give at least some evidence that we think there can be requirements to continue loving. However, we are perhaps quite a bit more likely to say "You would be crazy to leave her" than "You would be crazy to stop loving her." Leaving a person, unlike loving her, is, after all, under one's voluntary control and so a more natural candidate for assessments of rationality.

It is thus not entirely clear whether we should say that rational obligations of this sort exist; but there is little if any reason, so far as I can see, to think that the vision view could not accommodate whatever the correct answer to this question might turn out to be. The real worry for the vision view is whether this view actually *requires* Alighieri to cease loving Beatrice if she comes to lose the qualities—her beauty, her charm, and so on—on which his love has been grounded. For the objector is quite right to point out that qualities of this sort are very often impermanent, whereas love is frequently understood as a kind of commitment that is meant to persist even through significantly changed circumstances. Even though we recognize that there is no guarantee that we will continue to be loved as we grow older and change, at the same time we know that people often do manage to continue loving their beloveds, sometimes over the course of quite significant changes. Moreover, we tend to approve of such stability, to desire it for ourselves, and to think that something like this is what love requires. A theory implying that rationality mandated inconstancy of the sort we are considering would thus be both implausible and somewhat unpleasant.

How might the vision theorist respond? We have already considered the possibility that the vision view might reject the idea of rational requirements to *continue* loving in cases where the beloved's features do *not* undergo significant change. One possibility for responding to the inconstancy objection, then, would be to continue and extend this line of thought all the way to the denial that there are any rational requirements to love at all. This may at first seem contrary to the spirit of the vision view, which is supposed to see love as largely a matter of reason. But even in emphasizing and focusing attention on the role of reason in love, I have consistently and repeatedly de-emphasized the role in that context of *rational obligation*, and repeatedly emphasized that considerations that generate reasons for lovers tend to do so by making certain options and patterns of behavior eligible rather than required. Love is rational in the sense that when it is working as it should, the lover is responding to the properties of the beloved, which implies that there are reasons for love and that the lover has a justification. But reasons for love are not reasons that force a person to do one thing rather than another, on pain of irrationality; an agent is not irrational for failing to act on some of the reasons available to her or for failing to promote or fully appreciate some of the values that she might have promoted had she chosen a different course in life. Indeed, as chapters 4 and 5 are meant to establish, the world presents an agent with far too many values and reasons for her to respond fully to them all, and this makes the ability to choose from among a wide array of options one of the most significant elements of agency. One can hold, then, that love is a matter of reason in the appropriate sense—that it is a response to certain real values and is rendered appropriate and justifiable by those values and the reasons they generate—without feeling any pressure to add to this the claim that such reasons and values involve obligation. On this view, a person can never be criticized for being irrational on account of his failure to love someone whom he "ought" to love.

Considered in this light, our response to the inconstancy problem is very similar to the proper response to the trading-up problem. There, too, the worry is that the vision view rationally obligates a lover to stop loving her beloved under certain conditions. Trading up suggests that the lover ought to stop doing so when somebody with more attractive or valuable properties comes along. But this is so only if the lover is comparing her current beloved with the new candidate in an objective way, and this sort of objective, cool-minded comparison is precisely what love forbids. With respect to the inconstancy problem, the relevant comparison is not between the beloved and some other person, but with the beloved as he is now and as he was before. Once again, although a hyper-rationalistic view might well demand that one's beloved be constantly scrutinized in this way, and that the beloved be abandoned if the assessment does not come out in his favor, the kind of valuing involved in love, properly understood, simply will not have the lover perform the comparison to begin with.

That is the first point that many vision theorists will want to make. The second and related point is that on the vision view as I have developed it here, love does indeed involve an appreciation of the beloved's qualities, but it also and simultaneously involves an identification with the beloved—so much so that it would not be much of an exaggeration to say that a genuine lover is committed to trying to appreciate the qualities of her beloved, *whatever they might be*. To forestall misunderstanding, let me say that this is very different from saying that the lover is committed to responding positively to the properties, whatever they might be; *that* formulation strongly suggests that the lover is not responding to the properties at all, but rather is forcing a predetermined interpretation upon them. As I argued in chapter 3, what love requires is not that sort of predetermined attitude—an insistence on viewing what one encounters as valuable whatever turns out to be there—but rather an openness to finding whatever value might be there, even if it is difficult to see. Without a commitment of *this* sort, what one feels, no matter how intense it may be, is simply not love.

Moreover, it is important to keep in mind that people do not tend to lose all of their attractive properties at once; and although some are typically lost over the course of a lifetime, other valuable properties tend to be gained or to increase in strength or visibility. Indeed, it is exceedingly rare for a person to lose all her attractive properties without these being compensated by a gain or increase in another area. If one's lover is truly committed, in the manner suggested, to finding value there, only in the rarest and most unfortunate circumstances will there be no value to find.[17]

Finally, there is a third and very important point to be made, one that is all too often overlooked. Although it is commonly assumed that vision views place value only on the *current* properties of the beloved, there is no need to saddle such theories with this restriction. Holding that what one does when one loves is largely a matter of responding to the valuable qualities of the beloved is perfectly compatible with holding that one is responding not only to current qualities but also to past qualities—particularly those that the beloved possessed during previous stages of his relationship and that one was therefore able to have direct experience of at the time.

People are often loved for being beautiful, but it is also possible to love someone for having been beautiful.[18] As McTaggart observed, one might love somebody, in part, because she has beautiful eyes; but one might also love someone, at least in part, because she *used to* have beautiful eyes. Such love may well be tinged with regret, but that hardly keeps it from being genuine. Moreover, a lover is often able to see, in a way that no one else can, the vestiges of former beauty in the face the beloved has today. She may well be able to see that face as beautiful, and thanks to love's blindness, she may be largely unaware of the effects that time has had on it. "Even the very simple act that we call 'seeing a person we know' is in part an intellectual one," Proust wrote. "We fill the physical appearance of the individual we see with all the notions we have about him, and of the total picture that we form for ourselves, these notions certainly occupy the greater part."[19] Proust might have added that although some of the notions one has about one's beloved come from imagination, a great many come from the lover's memory; past events, deeds, and experiences shape one's perception of a person so that there is a quite literal sense in which it is frequently the case that two people looking at a third person are not seeing the same thing at all.

Given this role of memory in perception, there is no reason for restricting the vision view to qualities that the lover currently possesses. One may well be loved, valued, honored, respected, and admired not only for what one is at the present moment but also for what one has been and done. This is particularly clear when speaking of deeds and achievements; having been the person who made a discovery that saved many lives or who risked her career, reputation, or life in taking a courageous stand is something one may well be admired for the remainder of one's days. But there is no reason why other sorts of admirable or likable traits and characteristics may not work in this way also—particularly from the perspective of the lover who, again, will be especially inclined to see the image of the past in the face of the present.

Valuing for past properties is common with respect to certain types of inanimate objects. A certain copy of a book is a first edition and thus more valuable than other copies because it was one of the first copies of that book to appear on the market. A certain otherwise ordinary pen may be valued because it was owned by a significant person or used to sign an important historical document. Of course, one might object that such sentimental attachments are irrational; only differences in current qualities ought to be allowed to affect one's estimation of a thing's current value. But although it is clear why this rule may be reasonable with respect to, say, instrumental valuing—the fact that this piece of metal was once a key that would open my front door is hardly relevant to its value if it is now so worn down that it can no longer perform that function—it is not at all clear why it should be taken to apply to all forms of valuing. And indeed, whatever our ultimate position with respect to the values of inanimate objects, the necessity of such a limitation will be very hard to convincingly demonstrate in connection with individual persons, who, after all, inevitably conceive of *themselves* as objects whose deep nature it is to persist through time and to act and develop in a manner best described as narrative, and whose estimates of their own worth are arrived at in accordance with this mode of self-conception. A pen or other inanimate object will not think of itself as important because of who owned it, but a person might well think more highly of herself because she once was physically attractive, made an important discovery, or used to possess a razor-sharp wit. And there is no clear reason why our appreciation of the values of others ought to diverge in a deep way from the manner in which they tend to conceive and appreciate themselves.

Allowing love to be grounded by past as well as present qualities enables us to drive a conceptual wedge between *accidental* properties—properties one might not have possessed had one's life gone differently—and *impermanent* properties—properties one will not, or might not, always be in possession of. Proponents of the inconstancy problem tend to treat these as the same and so to assume that if Alighieri's love for Beatrice is grounded by her beauty, he will be obliged to withdraw it if she ceases to be so beautiful. I have suggested that there are several reasons for doubting either that the vision view would oblige him to withdraw his love or that it would recommend his doing this; the most forceful, I think, is the simple fact that such a view can and should allow past properties to count as well as present ones. Beatrice may perhaps cease at some point to be beautiful, but she will never lose the property of having been beautiful, and this will always be a (potential) reason—one among many—that Alighieri, as her lover, will have for continuing to love her.

As I suggested earlier, our fictional Beatrice (who, let us stipulate, is going to live a much longer life than the historical Beatrice) will, if she is like most people, develop compensating virtues and attractions as she ages, so that in his old age Alighieri will not end up loving her *only* on the basis of what she once was; he will love her in part for that and in part, as ever, on the basis of what she is. Physical beauty is by its very nature impermanent; over time nearly every physically beautiful person will become less beautiful, and many will lose their beauty altogether. If Alighieri's love for Beatrice were based *only* on Beatrice's beauty and could not expand beyond this one feature of hers, then Beatrice would indeed have reason to worry—even if, as I have suggested, he would be able to continue to value her for having been beautiful once she has ceased to be beautiful. But the account of love I have developed not only allows but indeed strongly suggests that a love based *only* on the beloved's physical beauty would not only be highly unusual but would most likely not count as genuine love. This is not to say that love cannot be inspired by a person's beauty; in the early stages of a relationship, a person's beauty can constitute one of the most powerful enticements. But if the initial attraction is to develop into full-fledged love, it must generate the sort of commitment discussed earlier: a commitment to coming to be able to see and appreciate all of the values instantiated by the beloved. And if this development can take place, the result will be an emotional attachment and appreciation that ought to survive significant changes in the beloved—including, one would hope, the loss of his beauty. An attachment of this sort will make it likely that the lover will continue to see her beloved as beautiful even under conditions when others would be more likely to judge that his beauty has faded, while also encouraging the lover to see and appreciate the other species of value her beloved instantiates.

Sad cases do occur, however, in which a person loses all or nearly all of the qualities that made her who she was while gaining little by way of compensation. I think the vision theorist should acknowledge that in a situation in which the *only* remaining grounds of love are those based in past rather than present qualities, love, although it may and perhaps should persist, will not persist unchanged. Consider the real-life example discussed by Derek Edyvane of Iris Murdoch, who was a brilliant philosopher and novelist for much of her life but whose mind was in her later years destroyed by Alzheimer's disease.[20] The inconstancy problem, as originally presented, would have held the vision view to imply that if Murdoch's husband, John Bayley, loved Murdoch primarily for her amazing philosophical abilities, then he ought to have stopped loving her when she lost those abilities (and most of the rest of her mental attributes as well). This seems quite the wrong thing—certainly it would be cold-hearted to say that Bayley ought to have abandoned Murdoch when she was at her most vulnerable—and as we have seen by now, the vision view need not say it. Rather, it can hold that Bayley might have been justified in continuing to love Murdoch for the brilliance she used to possess, even after she had stopped possessing it.

At the same time, though, it seems to ask too much to require that Bayley's feelings for Murdoch not alter at all. I tend to agree here with Neil Delaney, who argues that in such a case it is really not clear that we do think the lover ought to continue to love the beloved *romantically*. (Delaney suggests that in such a case, romantic love ought to be replaced by what he calls a "loving commitment.")[21] The idea that love should be so unresponsive to the qualities of the beloved that it could persist essentially unchanged even after the beloved's loss of *all* of her attractive qualities, a catastrophic change that might well be expected to render her very nearly unrecognizable, seems to make love into an arbitrary, even neurotic attachment. Indeed, what it suggests is that the lover was never really interested in his beloved as a particular person. "I would love anyone you might conceivably become" seems, in the long run, nearly as impersonal and alienating as "I would love anyone who had your name and social security number."

Suppose one's beloved were to become evil—transforming into, let us imagine, a devoted adherent of the Nazi Party or the Ku Klux Klan. Would we really want to say that love demands a commitment so unyielding and inflexible that it would require even *this* unfortunate lover to continue to display loyalty to her partner? One might well think that to love *this* version of him would necessarily be a betrayal of her *previous* commitment to him, in which case her love for him might require its own extinction. At any rate, the possibility of avoiding the inconstancy problem in the way suggested—that is, through an appeal to past properties—ought not, I think, lead us too quickly to assume that love should *never* "alter when it alteration finds."

Conclusion

"To love one person above all the world for all one's life because her eyes are beautiful when she is young, is to be determined to a very great thing by a very small cause," McTaggart wrote. Indeed. In fact the cause here is surely too small—the person who fell in love with a woman on account of her beautiful eyes, *and her eyes alone*, would be a fetishist, a quirk lover, in an objectionable sense. (Imagine him saying: "It turned out that she was incapable of speech, rational thought, or social interaction—but who cares? Those eyes!") Still, one commonly has the thought that *whatever* the qualities that go together to form the lover's set of reasons for loving, they will constitute "a very small cause" that determines "a very great thing." And this is right—for as the incompleteness thesis shows, that set of reasons is never in itself sufficient to make it the case that the lover, or for that matter anyone, had to fall in love with that particular person.

But it is an error to draw from this the conclusion McTaggart draws, that "the determining qualities are not the justification of that emotion, but only the means by which it arises." Beatrice's qualities are not enough to provide Alighieri with a complete answer to the question, why did you fall in love with her, and not somebody else? Since Beatrice was not the only beautiful woman in Florence—nor the only charming woman, the only intelligent woman, and so on—there will always be an element of "that's just the way it happened" in any answer Alighieri, or any lover, might give. (He might well have little to say if another comparably attractive woman asked him, "Why her, and not me?") But the fact that Alighieri was not rationally compelled to love Beatrice instead of anyone else does not imply or even support the claim that his love is unjustified or even that it was not fully justified. The justification for Alighieri's love is that Beatrice is beautiful, charming, and so forth, and this is sufficient. The object of his love possesses valuable, attractive qualities of the sort that render love an appropriate emotional response, and since it is the nature of love to focus on particular individuals and not to try to spread itself around on as many appropriate objects as possible, this is all that is required for justification here.

It is sometimes assumed that there must exist considerable tension between loving persons and valuing the qualities and other properties that attach to persons. I have argued that this tension is largely ungrounded. In particular, we need not worry that valuing those properties must necessarily imply that the person herself is not being valued or that in valuing a person for assessable contingent properties we are, in any objectionable or worrisome sense, objectifying her. Rather than regarding themselves as alienated from their (attractive) "accidental" properties, persons who have them typically identify with them and want to be perceived by others as possessing them. Individuals conceive of *themselves* as entities in possession of certain features that are observable by others and assessable in terms of value and attractiveness, and almost all of them strongly desire that at least some of these features be judged by others to be attractive and desirable. It is not as if our observable qualities appear only in the way in which others conceive of us but do not infect our own self-understandings. Rather, they figure prominently in both contexts.

Admittedly, most people do want very badly to be loved, and if we fear that our qualities are not worthy to provoke such love, we may well find ourselves desiring to be loved *despite* our flaws. Indeed, since such insecurity, at least to some extent, is part and parcel of ordinary human psychology, most if not all human beings will find themselves experiencing some version of this desire, at least on occasion. But it remains, at least in most cases, a secondary desire, the desire that takes over when our confidence fails. Although people may sometimes say that they want to be valued, desired, or loved "unconditionally," I think the more plausible view is that what each of us *really* wants is not to be loved despite our flaws, but to be attractive and worthy enough that someone will love us, reasonably and justifiably, for precisely the person we are.

None of this is to say that there is no distance between the lover's view of the beloved and the beloved's view of himself. A person's features are sometimes easier to perceive from the internal standpoint than the external one or vice versa. As an outside observer, I might be able to see that a person who thinks of herself as awkward and shy is actually quite charming and even desirable—or, conversely, that someone who believes he is charming is rather obnoxious, or that someone who thinks her integrity is unassailable is less committed to her principles than she believes. Or I might be able to see, and confirm, that what the beloved hopes is true— that she is charming, beautiful, funny, or compassionate—really *is* true, despite her fears and insecurities on the matter.

All of this is perfectly consistent with and in a sense even helps to reaffirm the main point, which is that ordinarily, the terms in which the lover will conceive of, and appreciate, her beloved will be very much the same terms as those in which the beloved conceives of and appreciates *herself*. Contra Velleman, there is no necessary deep divide separating a person's externally visible qualities from her "inner self," in a way that would imply that an appreciation of the former, a valuing of that person's perceptible qualities (or, for that matter, of that person for her qualities), would have to "eclipse" the latter and so preclude identification with that person's subjectivity. The gap that does exist is of a different sort. It is a gap between a person's properties as they ordinarily appear to the world—a world that is for the most part too self-obsessed, too distracted, and in too much of a hurry to give those properties anything but the most superficial glance—and her properties as they really are, that is, her properties as they reveal themselves to a sympathetic observer who is willing to take the time and effort to *really look*.

In some cases the lover's view of the beloved, and the beloved's view of himself, can come apart. Such an occurrence can be a source of serious trouble, and it may lead to, among other things, objectionable forms of objectification. But the fact that identification can fail does not imply that it must fail in all cases. Indeed, we are able to understand the failures as instances of the wrong sort of valuing precisely because we view them against a background of valuings of the right sort. And when the valuing is of the right sort, we are appreciated and loved as precisely what we are: persons with properties, that is, objects that are also subjects.

seven

Love and Morality

> It is a drastic reduction to think that we can capture the moral by focusing only on obligated action, as though it were of no ethical moment what you are and what you love. These are the essence of ethical life.
>
> —Charles Taylor, "Iris Murdoch and Moral Philosophy"

Introduction

It is human nature to have high hopes for love: to expect it to save us or transform our existence, to make us into complete, fulfilled people, to fill the gaps in our characters, our lives, or our souls. And when it turns out that love cannot live up to these expectations (and really, what could?), some people turn angrily and resentfully against it, declaring it a sham and a hoax, writing it off as worthless. Both attitudes—expecting everything and expecting nothing—are unreasonable, and we would do better to learn to avoid them. Love is unlikely to give us *everything*. Surely, though, it is good for *something*.

This tendency to gravitate toward extreme views of love extends into our moral discourse. What we find there, as elsewhere, is a tendency to ask "Love: good or bad?" and to forget that love's tendency is to be "something in between." In fact, there are strong reasons for seeing love as a kind of moral emotion, and in this chapter I will defend the view that it is a moral emotion. But this is not to say that love inspires *only* moral behavior or to deny that on occasion it can motivate quite clearly immoral actions. Love may move us to regard our beloveds through rose-tinted lenses, but we should avoid, if we can, taking an excessively rosy view of love itself.

My position on the love-morality relationship is similar to the position I defended in chapter 3 on the relation between love and epistemic rationality. There I argued that love carries its own epistemic standards, grounded in partiality, attachment, and engaged attention—standards that might conflict with those promulgated by a competing set of epistemic practices, grounded in impartiality, detachment, and disengaged, neutral observation. Each set of practices is appropriate in some contexts and inappropriate in others. Thus, love is an epistemic phenomenon that poses epistemic dangers. I now suggest that we say the same thing about love's moral status: love, that is, is a genuinely moral phenomenon that poses genuine moral dangers.

Love's Dangers: Is Love an Immoral Emotion?

> The danger in passionate love is that it obscures the evil that may be caused in its name.
>
> —John Kekes, *Facing Evil*

As we saw in chapter 1, the moral case against love is not especially difficult to make. One way of doing so begins with the idea that the main purpose of morality is to keep the natural, spontaneous passions and urges of human beings in check. If left to their own devices, such urges and passions often tend to destroy and create chaos. Love, which involves some of the strongest and most intense feelings that human beings experience, is precisely the sort of emotion that morality is intended to govern. On such a view the natural tendency of love will inevitably be presumed to be an antimoral one.

Love's potentially destructive passions and urges are not directed only toward people who stand outside the relationship. As we noted in chapter 1, lovers are sometimes motivated to harm their beloveds. Spurred by jealousy, possessiveness, or insecurity, emotional and physical cruelties are all too common. As Plato wrote in the *Phaedrus*, "You have to realize that a lover's friendship is without goodwill. You are like food to him when he is hungry. As wolf loves lamb, so lover loves his boy."[1] Plato is surely over-universalizing; not *every* relationship based on love or sexual passion meets this description. But sadly, too many do.[2]

The more salient danger, though, is not that of harm to the beloved but of harm to those who stand outside the relationship and are excluded by it. A central element of the vision view is that love involves a kind of blindness to the needs and interests of persons other than the beloved; the lover's attention is so focused and fixated upon her that he might not notice the plight of vulnerable others in his vicinity. "Lovers do not look around at the entirety of their world," Martha Nussbaum writes, "but are exclusively wrapped up in one another. They do not enter into anyone else's predicament; their imaginations do not see out."[3]

A central plot in Michael Ondaatje's novel *The English Patient* and in the 1996 film adaptation of that novel concerns the Hungarian count and desert explorer Laszlo de Almásy, whose passionate love for the wife of a fellow explorer during the Second World War leads him to perform a morally reprehensible action: he gives members of Rommel's northern

African army maps of the desert, thus helping them reach Cairo. The action is an attempt to save his beloved's life,[4] and so far as we can tell, no moral consideration of any sort enters his mind. Almásy truly occupies a universe of two; it is as if other people do not exist for him. As he explains his actions in the film: "I had to get back to the desert. I made a promise. The rest meant nothing to me."

The film version in particular was criticized by various commentators who took it to be endorsing Almásy's action. The philosopher Thomas Hurka, for example, complained:

> In *The English Patient* the personal is more important than the political. Whatever the effects on the outcome of a coming war, the movie suggests, it's understandable to give priority to your personal relationships. . . . This is the immorality at the core of *The English Patient*: It exalts personal emotion at the expense of everything else. In *Casablanca* Rick's love doesn't blind him to larger issues of politics. On the contrary, only after Ilsa returns that love can he care about those issues properly. But Almásy in the desert thinks only of his own small affair. And the movie presents this as making his betrayal not only forgivable but even, as the background music swells, inspiring. . . . Almásy's blindness to the reality around him is presented not as irresponsibility but as a sign of profound and wonderful love.[5]

Regardless of whether we read the film, ultimately, as endorsing Almásy's decision,[6] there is no denying that his action is highly romantic; and in a society such as ours, which lionizes and valorizes romantic love to a very high degree, there will be many who will extol it as an example of ideal behavior. As Aaron Ben-Ze'ev and Ruhama Goussinsky point out, romantic love, like religious faith, "is treated not only as the ultimate significance but also as the ultimate justification. Love made me do it—these are the magic words that win social applause. Love seems to be the only ideal that is not controversial.[7]

I have been pursuing the moral worry about love that begins with a certain picture of morality, according to which its function is to control our irrational or arational passions and urges. Alongside this we can add a second sort of picture, one that fastens on the popular idea that morality is fundamentally impartial and that this indeed is what characterizes it. The two pictures are not identical, but they are related; it is common to think, at any rate, that the passions are chaotic and destructive in large part because they involve and encourage partiality, by fixing on certain individuals obsessively and to the exclusion of all others. It is, after all, precisely Almásy's mad passion for Katharine that leads him to do what he does while suppressing any thought about the consequences or the rightness of what he is doing. On the combined picture, then, love runs the risk of immorality both because it is a matter of unreasoned passion and because it involves unjustifiable partiality. As Robert Ehman writes, "There is always something immoral in the privilege and attention that the lover gives to the beloved at the expense of others who might have had an even higher moral claim."[8]

This is a significant point, for it strongly suggests that the moral worries we have been developing extend beyond romantic or sexual love and apply to the typically cooler but nonetheless powerful attachments of friendship as well. Even a love that is not passionately romantic will be thought by some thinkers to be morally dangerous, precisely because it involves partiality. Love endangers us, then, not only by filling us with mad passion but also by urging us to trade the value system recommended by impartial morality for one that would allow and even encourage us to be unequal and partial, to bend or entirely ignore ordinary rules of conduct, and to prioritize the needs or well-being of one's beloved or the demands of one's relationship with her. Insofar as romantic and friendship love make demands of us that can conflict with the demands of the larger community or those of impartial morality, both of them seem entirely capable of making us into worse people.

Love's Justice

> Love is the extremely difficult realization that something other than oneself is real.
> —Iris Murdoch, "The Sublime and the Good"

Why, in the face of the undeniable fact that love poses such dangers, do I want to insist there is a very real sense in which love is a moral phenomenon? We might start by observing that friendships and romantic relationships carry obligations that in many ways look like moral obligations. We aspire to be good friends, good lovers, good husbands and wives, and we praise ourselves when we succeed and criticize ourselves, feel guilty and shamed, when we fail. Such relationships involve and encourage various virtues: compassion and sensitivity, honesty and integrity, loyalty, resolve, and on at least some occasions courage. Love can demand significant, at times tremendous, sacrifices. Most significant, love relationships take us out of ourselves, freeing ourselves from excessive self-concern and narcissism. Love helps us grasp the full force of the obvious but elusive fact that the world is larger than ourselves, that other people are just as real as we are. Thus, as the narrator of John Banville's novel *The Sea* reminds us, one's first experience of love frequently constitutes a watershed moment in one's personal moral development.

She was the one on whom I had chosen, or had been chosen, to lavish my love. . . . In her I had my first experience of the absolute otherness of other people. It is not too much to say—well, it is, but I shall say it anyway—that in Chloe the world was first manifest for me as an objective entity. Not my father and mother, my teachers, other children, not Connie Grace herself, no one had yet been real in the way that Chloe was.[9]

Like morality, love calls the agent out of herself and demands that she focus her attention on the needs, interests, desires, and well-being of other people, rather than on her self-interest. It prohibits excessive self-concern and calls for attention, empathy, and care. As we saw in chapter 3, love requires that we view people in the best possible light, that we struggle to understand choices and actions that do not immediately make sense to us and might even baffle or repulse us, that we question our presuppositions and attempt to see the world from another point of view. And love, like morality, can ask for sacrifices that are neither pleasant nor easy—a point that has been emphasized both by such antireligious philosophers as Nietzsche and by Christian thinkers like C. S. Lewis, who wrote: "Eros does not aim at happiness. . . . It is the very mark of Eros that when he is in us we had rather share unhappiness with the Beloved than be happy on any other terms."[10]

Still, the sacrifices demanded by love do not always feel like sacrifices; where the love is true and strong, the demands of *we* tend to silence the demands of *I*. The moral notions of impartiality and impersonality are frequently associated and almost as frequently conflated; although the notion that love for individual persons must involve *impersonality* is deeply misguided, it is quite true that love often demands of us a kind of *impartiality—impartiality*, here, in the sense of fair-mindedness, of putting aside one's biases and preconceptions and viewing the person standing before us with close attention and with open eyes and of taking their needs and interests as seriously as we do our own. At the very least, love demands that we struggle to overcome the partiality to *self*, which tends to exert such a powerful influence on the behavior of humans.

The sort of focused and devoted attention involved in love is a profoundly moral phenomenon insofar as it both enables and takes as its goal the full, unrestricted recognition of a human individual. We find a sign of this in the experience of grief. The deaths of most people will affect a given agent little or not at all; after all, many people die every day, and a person who is incapacitated by grief over every single death will be unable to function as an agent. But the death of each person is nevertheless a deep and tragic loss. And when a loved one has died, the magnitude of this loss is fully experienced. In such circumstances one is devastated, one's experiences of other aspects of life are muted or pushed to the side, and one simply *cannot,* for a while, go on as one did before. And this is as it should be. If a person is genuinely loved, when she dies, there will be *someone* who responds with the full recognition of what has happened. Love opens a window on reality, allowing us to experience and to feel that from which we are ordinarily alienated and, thus, protected.

The kind of moral relation demanded by this sort of full recognition, then, is very different from the kind of moral relation an agent will have toward most of the people in the world. The typical agent's moral duties toward strangers are, in large part, discharged simply by his leaving them alone. Given that we do not know these persons, in most circumstances this is the best we can do; we respect them, on the whole, by keeping our distance and refraining from interfering with their pursuit of their good.

In chapter 4 I spoke of the love relationship as an "ethically ideal relationship." The idea is that relations with strangers, from the point of view of love, are at best rough simulacra of the *ideal* ethical relationships we find obtaining between those who genuinely love one another. I simply do not know a stranger well enough to treat him in a genuinely moral manner. I cannot take part in, or even encourage, his projects, as I do not know what they are. If he suffers, I may perhaps feel compassion for his suffering in an abstract way, though even this presupposes *some* knowledge of him; but I cannot truly *empathize* with the sufferings of a stranger, for as long as he remains a stranger he represents at best an abstract representation of humanity in my eyes. As Aldo Leopold has written, "We can be ethical only in relation to something that we can see, feel, understand, love, or otherwise have faith in."[11]

Relationships of love, by contrast, are anything but abstract; indeed, they manifest a deep opposition to abstraction. Such relationships focus the lover's attention on the beloved as a concrete, particular individual and call for intimate, committed relationships in which, ideally, the lover's appetite for knowledge of the beloved will increase in proportion to the knowledge he acquires. As Nussbaum writes, true understanding of another person "could not possibly be acquired through a general description. . . . It requires the experience of shared activity and the cultivation, over time and through the trust that comes only with time, of an intimate responsiveness to that person in feeling, thought, and action."[12]

To respect someone's autonomy by leaving her alone, or otherwise treat a stranger as impersonal morality demands, one need not know much about her. To attend to her as love requires, though, one needs to know a great deal. In viewing an individual with love, we say that we do full justice to her; and the use of the word *justice* here is not metaphorical: the lover does, indeed, view her beloved justly, which is to say, both accurately and generously. The charity of her vision leads her to strive for explanations and interpretations of her beloved's behavior and character that are deeper than the easy and shallow interpretations with which, at least when faced with strangers or mere acquaintances, we ordinarily rest content.

The case in favor of connecting love with this sort of moral vision has been most persuasively articulated and elaborated by Iris Murdoch. In Murdoch's view, which is highly influenced by Plato, becoming moral is a matter of becoming enlightened by learning to transcend what she calls "the tissue of self-aggrandizing and consoling wishes and dreams which prevents one from seeing what there is outside one" and learning to perceive the truth about the world.[13] Thus, on this account, "It is a *task* to come to see the world as it is."[14] But the task is necessary for morality, since it is necessary for action and choice: "I can only choose within the world I can *see*, in the moral sense of 'see' which implies that clear vision is a result of moral imagination and moral effort."[15] The culmination of the project is the ability to achieve "a just and loving gaze directed upon an individual reality"[16]—an ability that, on Murdoch's view, lies at the very foundation of morality.

> We use our imagination not to escape the world but to join it. . . . The authority of morals is the authority of truth, that is of reality. We can see the length, the extension, of these concepts as patient attention transforms accuracy without interval into just discernment. Here too we can see it as natural to the particular kind of creatures that we are that love should be inseparable from justice, and clear vision from respect for the real.[17]

How is this instantiated in the demands love makes of us? I have concentrated on the way that love prompts the lover to open her eyes to her beloved: that is, to pay close attention to him, to try to see him as he truly is and at the same time see him in the best possible light. But there are other aspects to a love relationship: making the beloved a partner in the formation and carrying out of one's plans; taking the well-being of the beloved to constitute part of, or to be inseparable from, one's own well-being; taking the beloved's thoughts, judgments, and opinions seriously in one's deliberations; caring about the beloved's assessments and opinions of oneself and undertaking attempts at self-improvement as suggested by these; wanting one's feelings of love to be reciprocated; and publicly acknowledging the existence and significance of the relationship. All of these are, typically, elements of a committed love relationship, and each expresses, in its own way, the lover's taking seriously the individuality and individual value of her beloved. To make a human being a partner in one's ongoing projects and endeavors, to open oneself to him and orient one's very life around him, is to recognize in a most fundamental way his value and significance as an individual—and, indirectly but nonetheless profoundly, the value and significance of humanity itself.

Love, Morality, and Conflict

Opening one's eyes to another individual and seeing him as he really is, without a vision clouded by presuppositions and prejudices, is a challenging task. Love's demand that we undertake this task, in the interest of striving for a full and genuinely complete recognition of another human being, grounds a strong case for the claim that love is in a very deep sense a moral phenomenon. Those who, like Murdoch, see love as a powerful moral force, an emotion that embodies and represents a genuine way of responding to the value of human individuals, are perfectly correct. But those who see love as morally dangerous are also quite right. In the complex world in which we live, a world where goods and goals inevitably conflict with one another, it is perfectly possible for an emotion that represents a deeply moral attitude to motivate morally unjustifiable, even deeply immoral, actions. Indeed, such a state of affairs is more than possible; it is part of the reality with which we ethical agents are faced on a daily basis.

Murdoch herself is probably a bit too optimistic about love's powers. In part this is because she is, in a way that is heavily influenced by Freud, deeply pessimistic about the human situation, holding that human beings are constantly subject to self-delusion and are therefore rarely if ever able to achieve unclouded epistemic contact with the world. ("Objectivity and unselfishness," she writes, "are not natural to human beings.")[18] Given such assumptions as to how inept human beings ordinarily are at perceiving reality, and how deeply selfish and pervasively self-deluded they are, it will seem reasonable to think that *any* emotion or force capable of directing their attention outside themselves—if nothing else, love is at least *that*—ought to be commended.

Love should, of course, be commended, at least much of the time; but we should also allow for a possibility that Murdoch is perhaps overly hesitant to entertain: love, rather than always leading us closer to a correct apprehension of reality, might on occasion lead us away from it. Much of chapter 3 was devoted to the argument that love's epistemic critics (represented there by Simon Keller and Sarah Stroud) tend to overemphasize love's tendency to lead lovers to believe false things. But as I explicitly argued there, my claim was not that love *never* has this effect on lovers. There is no one way of seeing that is always guaranteed to lead agents to the truth. Some epistemic standpoints are better suited than others to certain situations, but at the end of the day our belief-forming conduct, like so much of the rest of life, is largely a gamble.

Another recent thinker, much influenced by Murdoch, who adheres to a somewhat one-sided and ultimately misguided interpretation of love's moral nature is David Velleman. Velleman follows Murdoch in emphasizing the way in which the successful completion of the task of "really looking" calls for the lover to transcend his own ego, to put aside many of his own desires, and to be responsible to an independent reality in a way that makes him both emotionally vulnerable and open to a kind of enlightenment.[19] All of this—including the implied claim (which Velleman goes on to make explicit) that the larger reality of which the lover is made aware will often include many persons, and not just the beloved—seems quite right. But we should not be led by this, as Velleman is, to insist that love's appearance of partiality is therefore an illusion or, at most, a thin veneer laid over the top of a more profound and pervasive impartiality—a position that leads him to make some highly implausible remarks about Williams's Drowning Wife case.

> I do believe that the man's love for his wife [in Drowning Wife] should heighten his sensitivity to her predicament. But I cannot believe that it would leave him less sensitive to the predicament of others who are in—or perhaps alongside—the same boat. My own experience is that, although I may be insensitive to suffering until I see it in people I love, I cannot then remain insensitive to it in their fellow sufferers. The sympathy that I feel for my wife's difficulties at work, or my children's difficulties at school, naturally extends to their coworkers and classmates.
>
> The idea that someone could show love for his own children by having less compassion for other children strikes me as bizarre. Whatever caused someone to favor his own children in this manner could hardly be love. Of course, a person's love for his children shouldn't necessarily lead him to *love* other children. Ideally, he will find his own children especially loveable—that is, especially expressive, in his eyes, of an incomparable value. But when his children awaken him to that value as only they can, they awaken him to something that he recognizes, or ought to recognize, as universal.
>
> . . . Of course the man in Williams's story should save his wife in preference to strangers. But the reasons why he should save her have nothing essentially to do with love.[20]

Erich Fromm sometimes expresses a similar idea: "If I truly love one person I love all persons, I love the world, I love life. If I can say to somebody else, 'I love you,' I must be able to say, 'I love in you everybody, I love through you the world, I love in you also myself.'"[21] But this is nothing more than a pleasant fantasy.[22] I imagine that Sam—or, for that matter, Andrea—would want to reply to Velleman by saying,

LOVE AND MORALITY 155

Well, *of course* the lover's sympathy for his beloved will "naturally extend'" to other people *in some cases*. But in cases where the beloved's well-being, for that matter *her very life*, is pitted against that of others, it's simply absurd to expect the lover to feel, or show, the same concern for everyone. The concern that the lover feels can extend to a broad group, sometimes very broad. But it is foolish to pretend that it will always do so, or to view love as deficient wherever it does not. The world simply isn't set up to allow for that sort of concern—in the world as we encounter it, a person could be prepared to respond equally to *everyone* only if he wasn't especially inclined to respond to *anyone*.[23]

We must deal carefully, moreover, with Velleman's skepticism toward the idea that, as he puts it, a parent "could show love for his own children by having less compassion for other children." As written, this is ambiguous. Does Velleman mean that the parent, by virtue of being a parent, tends to feel less compassion for other people's children than he does for his own children, or that he feels less compassion for other people's children *than he otherwise would* (i.e., if he were not a parent)? The latter claim is indeed bizarre, but no one holds this. (It is not as if, had his own children not come along, he would have loved all other children in the world *as if* they were his own.) The former is the essential claim, and it is innocuous: *of course* parents will feel a special degree of compassion for their own children that they will not feel for the children of others. If Velleman doubts this, then he is the one defending a deeply radical claim: that good parenting does *not* involve feeling more compassion for one's own children than for the children of others.

Rather than concluding, as Velleman does, that love must be fundamentally impartial (since love is moral, and morality is fundamentally impartial), we should draw a different conclusion: since love is moral, there are ways of seeing that are moral and yet, at the same time, deeply partial. Of course, one might object; how can it be that love is deeply moral, one might ask, if such a way of seeing can lead us morally astray? The answer to this question is essentially the same as the answer I suggested in chapter 3, where the objection was that since love sometimes leads people to form false beliefs, it cannot be commended from the standpoint of reasonable epistemic practice. If there were any such thing as *the* standpoint of reasonable epistemic practice, this argument might be convincing; but the world is too messy to allow any such thing. Rather, there are multiple sets of practices, none of them universal or guaranteed to give the correct answer. Some sets of practices—"believe whatever your parents tell you," to take an exceptionally simpleminded example—are so bad that they can be ruled out. But after ruling out every practice that fails to pass the bar of minimal reliability, there will remain more than one way of being, or attempting to be, a reasonable epistemic agent. That this is so is simply inevitable, given the nature of the world and the limits of human ability.

We can say the same in the moral case. Indeed, here we can go a bit further, for moral reasons seem to be subject to a more thoroughgoing pluralism than is present in the theoretical sphere. There may be various ways of being a responsible epistemic agent; but still, at the end of the day, one is tempted to say one's picture of the world is either accurate or inaccurate. Things seem to be very different, though, in the moral realm. Although in certain situations an agent's moral options may be limited to one—the other alternatives may be too costly or impermissible for some other reason, and perhaps even unthinkable—there is no reason to expect this in every case; rather, we are quite comfortable with the idea that agents will typically have a variety of options available to them from which they may choose. The guaranteed existence of a single right answer seems commonly to be the case in the realm of theoretical reason (there, after all, a belief is either true or false), but it is the exceptional case in the practical sphere.

It is all too common, though, for philosophers to assume that there must be one response to any morally challenging situation that is *the* morally required response, and thus to find plausible the idea of a single, unified "moral point of view"—a point of view that need not be, but is very easily and frequently, identified with the *impersonal* point of view taken as morally decisive and authoritative by utilitarians and others. In an essay entitled "The Moral Philosopher and the Moral Life," William James wrote that the aim of the moral philosopher "is to find an account of the moral relations that obtain among things, which will weave them into the unity of a stable system, and make of the world what one may call a genuine universe from the ethical point of view. So far as the world resists reduction to the form of unity, so far as ethical propositions seem unstable, so far does the philosopher fail of his ideal."[24]

Predictably enough, perhaps, the ethical view James arrives at is one in which right action consists in satisfying as many individuals' demands as possible. But although the effects of an adherence to this view might be supported by a majority of people in a majority of cases, there is little reason for thinking that every one of its deliverances will be ethically just or for writing off the concerns of those who do not find themselves in the majority on important matters and whose judgments and interests are, as a result, given short shrift. Indeed, James himself is clear that the demand that we satisfy as many preferences as possible is a compromise; a genuinely moral universe, on James's conception, would be one in which it was always possible to satisfy *everyone's* preferences. To the extent that our universe falls short of that privileged state of being, genuinely moral action, as James understands it, simply lies beyond the bounds of human possibility.

The desire for a universe that contains no conflict, or in which all apparent conflicts are superficial and can be reconciled at a deeper level, is surely understandable. But given the deeply problematic nature of many of the moral puzzles we face and the significance of the individual claims that are in conflict in these situations, a set of elegant and fully satisfying solutions that manages somehow to fully accommodate all these claims is precisely what we should *not* expect to find. Indeed, any putative solution that does lay claim to all of these virtues will almost certainly be found to be guilty of simplification or falsification in some respect.

As Murdoch herself perceptively writes, "It is the traditional inspiration of the philosopher, but also his traditional vice, to believe that all is one."[25] It is Murdoch, too, who suggests the proper antidote to this desire for unity—and who links it to love: "The direction of attention is, contrary to nature, outward, away from self which reduces all to a false unity, towards the great surprising variety of the world, and the ability so to direct attention is love."[26]

We should do our best to avoid any theory or pretheoretical commitment that would force us to consider love purely moral or to see love and morality as one and the same. But we should just as strenuously resist any theory or commitment that would force us to deny that love and morality overlap at all. Both of these fundamental presuppositions have the virtue of simplicity, and both capture part of the truth, but neither is adequate to the complex and morally messy world in which we live.

Two Attitudes toward Human Value

With respect to love, then, what we should say is something like the following: To encounter a human individual is to be confronted with an object that is capable of bearing various sorts of value, including a type of value that may well be unique in the universe, the value of being an object that is also a subject, an object that has a perspective on the world, something for which a world exists. These various perspectives are metaphysically distinct and cannot be reduced to one another. (Since one person cannot have another person's experiences, one person's pain cannot be genuinely compensated for with a benefit experienced by someone else.) As such, individual human beings ought to be treated with respect, as ends in themselves, so that one may not trade one human for another in the straightforward manner in which one may permissibly and fully reasonably trade most value-bearing objects. This helps to explain why the sacrifice of a smaller number of persons for a greater number is an occasion for regret and leaves an irreducible moral remainder. If to save one person is to save the world, then to sacrifice one person is to destroy the world, and what could possibly compensate for the destruction of the world?

Two attitudes can be taken toward the value of human beings. The first and broader stance, which we can call the impersonal attitude, recognizes that all human beings have roughly equivalent claims on life and well-being. In striving to acknowledge the equal standing of all human beings, this attitude asks us to refrain from attending so closely to the affairs of any particular human being that our grip on the overall equality might be threatened.

The second attitude is what we can call the personal attitude. The personal attitude eschews the broad view of the impersonal attitude and focuses instead on particular individuals, striving for a complete appreciation of a small number of such individuals to the exclusion of others. This necessitates placing some individuals in the foreground of one's concern while relegating others to the background. This attitude does not deny that all persons are equal in all fundamental respects, including in respect of being deserving of this sort of close attention and engagement; but it does not call on us to embody the recognition of this general equality in our emotions or in our actions. For doing so—that is, doing what the impersonal attitude calls on us to do—is incompatible with the full recognition of the value of a person. The central emotion of the impersonal attitude is a broad-minded, disinterested beneficence. The central emotion of the personal attitude is love.

Neither of these attitudes is reducible to the other. Indeed, fully adhering to one makes it impossible fully to adopt the other—a single agent cannot simultaneously and wholeheartedly hold both of them. It is nevertheless the case that each of these attitudes represents a valid and intelligible form of response to the value of human individuals. While they represent *different* modes of recognition, both are modes of recognizing the same general value, and each embodies a valid insight that the other cannot fully capture.

The reality of two distinct and irreducible attitudes helps explain the existence of moral dilemmas. Consider, for instance, a situation related to Drowning Wife, in which an agent must choose between rescuing one endangered stranger or rescuing five. Many people take it as obvious, when presented with the situation in its abstract form, that one ought to maximize by saving the greater number; this, at any rate, is surely the moral thing to do. And yet the choice in real life would not necessarily be quite so easy. Imagine that you, the agent who must make the choice, are close enough to the one stranger to look him in the eye; in choosing to save the five you must literally turn your back on him. Or imagine that afterward you will be called on to explain why you made the choice you

did to the family of the person you allowed to die. John Taurek has offered a powerful argument to the effect that morally speaking, the choice
is not at all clear. In Taurek's view the best moral policy would be to flip
a coin, thus giving each person an equal chance of survival.

> For each of these six persons it is no doubt a terrible thing to die.
> Each faces the loss of something among the things he values most
> . . . should any of these five lose his life, his loss is no greater a loss
> to him because, as it happens, four others (or forty-nine others)
> lose theirs as well. And neither he nor anyone else loses anything
> of greater value to him than does David, should David lose his life.
> Five individuals each losing his life does not add up to anyone's ex-
> periencing a loss five times greater than the loss suffered by any one
> of the five. . . . My way of thinking about these trade-off situations
> consists, essentially, in seriously considering what will be lost or
> suffered by this one person if I do not prevent it, and in comparing
> the significance of that *for him* with what would be lost or suffered
> by anyone else if I do not prevent it. This reflects a refusal to take
> seriously in these situations any notion of the sum of two persons'
> separate losses.[27]

This "refusal to take seriously . . . any notion of the sum of two persons'
separate losses" makes no sense whatever from the perspective of the
impersonal attitude. But a person who leans more toward the pole of the
ethical continuum expressed in the personal attitude will have no trouble
understanding the idea Taurek is getting at here. Each of the persons at
risk in this situation is, after all, a *person*—a subject for whom a world
exists—and each has as much to lose as any of the others. "The whole
earth can suffer no greater torment than a *single* soul," as Wittgenstein
claimed—a sentiment echoed in Graham Greene's statement that "suffering is not increased by numbers: one body can contain all the suffering
the world can feel."[28] Of course, this is true not only of the one but of
each of the five as well. But Taurek's point is precisely that the fact that it
is true of *each* of the five does not make "the five" into a metaphysically
distinct entity with a claim to being rescued that is somehow five times
as strong.

My intention is not to defend Taurek's conclusion. Indeed, I tend to
think that there *is* a fairly strong reason, in a case of this sort, to save the
five endangered people rather than saving only one. But this reason is not
one that necessarily forces itself on a moral agent faced with this choice;
and although we would probably be surprised by a person who flipped a
coin in order to give the single person a chance of being saved, I do not
think that such a choice is unintelligible. I take this as evidence for my
main claim about the relation between the two attitudes, for it is the

possibility of taking either attitude, and the fact that which one to take cannot be determined for us by any objective fact or neutral decision-making process, that explains the nature of our intuitive responses in such cases, and why, in particular, those responses tend to be complex and to some degree mutually irreconcilable.

Similar responses are at play in Drowning Wife, with the difference that here, of course, the one who is in danger is not a stranger, but someone whom the agent loves. From the perspective of the purely impersonal attitude, this makes no difference; it is still a matter of five versus one, and the five ought to carry the day. Here, though, more people will find their intuitions somewhat conflicted, and the majority of people whose intuitions are *not* conflicted tend to go the other way and agree with Williams that love trumps morality and that one ought to save one's beloved without a second thought. Here too, though, there is an intelligible, even powerful case for *either* response: choosing to save five strangers rather than one's own beloved does manifest a certain concern for the value of persons in a way that we can all understand, even if we ourselves cannot imagine making that choice.

And indeed, despite its representing an intelligible response to the value of human individuals, the impersonal attitude, taken to such extremes, does strike many people as repellent. In at least some sense, it seems, a person who is equally concerned with the interests and well-being of everyone cannot really care very much about anyone. This is not only due to human agents' limited capacities for empathy and identification. The deeper point is a conceptual one: by its very nature genuine concern for another involves empathy, which requires entering into the subject's point of view; and to occupy one person's point of view is by definition *not* to occupy someone else's. Even a godlike entity that was not subject to human psychological limitations would be unable simultaneously to empathize with *everyone*: the state of universal empathy is not simply inaccessible to creatures like ourselves; it is conceptually incoherent. (Imagine trying to empathize, at one and the same moment, with a torturer and his victim.) Thus, while we might admire a person who takes the impersonal attitude for her ability to extend her concern so broadly, at the same time we are likely to have our doubts regarding the depth and genuineness of her concern: against the backdrop of the wider world, how significant can the interests or suffering of any *particular* person be?

The only way to truly understand suffering is to understand it from the point of view of the particular person who suffers—a point of view from which the suffering, if serious, will appear to be the most significant fact in the universe. It is quite useless to tell a person in serious pain to consider the *insignificance* of such suffering in the grand scheme of things as a way of gaining perspective. Consider the following passage from William Boyd's novel *Any Human Heart:*

Hodge lectured me again on Freya and Stella. Thirteen other people died when that explosion happened, he said. Thousands of Londoners died from bombs or rockets, many of them women and children. Millions of people died in the war. You could have been a German Jew—lost your entire family in the gas chambers—wife, children, brothers, sisters, nieces and nephews, parents, aunts and uncles, grandparents. It's an awful bloody terrible tragic thing, but you have to see them as victims of a global armed conflict, like the millions of other victims. Innocent people die in a war. And now we're casualties too. I said, you can't equate my wife and child with your fucking leg. Yes I fucking well can, he bellowed at me. To me—to me—my lost leg is more important than your lost wife and child.[29]

It would be inhumane to demand that Hodge not feel this way—to demand that because it is true in some sense that a lost wife and child are worse than a lost leg, Hodge must take the identities of the persons involved to be irrelevant and feel that *his* loss of a leg matters less than someone else's loss of a wife and child. And yet there is undeniably a kind of inhumanity present in Hodge's position as well, not only in the implied lack of sympathy for his friend's loss, but more disturbingly in his insistence on treating those two deaths as *his friend's* loss, rather than as losses to the people who died, his failure, that is, even to consider the perspectives of his friend's wife and child. When tallying such losses, it is perhaps inevitable that the dead receive short shrift: after a person has ceased to be, the perspective from which that event would be seen as the most significant loss—the loss of *everything*, the loss of the world itself—is no longer occupied. No one remains to press these claims. And yet for all that it still seems absurd to see Hodge as committing any sort of error in caring more about the loss of his leg than about any of these other losses; *to him*, as he says, it really is the most important. Among the moral facts that populate our universe, this—the impossibility of eliminating the variety and fundamental distinctness of these competing perspectives—is perhaps one of the hardest ones fully to face.

"This Wild Gaping after Just One Body": Monogamy versus Promiscuity

> When I put the rose in my hair like the Andalusian girls used or shall I wear a red yes and how he kissed me under the Moorish wall and I thought well as well him as another.
>
> —James Joyce, *Ulysses*

The tension between the personal attitude and the impersonal attitude exerts a significant influence on the issue of whether, and to what degree, we think love relationships ought to be exclusive. It is often thought that sexual and romantic love ought to be very exclusive: one lover at a time, if not one lover for one's entire life. Friendship, on the other hand, is also exclusive but to a considerably lesser degree. On this promonogamy view, as I will call it, a person who has a regular romantic lover is committing a betrayal if he starts up a romantic relationship with someone else, whereas a person who has a friend and who makes a second friend ordinarily is not.

The vision view accepts that some degree of exclusivity is essential to love. An orientation toward exclusivity is one of the main things, perhaps the main thing, that distinguishes the personal from the impersonal attitude. And much of my argument has been devoted to showing that we can make sense of exclusivity without turning love into something deeply irrational; that we can make a place for reason(s) in love without being driven to Socrates' view that a rational person "must become a lover of all beautiful bodies, and he must think that this wild gaping after just one body is a small thing and despise it." And one might well be tempted on this basis to assume that the vision view will require romantic lovers to be monogamous.

But there are three reasons for resisting this quick assumption. First, monogamy involves a certain degree of exclusivity: one is limited to a single partner. But one might well hold the view that love must involve some degree of exclusivity without holding that it requires quite *this* much. Again, friendship is an exclusive relationship—one cannot be *everyone's* friend, as C. S. Lewis observed[30]—but a person who had as many romantic lovers as most people in our society have friends would be considered quite promiscuous. One can hold that love requires exclusivity, then, while denying that the exclusivity involved is of the highest degree imaginable. What is required is that some people be in the club and others not, but we need not require that the club have only *one* member.

Second, one might hold that romantic love must involve *some sort* of exclusivity while rejecting the idea that the exclusivity must be of a sexual nature. There might, after all, be other conceivable ways (shared living spaces, shared financial arrangements, children, etc.) of signifying the special attachment that exists between two romantic partners—ways that would leave them free to pursue sexual relations with as many willing partners as they would like.

Of course, in our society it is sexual exclusivity that is typically taken to matter most, and in this book I have for the most part proceeded on the assumption that that sort of exclusivity would be felt for, and desired by, typical lovers and beloveds. But here the third point becomes relevant, which is simply that there is a difference between what is *typical* and what is *ethically required*. It seems highly likely that, at least in our own society and in others like it, most people will continue to regard some degree of sexual exclusivity as a central element of romantic love. People are naturally inclined to feel this way, and most people's inclinations are reinforced by the expectations embedded in the practices of their society; and I have written most of this book with these people, and these inclinations and expectations, in mind. Nonetheless, it is also worth considering those people who find that they do not feel this way or who are capable of other forms of romantic love. Must a lack of sexual possessiveness or jealousy be an indication that one's love is somehow deficient? Is there something morally suspect about the romantic lover who wants to have sexual relations with more than one partner—or, for that matter, the lover who does not mind if his partner does?

It is not at all clear that we must answer yes. As I have suggested, the vision view ought to be found amenable by people who also accept the promonogamy view. But it does not seem to me that the former in any way implies the latter; to say that love involves *some* degree of exclusivity in *some* area is quite compatible with stating that it is both permissible and reasonable to have, at one time, not one but several sexual partners. It may even be compatible, at least for some people, with having more than one romantic lover at a time (though this, I suspect, may be somewhat less common).

Why is it so commonly thought that having sex, which is the main thing that separates romantic relationships from friendships, automatically requires such a high degree of exclusivity? The explanation of the fact that we *do* often tend to regard demands for sexual exclusivity as reasonable is in large part historical and has to do with the way in which our understanding of love and the institution of marriage has been shaped, at least for Westerners, by the Christian tradition. As suggested by Pope Benedict XVI, one person's romantic love for another is, on the Christian tradition, supposed to be a mirror of our love for God; a similar species of fidelity and exclusive devotion is required in each case and is thought to constitute an honoring of the beloved: "Corresponding to the image of a monotheistic God is monogamous marriage. Marriage based on exclusive and definitive love becomes the icon of the relationship between God and his people and vice versa."[31]

But a historical explanation of this sort does not amount to a justification. Indeed, historical explanations tend to be undermining; once we are aware of the contingent historical processes that have led to our current assumptions, those assumptions come to appear themselves contingent and so less compelling. This will be particularly true, here, for those who no longer believe in God or whose religious or spiritual practices fall outside the Catholic Church. (Moreover, the model seems to invite a troubling question: if God is permitted to love not one person but many, why should we, whose love is supposed to be an image of God's, not be granted similar permission?)

A different answer refers to biological human nature. Evolutionary biologists will claim that we have evolved to be creatures who experience jealousy and possessiveness as part of sexual love. If this is a deep and immutable feature of human nature, then we do seem to have a strong reason to be faithful to our partners: *not* being faithful to them may cause them pain. But we must be careful not to overestimate the influence of biology at the expense of culture and socialization. Our proclivity toward such pain is not entirely a matter of biology, and it is overly pessimistic to view it as a deep and unalterable element of our psychological constitution. To some degree, at least, tendencies to sexual jealousy and possessiveness are surely cultural, the effects of socializing processes. We are taught to expect our lovers to be monogamous and to expect them to expect this of us. Some individuals, moreover, have shown themselves able to overcome these tendencies to a considerable degree. It seems quite possible, then, that individuals brought up in a society in which nonmonogamy was presented as an acceptable norm might find themselves free of these feelings.

Of course, the mere possibility of this is no argument that society should be changed in this way. Still, if such an option is possible, then it will not be hard to come up with reasons that speak in its favor. Since different things make different people happy, making nonmonogamous sexual arrangements a possibility would seem likely to increase overall happiness. And with respect to most goods and values, we do tend to think that at least a certain amount of freedom to investigate, explore, and try things out is a good thing. (The promonogamy view, except in its strongest forms, typically allows a period of exploration and investigation before marriage, but puts a stop to it thereafter—as if one could "eat around" until the age of twenty-five but then had to commit to a single type of cuisine, or perhaps even a single restaurant, for the rest of one's life.) Allowing extramarital sexual relationships would not only provide opportunities for married people who are sexually dissatisfied but might ease the pressure on their partners who are experiencing diminished desire. Here as elsewhere it is not difficult to find reasons that speak in favor of increased liberation and a lessening of traditional restrictions on behavior.[32]

Still, some may be unable to escape the suspicion that there is necessarily a deep tension between the propromiscuity position and the general spirit of the vision view. On the vision view, to love someone is to place him at the center of one's field of vision: the world is oriented around him, so that "everything else lives in [his] light." But a field of vision has only one center; so true love, complete love, must be directed to only one person. An initial response to this suggestion might be that it indicates a problem for the vision view; it *is*, after all, clearly possible to love more than one person. Many parents have more than one child, and it is not ordinarily the case that the love for each diminishes as more children are added, let alone that having more than one child necessarily implies that at least some of them are not genuinely loved. And the same seems to go for friendship. There may be a limit as to how many friends a person can have before her affection is stretched too thin, but the limit is surely considerably larger than one.

Or is it? At least some people—Montaigne, for instance—have thought that a person could have only one friend in the complete sense; to have more would result in diluted, less than ideal friendships and would mean giving up on the possibility of the real thing.[33] This seems to me too strong to be plausible, but it points us in the right direction by reminding us that the correct way to think about these matters is not so much in terms of an absolute cutoff but rather in terms of a continuum, with full monogamy occupying one pole and promiscuity the other. Montaigne demands too much of friendship, but he still has a point: the most complete, most powerful recognition and affirmation of the value of a human being would be to devote oneself to that person to the exclusion of all others. Just as most people attempt to reach a reasonable balance between the demands of love and those of impersonal morality, so too, within the context of love, we aim for a proper balance between a very demanding ideal of exclusive love and a more capacious notion that remains an expression of the personal attitude, insofar as it is focused on a number of particular persons but does not carry one all the way to a fanatical, obsessive devotion to a single human being.

Once again, moreover, we must recall the importance of the fact that human beings are historical entities. A loved person need not *always* occupy the center of one's field of vision; what love requires, rather, is that she get *enough* attention. If I am never—or rarely—the object on which my lover's attention is focused, then it is not really true that she loves me at all. But she need not always be looking at me, thinking of me, or fixated on me in order to love me. And it is not obvious why during those times when she is not, she might not be looking at, thinking of, even to a degree fixated on, somebody else. Again, the love that seems to exist between friends and between parents and their children suggests the opposite.

In one sense, then, it is not true that there is only one center in a person's field of vision; what is true is that there is only one center at any given time. But this seems to allow the possibility of a plurality of lovers,

unless and until an argument is made to show that with respect to romantic love, getting *enough* attention from one's lover not only means that
her attention must frequently be fixed on the lover but that it may *never*
be fixed in this way on anyone else.

The ideal of exclusivity seems to arise, in part, from the nature of infatuation. Infatuation, as a psychological phenomenon, encourages just
this sort of silencing: obsessive thinking about the beloved, to the exclusion of nearly everything else. And this has led many people to think that
this ought to be a part of all love, not just of love in its early stages. This
stage of love is undeniably thrilling, pleasant, and affirming. And the romantic ideology that dominates our current discourse about love strongly
encourages us to see love as an extension of that initial infatuation phase,
as if what love gives us in those early weeks and months included a promise of more of the same, forever and without limit.

The expectation is, sadly, unreasonable. Psychologically speaking, we
are just not designed to remain obsessed with one person for the rest of
our lives. Yet one sees, again, how even in its very unreasonableness such
a thought expresses a certain way of responding to the value of human
individuals; and this, perhaps, is why it continues to speak to us and
strike us as both intelligible and attractive, even when we have come to
be somewhat aware of and skeptical about the romantic ideology sur-
rounding us. Think again of Hana in *The English Patient* and her decision
to "care only for the burned patient," so that "her only communication
was with him." As I suggested when I introduced this example, this can
be taken to represent an ethically ideal relationship. Precisely because she
chooses not to balance the needs and interests of her patient against those
of other people, Hana expresses a kind of intense and uncompromising
appreciation of his value and by implication of the value of humanity
at large. Of course, very few people will feel this way, spontaneously
and permanently, without ever lapsing. Nearly everyone, no matter how
committed in principle to the value of monogamous love, will have romantic, sexual, or otherwise troubling thoughts about other people at
some point. Still, one who takes this ideal as her own may choose to act,
or attempt always to act, *as if* she actually felt the way it asks us to feel;
and not only her actions but her feelings may be shaped in large part by
her decision to do so.

It is not difficult to understand why a person who loves another
should want to give him "everything"—why this, at least, represents a
kind of ideal of love, even if it is extreme and demanding enough that
many of us will not pursue it but will choose a recognizably related but
somewhat less demanding pattern of behavior instead. But even for those
who do accept it as their ideal, the question remains open about why it
must be interpreted as a *sexual* ideal: why, that is, must the "everything"

that one lover gives to another include, or have anything to do with, *sex*? We do not *literally* think lovers ought to give each other everything, after all; most of us do not think that I ought to show my love for my wife by refusing to engage in conversation or play table tennis with other women. Why is sex supposed to be so different? Love is exclusive by nature—that it has us focus on some individuals rather than others is what makes the personal attitude personal. But even if we decide to make love *maximally* exclusive and restrict it to a single other person, it is still not obvious that sex, rather than conversation or table tennis, must be the primary domain in which this exclusivity is manifested.

A final argument states that monogamy has one advantage that promiscuity cannot claim: it has been tried in practice and has proven to be, if not ideal, at the very least workable. This, though, overstates the case. Those societies that have claimed to accept monogamy as their sexual norm have nearly always accepted it in a very impure and halfhearted form; the amount of infidelity that takes place in societies where infidelity is officially condemned is, typically, very large.[34] Perhaps at the end of the day it is this—"official" monogamy combined with a reasonably high degree of covert promiscuity—that will stand revealed as the truly workable policy, perhaps even the policy that best contributes to human flourishing. A pessimist about human nature might well say so. A more idealistic person might be forgiven for wondering whether we might not find a way of reconciling the moral ideals we approve in public with the views we show allegiance to in private. At any rate, it seems to me still unresolved whether exclusivity and fidelity with respect to sexual activity in particular is the best means of expression for those who, having adopted the personal attitude to some significant degree, are in need of *some* manner of expressing the role that love's exclusivity plays in their lives. Like the personal and impersonal attitudes, each of the contenders here—monogamy on the one hand and promiscuity on the other—represents an intelligible way of expressing one's attachment to and respect for certain values that are deeply connected to the value of the human individual and of humanity itself. One must choose on the basis of one's character and on the basis of what one wants one's character to be, and one ought to acknowledge that regardless of which one is chosen, something significant will have been lost.

Conclusion

To love a person is to treat him as an end in himself and to fully recognize his existence as an individual. It is to take his needs and concerns as one's own, to regard him charitably and justly, and to place him at the center of one's life. All of this speaks to the fact that love is a deeply moral emotion.

Yet this moral emotion can blind us to the needs of others, and the passion it inspires can cloud our judgment and provoke deeply immoral actions. Even here, love does not cease altogether to function as a moral force, for in such cases it is precisely the commitment to a particular individual that leads the lover to neglect or harm someone else. Ours is a difficult, complex, and occasionally tragic world in which moral forces sometimes lead to immoral actions—and vice versa.

The danger that love may inspire immorality may lead some to wish that love and its passions could be expunged from human nature. But even if this were possible, the costs of doing so might be greater than love's critics realize. A case can be made for the impersonal attitude, which represents an insight about the nature of the value borne by individuals. Perhaps we should even allow that a person who lives her life *entirely* according to the impersonal attitude might be viewed as a kind of moral saint—not the *only* possible kind of moral saint, but one kind. It may be, though, that such saintliness is parasitic—in a way that might not be immediately apparent—on the existence of love and the experiences involved in love. The impersonal saint knows that human beings are valuable, but how does she know that? If her relations to others are genuinely and pervasively impersonal, she cannot know it through direct experience, for the direct experience of that value, or of any value, is always particular. She would have to know it, then, through the experiences of others: the experiences, that is, of lovers.

If this is correct, then the personal attitude is, in one sense, more fundamental than and prior to the impersonal attitude: the ethical ideal expressed by the latter is dependent on knowledge of value that can be gained only by people who adopt, to a significant extent, the former. If so, then it seems that human moral agents need and will continue to need love—not only as a source of moral motivation but more fundamentally as a source of moral knowledge.

afterword

Between the Universal and the Particular

One of the large questions left hanging at the end of chapter 1 was whether love and morality can be reconciled. My answer may be seen as a qualified yes. Love is an inherently moral phenomenon and so in that sense is more than reconcilable with morality—it is a part of morality and expresses a profound moral insight. But there are other parts of morality, based on other insights, with which the morality of love cannot be reconciled. When we love, we recognize and respond to certain moral values, those connected to the individual considered in herself, while closing our eyes to certain other moral considerations: the value of universal equality, for instance, or the demands of the impersonally determined good. Love's reasons, then, do have the potential to conflict with demands arising from other standpoints that are also, in their own way, profoundly moral: in particular, the impersonal standpoint that exists outside and apart from all personal relationships and special obligations and mandates a strictly equal regard toward all individuals. The potential for conflict between these two ways of seeing the world, each of which expresses an important moral truth, is both real and deep.

It must be kept in mind, though, that the existence of *potential* conflicts does not necessarily mean that every agent will inevitably find her practical life pervaded by irresolvable dilemmas. A few unlucky agents will find themselves facing deeply conflicting and irreconcilable demands that lead to tragic outcomes and painful, perhaps unbearable, regrets. The practical experience of most agents, though, seems marked not so much by dilemma and crisis as by vagueness and uncertainty. One must find a way to balance the competing demands that make claims on one's agency, and it is often not clear just what the proper balance should be. Still, there seems to be little if any reason to shackle ourselves to the idea that there must be a single correct conception of what constitutes a proper balance that every agent must, on pain of error or irrationality, adopt.

The thought that there *is* a single conception of virtue and value that would provide clear and precise answers to questions of balancing conflicting values is nonetheless tempting. As Murdoch writes in *The Sovereignty of Good*:

> The mind which has ascended to the vision of the Good can subsequently see the concepts through which it has ascended (art, work, nature, people, ideas, institutions, situations, etc., etc.) in their true nature and in their proper relationships to each other. The good man knows whether and when art or politics is more important than family. The good man sees the way in which the virtues are related to each other. . . . We work with the idea of such a hierarchy insofar as we introduce order into our conceptions of the world through the apprehension of Good.[1]

I would not want wholly to reject this optimistic vision. At the very least it would be an overreaction to conclude from the facts that there is no single determinate answer to the question of balance and that there is often more than one acceptable and justifiable response to a particular moral situation, that there is never any such thing as a *wrong* answer, either to the general question about balancing competing demands or to some particular moral question about what to do in a given situation. Here, as elsewhere, pluralism does not imply nihilism. A situation in which many things might go—in which, that is, there is more than one option a reasonable agent could be justified in choosing—is not necessarily a situation in which *anything* goes. And in some cases, where there is a great deal at stake or where some particular moral consideration is especially compelling, there might be only one justifiable or permissible option.

Faced with an individual in great pain and great need, for instance, it is often hard to see as anything other than a moral failure the decision simply to turn away—even if one is a committed impartialist and turns away only to serve the greater good. Similarly, a commitment to the impersonal good ought not to lead an agent deliberately to sacrifice an individual or violate her rights. But neither should a commitment to some *particular* individual—the sort of commitment arising not from the standpoint of impersonal morality but from that of love—lead to such behavior. Rather, moral prohibitions on treating persons in ways that fail to show at least a minimal level of respect for them as individuals and as ends in themselves apply to all agents equally, regardless of the nature of their positive commitments.

We might think of moral agents as players engaged in a game or sport. The way in which players belong to different teams corresponds to the way in which different moral agents take different perspectives on the world. In the case of sport, the contrast is rather stark: what counts as a success for members of one team counts as a failure for members of the other. Even so, all of the players have a good deal in common. Everyone on the field, for instance, plays by the same rules. And there might well be general agreement about what constitutes a virtue in the context of the sport in question—what counts as a skillful or impressive play, for instance. The thought that morality might well be universalistic, and the moral universe in this sense unified, is not threatened by the idea that there are multiple perspectives from which competing demands arise or by any degree of reasonable skepticism regarding the existence of a single unified answer to the question of how to balance these demands.

In this sense it seems quite possible, even plausible, that morality may constitute a kind of unity and, to the extent that it is constituted by rules, that those rules are universally binding. Within the limits set by this, however, it seems more likely that there exists a wide variety of justifiable approaches to dealing with the challenge of responding to competing values and balancing conflicting demands than that there is a single correct pattern of life to which all moral or rational agents must adhere. It is possible that Murdoch may have meant to allow as much, but the language she chooses ("The good man sees the way in which the virtues are related to each other") seems to carry the suggestion that there *is* a single way in which the virtues are interrelated and which the wise agent sees. And if this is what she means, then I am more skeptical than she. Whereas Murdoch frequently seems to theorize as one would in a universe that presented us with various expressions and instantiations of a single "Good," my own experience is that of a complex world that contains multiple and not infrequently conflicting goods.

As moral and rational agents, we want our actions and choices to be intelligible and justifiable to one another. But this is not at all to say that we want everyone to act in the same way—how much less interesting the world would be if *that* were the case! Similarly, while I may want others to be able to see what it is that I see in my beloved, there is also a sense in which I want to occupy the only perspective from which her best qualities can *really* be seen. (And I would certainly prefer that my beloved *not* see other people the way their lovers see them.) In responding to my beloved's great and incomparable value, then, I take myself to be acting for reasons; and reasons, by their very nature, cannot be entirely idiosyncratic but must be conceived as being at least potentially available to all. Yet these are not reasons that I would want to be actively appreciated by everyone or to move everyone in the same way. I have my beloved, and they, with luck, have theirs; and I am, at least ordinarily, happier and better off if other people at least mostly ignore the reasons of love on which I act and around which I structure my life—just as they are better off if they, and not I, recognize and act on theirs.

One cannot love generally; when we love, we love some particular persons rather than others. And it is no denigration of reason to deny that reason alone can decide *which* particular persons one's love focuses on, any more than it insults reason to point out that reason alone cannot decide how I ought to balance the demands of love against the demands that arise from other practical standpoints, including competing moral standpoints. Reason can take us some distance toward the answers to such questions, but past that limit it becomes something else: a matter of deciding, and also of discovering, what kind of person one wants to be.

Love, it seems, lies somewhere between reason and unreason, just as it lies somewhere between the particular and the universal. It places a particular individual at the center of my field of vision, and in doing so makes my experience of my life very different from what it would otherwise have been and very different from other people's experiences of their lives. It even makes my experience of life different from that of my beloved. After all, when I look into her eyes and she into mine, we see different things. I see her, and she sees me. It is sometimes suggested that the most unified lovers are not those who gaze lovingly into each other's eyes but those who are perceiving some third thing, who share some object of attention and thus share an experience: a pair of lovers regarding a sunset or a painting, listening to a symphony, or watching a movie. However, we can surely say that even if the particular details of the experience are different, there is undoubtedly a *kind* of experience—*seeing one's beloved*—that is shared by lovers who are looking at each other.

In pulling me deeply into its small communities—at its most exclusive, a community of two—love pulls me out of the larger world and away from many other communities I might have entered more completely. But at the same time the people around me are living out their own particular experiences of love and are being pulled away from me by their loves. The experience takes somewhat different forms in different cultures and societies. Still, the basic experience of love's particularity, and of being isolated from the world by love, may be as close as we will get to a genuinely common and distinctively human experience. Love, in separating us from one another, unites us all.

NOTES

Preface

1. Proust, *Swann's Way,* p. 102.
2. Frankfurt, *Reasons of Love,* p. 43.
3. My claim is not that an attitude must be reciprocated in order to count as personal love, but rather that part of what distinguishes personal love from other forms of love is the fact that it is directed toward an object that is capable of reciprocating it.
4. And there are some such cases, of course, in which a good deal of soul-searching is required to determine whether, and to what extent, one's apparent feelings about one's family members are genuine. It is not only relations between romantic and sexual partners, then, that are rendered complex and confusing by the influence of factors that have nothing essential to do with love.
5. Alan Soble, introduction to *Eros, Agape, and Philia,* p. xxii.
6. As Richard Moran writes,

There are more ways of changing someone's mind than changing his or her beliefs. Although this may be most easily seen in the case of rhetoric, it is quite generally true for both philosophy and literature that much of what they aim at is not on the level of specifically altered beliefs but rather such things as changes in the associations and comparisons one makes, differences in the vivid or "felt" appreciation of something already known, or changes in one's habits of attention and sense of the important and the trifling. ["Seeing and Believing," pp. 100–101]

7. My conversations with Linda Zerrilli were especially useful in helping me see, in the early stages of this project, that this was the way to proceed.

Chapter One. "Something In Between": On the Nature of Love

1. Broyard, *Kafka Was the Rage,* pp. 51–52.
2. Armstrong, *Conditions of Love,* p. 1.
3. Solomon, *About Love,* pp. 16, 9.
4. Krauss, *History of Love,* pp. 126–27.
5. Armstrong, *Conditions of Love,* pp. 118–19.
6. Coetzee, *Youth,* p. 3.
7. Lear, *Love and Its Place in Nature,* pp. 3, 238, 140.
8. Iris Murdoch, "The Sovereignty of Good Over Other Concepts," in The *Sovereignty of Good,* p. 103.
9. Teilhard de Chardin, *On Love,* p. 7. He goes on to suggest that love is "the attraction exercised on each unit of consciousness in the universe in the course of taking shape . . . love is the primal and universal psychic energy" (p. 9).
10. Ortega y Gasset, *On Love,* p. 10.

11. Buber, *I and Thou*, p. 126.

12. Dilman, *Love and Human Separateness*, pp. 80–81.

13. Plato, "Phaedrus," in *Symposium and Phaedrus*, 239e.

14. Cited in Wilson, *Iris Murdoch as I Knew Her*, p. xi.

15. Nussbaum, *Upheavals of Thought*, p. 461. It is worth saying, perhaps, that while Nussbaum takes this line of thought seriously, it does not represent her ultimate position on the value of love.

16. Kundera, *Identity*, p. 38.

17. "According to the 'quality theory,' for example, reasons for love are the beloved's personal attributes, such as her wit and beauty." (Kolodny, "Love as Valuing a Relationship," p. 135.)

18. Stendhal, *On Love*, p. 45.

19. Ibid., p. 48; my emphasis.

20. Tennov, *Love and Limerence*, p. 31.

21. Adam Smith writes that love "appears to every body, but the man who feels it, entirely disproportioned to the value of the object; and love, though it is pardoned in a certain age, because we know it is natural, is always laughed at, because we cannot enter into it." (*Theory of the Moral Sentiments*, p. 38.)

22. Keller, "Friendship and Belief," p. 333. See also Stroud, "Epistemic Partiality in Friendship."

23. Plato, *Phaedrus*, 238b.

24. Shaw, *Getting Married*, p. 25.

25. Shakespeare, *A Midsummer Night's Dream*, 5.1.7–8.

26. Austen, *Pride and Prejudice*, p. 108. Admittedly, Mr. Collins is thinking more of marriage than of love. For a case that explicitly concerns love, we might turn to Kip Lurie (David Wayne) in the film *Adam's Rib* (George Cukor, 1949):

> Mrs. Bonner, I love you. I love lots of girls and ladies and women, and so on, but you're the only one I know why I love. And do you know why? . . . Because you live right across the hall from me. You're mighty attractive in every single way, Mrs. Bonner, but I'd probably love anybody who lived right across the hall from me. It's so convenient. Is there anything worse than that awful taking a girl home and that long trek back alone?

27. Delaney, "Romantic Love," p. 343.

28. Frankfurt, *Taking Ourselves Seriously*, p. 25. A similar view is held by Irving Singer, who writes that love bestows value rather than creating it: "It is the valuing alone that makes the value." (*Plato to Luther*, p. 5.)

29. Such talk may seem more appropriate in the context of family love. One is, perhaps, obligated to love one's parents and one's children—at least under the right conditions. But although this is a common belief, explaining how such obligations can be justified turns out to be very difficult, leaving open the possibility that the widespread view that these obligations exist is simply mistaken.

30. Smith, *Theory of the Moral Sentiments*, p. 38.

31. Frankfurt, "The Importance of What We Care About," in *The Importance of What We Care About*, p. 90.

32. Note that this articulation of the incompleteness thesis is restricted specifically to the beloved's properties. Other versions of the incompleteness thesis,

having to do with other possible justifications for love, could in principle be constructed, but since the version of rationalism I intend to defend takes the beloved's properties to be central, I will not be concerned with those other versions here.

33. Nussbaum, *Upheavals of Thought*, p. 461.

34. Scruton, *Sexual Desire*, p. 96.

35. Of course, this assumes that the qualities in question are all universalizable, and some philosophers have appealed to nonuniversalizable historical properties in an attempt to circumvent the problem. There is something correct about this response, but the matter is a bit tricky. See chapter 6 for a discussion.

36. Nozick, *Anarchy, State, and Utopia*, pp. 167–68.

37. Nozick, "Love's Bond," in The *Examined Life*, p. 75.

38. Cf. Erich Fromm: "To be loved because of one's merit, because one deserves it, always leaves some doubt; maybe I did not please the person whom I want to love me, maybe this, or that—there is always a fear that love could disappear." (*The Art of Loving*, pp. 41–42.)

39. According to Dorothy Tennov, who conducted interviews with several hundred subjects regarding their experiences of romantic love, a complete inability to articulate one's reasons for loving is uncommon, at least so far as attraction in the early stages of a relationship is concerned. "The question 'What did you especially admire in ———?' or 'What particularly attracted you?'" she writes, "generally yielded a definite and specific response." (Tennov, *Love and Limerence*, p. 27.)

40. Green, "Is Love an Emotion?" p. 211.

41. From Montaigne's *Essays* (various editions); cited in Lamb, "Love and Rationality," p. 36.

42. To borrow a pair of terms from Jonathan Dancy—terms I will go on to make greater use of in chapter 5—we can say that facts like "Bill is a person," "Bill is not a serial killer," etc., are enablers, rather than favorers. An enabler is a consideration that does not directly function as a reason (at least, it would not ordinarily be cited by an agent giving an account of her reasons) but whose role is to enable other considerations to count as reasons. See Dancy, *Ethics without Principles*, chapter 3.

43. Or at least one might come to love someone whom one does not at first find physically attractive. Once one is in love with someone, however, love will lead the lover to see the beloved as attractive—even in cases in which one might have thought this to be highly unlikely. I discuss this further in chapter 3.

44. Frankfurt, "Some Mysteries of Love," p. 4. See also *Reasons of Love*, chapter 2, especially pp. 38–41.

45. See Frankfurt's discussion of the Hitler example in his "Reply to Susan Wolf," pp. 245–52.

46. Plato, *Symposium*, 201e–202b.

47. Ibid., 202c.

48. Choosing to do what one has the most reason to do might be compatible with and even enable a certain important form of freedom for rational agents. But the form of freedom enabled by love goes beyond this. In using the word *choosing*, I do not mean to imply that loving is completely or even largely within the

lover's voluntary control. That Martin Luther spoke truly when he said, "Here I stand, I can do no other," need not be taken to imply that his acting as he did was not, in an important sense, a matter of choice.

Chapter Two. Love's Blindness (1): Love's Closed Heart

1. Plato, *Symposium*, 210a–c.
2. It should be clear from these comments that I would also place the Christian idea of agape in a category separate from friendship and romantic love. Agape might represent or involve any number of things—beneficence, goodwill, charity, etc.—but it involves no appreciation of or attention directed toward its object (indeed, the very idea of agape is that the beloved's nature and qualities are irrelevant to the question of whether she is to be loved) and so has little to do with our ordinary ideas of love. For reasons of space, however, I will mostly leave this issue aside.
3. The need for this stipulation is brought out by a comment by Harry Frankfurt, who wonders why Williams focuses on the fact that the man is the endangered woman's husband, rather than the more salient fact that he loves her. See *The Reasons of Love*, pp. 36–37.
4. I have named the persons involved for ease of discussion.
5. Fried, *Right and Wrong*, p. 227.
6. Williams, "Persons, Character, and Morality," p. 18.
7. Stocker, "The Schizophrenia of Modern Ethical Theories," pp. 453–66.
8. Baron, *Kantian Ethics*, p. 123.
9. Frankfurt, The *Reasons of Love*, p. 36, n. 2.
10. Neo-Aristotelian virtue theorists frequently tend to speak as if there were a single unified set of virtues, thus making it appropriate to speak of "the virtuous agent," but I do not think anything in the account prevents us from endorsing the less ambitious and more reasonable view that there are multiple mutually irreducible sets of virtues to which one might commit oneself. Indeed, the discussion of chapter 4 will suggest that there is considerable reason to accept precisely this view of virtue.
11. John McDowell, "The Role of Eudaimonia in Aristotle's Ethics," in *Mind, Value, and Reality*, p. 17. Cf. McDowell, "Virtue and Reason," at pp. 334–35.
12. Little, "Virtue as Knowledge," pp. 73–74.
13. John McDowell, "Are Moral Requirements Hypothetical Imperatives?" in *Mind, Value, and Reality*, p. 90.
14. Ibid., pp. 90–91.
15. See Seidman, "Two Sides of Silencing," pp. 68–77. Seidman takes a moderate position on the issue, accepting McDowell's claim that the virtuous agent ought to feel no temptation but rejecting the idea that she ought to deny there is any reason for her to do the nonvirtuous thing.
16. McDowell, "Are Moral Requirements Hypothetical Imperatives?" p. 91. As he writes elsewhere, the virtuous person "can be completely aware of the attractiveness of the competing course; it is just that she is not attracted by it." ("Incontinence and Practical Wisdom in Aristotle," pp. 102–3.)
17. See Seidman, "Two Sides of Silencing," p. 71.

18. McDowell, "The Role of Eudaimonia," pp. 16–17.

19. Kant, "Moral Philosophy: Collins' Lecture Notes," trans. P. Heath (in *Lectures on Ethics*), p. 388. Compare Robert Nozick's claim that romantic love involves "the desire to form and constitute a new entity in the world, what might be called a we." (Nozick, *The Examined Life*, p. 70.)

20. See, for example, Soble, *The Structure of Love*, and Deborah Brown, "The Right Method of Boy-Loving," in *Love Analyzed*, ed. Lamb. See also Delaney's helpful discussion of the issue in "Romantic Love and Loving Commitment," pp. 341–43.

21. Scarry, *On Beauty*, pp. 22–23.

22. Adams, *Finite and Infinite Goods*, p. 170.

23. Frankfurt, "Some Mysteries of Love," p. 4.

24. Frankfurt writes:

There is a surprisingly widespread tendency to attribute an exaggerated importance to uniqueness. . . . It is probably true that if people did not differ from one another they would be less interesting, at least in the sense that there would be less reason for getting to know more of them. It seems to me, however, that the moral value and the moral entitlements of individuals—as distinct from their value as specimens— would not be diminished or altered in the slightest even if they were all exactly alike. In any case, the reason it makes no sense to consider replacing what we love with a substitute is not that loving something entails supposing that it is one of a kind. ["On Caring," in *Necessity, Volition, and Love*, p. 169]

Chapter Three. Love's Blindness (2): Love's Friendly Eye

1. Krauss, *History of Love*, pp. 126–27.

2. Ortega y Gasset, *On Love*, pp. 49–50.

3. Cited in Murray, Holmes, and Griffin, "The Self-Fulfilling Nature of Positive Illusions," p. 1174.

4. Hall and Taylor, "When Love Is Blind," p. 755.

5. Murray, Holmes, and Griffin, "The Self-Fulfilling Nature of Positive Illusions," p. 1163.

6. Bartels and Zeki, "Neural Correlates of Maternal and Romantic Love," pp. 1155–66.

7. Armstrong, *Conditions of Love*, p. 114. Cf. Sarah Stroud: "The bias of a good friend will normally take the form of casting what she sees or hears in a different light, shading it differently, placing it in a different optic, embedding it in a different overall portrait of her friend. Where our friends are concerned, in short, we become spin doctors." ("Epistemic Partiality in Friendship," p. 508.)

8. Hall and Taylor, "When Love Is Blind," p. 755.

9. Ibid., p. 757.

10. Tennov, *Love and Limerence*, pp. 31–32. The properties listed by Harry (Billy Crystal) in the film *When Harry Met Sally* (Rob Reiner, 1989) also strike us, for the most part, as silly and yet somehow intelligible: "I love that you get cold when it's 71 degrees out. I love that it takes you an hour and a half to order a sandwich. I love that you get a little crinkle above your nose when you're looking at me like I'm nuts. I love that after I spend the day with you, I can still smell your

perfume on my clothes. And I love that you are the last person I want to talk to before I go to sleep at night."

11. Stroud, "Epistemic Partiality in Friendship," p. 499.

12. Keller, "Friendship and Belief," p. 331.

13. Ibid., p. 332.

14. Ibid.

15. Ibid., p. 333.

16. Keller's argument is somewhat complicated by the fact that he tends to alternate between the belief that Rebecca's poetry is good and the belief that her poetry will be published and to treat these two beliefs as if Eric ought to have the same attitudes toward both. For my part, I do not at all find plausible the claim that Eric, as Rebecca's friend, ought to believe that her poetry will be published; this, after all, involves not just the belief that her poetry is good but also a further belief—that the world, at least in this respect, is just—which he might well fail to hold; and it does not seem to me that the demands of friendship have anything to say about this belief.

17. Keller writes:

> Even if Eric listens sympathetically to Rebecca's poetry, even if he sees and interprets it in the best possible light, it is possible that he will end up believing that her poetry is without potential, and that she does not have a realistic chance of getting it published. And if that is what he concludes, then it is likely that he should, insofar as he is Rebecca's good friend, believe (and tell her) that this project of hers is best left behind. ["Friendship and Belief," p. 335]

18. Stendhal sometimes writes in a way that suggests that his position is this extreme (at least with respect to romantic love, though presumably not with respect to friendship), though it is not entirely clear from his writings whether and to what extent he would ultimately endorse this.

19. As I noted in chapter 1, Neil Delaney has suggested that a person typically wants to be loved for the qualities she takes to be central to her conception of herself. (Delaney, "Romantic Love and Loving Commitment.") Delaney has romantic love in mind, but the claim might be defended with respect to friendship as well. If this is so, and being a talented artist is central to my friend's self-conception, then it would perhaps be necessary for me to value her as an artist in order to be the type of friend she wants.

20. There is one sort of reason why he might: if he trusts Rebecca's judgment, then the fact that she thinks that her poetry is good is at least some reason for him to think so as well (both before he is directly exposed to it and after, if he trusts her judgment as much or more than he does his own). I will return to the possibility of this sort of reason in the following section.

21. Hirsch, *How to Read a Poem*, p. 29.

22. Mills, *On the Poet and His Craft*, p. 37.

23. Keller, "Friendship and Belief," p. 335.

24. Stroud, "Epistemic Partiality in Friendship," p. 514.

25. Ibid., pp. 505–6.

26. Wright, The *Evolution of God*, pp. 456–57.

27. Stroud, "Epistemic Partiality in Friendship," p. 513.

28. Ibid.

29. Ibid. Similarly, on page 518 she writes that "friendship positively demands epistemic bias, understood as an epistemically unjustified departure from epistemic objectivity."

30. Little, "Seeing and Caring," p. 124. Cf. Velleman, "Love as a Moral Emotion," pp. 360–61: "Many of our defenses against being emotionally affected by another person are ways of not seeing what is most affecting about him. This contrived blindness to the other person is among the defenses that are lifted by love, with the result that we really look at him, perhaps for the first time, and respond emotionally in a way that's indicative of having really seen him." Erich Fromm also suggests a connection but reverses the explanatory order, proposing that love presupposes clear vision (rather than being presupposed by it): "I have to know the other person and myself objectively, in order to see his reality, or rather, to overcome the illusions, the irrationally distorted picture I have of him. Only if I know a human being objectively, can I know him in his ultimate essence, in the act of love." (*The Art of Loving*, p. 31.)

31. Little, "Seeing and Caring," p. 130.

32. This is similar to the main case discussed by Stroud, in which "someone tells a damning story about a friend of yours. Your friend appears in a bad light in this tale; he is portrayed as having acted badly, even disreputably . . . [and] comes off looking rather bad from the information conveyed." ("Epistemic Partiality in Friendship," pp. 503–4.)

33. One could say, of course, that she ought not to choose at all; not having been there, she ought to remain agnostic. But it is not always possible to remain agnostic; life frequently calls on us to make moral judgments about events we did not witness or witnessed imperfectly. Agnes's choice to continue being Brad's friend, for instance, and to continue treating him as she always has might in part be an expression of her choosing to believe that he is not guilty of unacceptably rude behavior.

34. Keller, The *Limits of Loyalty*, pp. 50–51.

35. Frankfurt, of course, would be correct to say that it is not because he has noticed that his children are much more valuable than other children that he loves them more than he loves other children. But I doubt that anything much follows from this. I return to this issue in chapter 6.

36. One is reminded of the moment in the film *Junebug* (Phil Morrison, 2005) when Ashley (Amy Adams) expresses her frustration with her husband by telling him, "God loves you just the way you are, but He loves you too much to let you stay that way."

37. Nehamas, *Only a Promise of Happiness*, p. 57.

38. Ibid., pp. 57–59.

39. Armstrong, *Conditions of Love*, pp. 96–97.

40. Jarrell, *Pictures from an Institution*, pp. 13–14.

41. In chapter 5 I will have a good deal more to say about the distinction between judging something to be valuable and valuing it.

42. Keller, "Friendship and Belief," p. 351.

43. Cf. Nelson Goodman:

The most neutral eye and the most biased are merely sophisticated in different ways . . . something is wrong with the very notion of copying any of the ways an object is, any aspect of it. For an aspect is not just the object-from-a-given-distance-and-angle-and-in-a-given-light; it is the object as we look upon or conceive it, a version or construal of the object. In representing an object, we do not copy such a construal or interpretation—we achieve it. [*Languages of Art*, p. 8]

44. Iris Murdoch, "The Idea of Perfection," in *The Sovereignty of Good*, p. 34. I will have more to say about Murdoch's views on this matter in chapter 7.

Chapter Four. Beyond Comparison

1. James, "The Moral Philosopher and the Moral Life," pp. 203–4.

2. Descartes, "Letter to Elizabeth," 1 September 1645, A&T, IV, 286, Letters, p. 170. Cited in Charles Taylor, *Secular Age*, p. 135. Descartes is particularly concerned with the choice of a certain sort of good, namely, "perfections of body and soul that can be acquired by our conduct." It seems likely, however, that he would have been willing to extend his characterization of the "true function of reason" to the choice between other goods as well.

3. Hampshire, *Morality and Conflict*, pp. 146–47.

4. Ibid., p. 155.

5. Velleman, "Love as a Moral Emotion," p. 360.

6. Glück, *Proofs and Theories*, pp. 78–79; my emphasis.

7. Broome, "Incommensurable Values," p. 31.

8. Ibid., p. 32.

9. Nehamas, *Only a Promise of Happiness*, pp. 43–44. A similar point lies at the heart of C. S. Lewis's complaint regarding the obsession, among certain critics, with rankings: "The human mind is generally far more eager to praise and dispraise than to describe and define. It wants to make every distinction a distinction of value; hence those fatal critics who can never point out the differing quality of two poets without putting them in an order of preference as if they were candidates for a prize." (*Four Loves*, p. 12.)

10. Iris Murdoch, "On 'God' and 'Good,'" in *The Sovereignty of Good*, p. 65. Murdoch goes on to write of such looking as an exercise in "detachment." Although I agree with the point she is making, I would not have chosen that word. It is too likely to be misinterpreted as a claim against the idea that contemplation is a type of actively engaged perception. The correct sort of detachment exists not between contemplator and contemplated, but rather between contemplator/contemplated on the one hand and the contemplator's extraneous interests and purposes on the other. (The Kantian term *disinterestedness* might be less likely to lead us astray here, though I am sympathetic to Alexander Nehamas's insistence that this word, too, gets it wrong; full-bodied aesthetic engagement is quite interested, and there is nothing wrong with that! See *Only a Promise of Happiness*, especially chapter 1.)

11. Comparisons between the outcomes of such decisions are particularly difficult precisely because the initial decision often determines, in large part, what will count as a criterion of success.

12. Many animals, of course, can also appreciate the world, in ways that are perhaps not too different from our own. I do not have space here to consider the

interesting issues this raises: whether we can love animals with the same love that we give to humans; whether animals can love; and so forth.

13. Alice Munro, "Floating Bridge," in *Hateship, Friendship*, p. 56.

14. Ondaatje, *English Patient*, p. 14.

15. Chang, introduction to *Incommensurability, Incomparability*, p. 19.

16. This way of using the term *eligible* is borrowed from Joseph Raz. See, for instance, "Incommensurability and Agency," ibid., p. 65.

Chapter Five. Commitments, Values, and Frameworks

1. One might, perhaps, be able to imagine circumstances in which a person could be rationally required to try to keep loving someone. Imagine a married man whose best prospect of happiness is to remain with his wife, so long as he can continue to love her; and suppose, as is surely true in many cases, that there are actions he can take that will make it more likely that he will continue to love her and others that will make it less likely. In such a case the rationality of self-interest would seem to require that he try, for the sake of his well-being. But this is a long way from saying that love is here, or anywhere, rationally required.

2. Green, "Is Love an Emotion?" p. 222. He also provides (p. 211) a more general version of the argument: "To the extent that A's love for B is exclusive, A will have no reasons for loving B rather than C, who is believed by A to have the same desirable properties; nor will such beliefs provide any basis for thinking that A loves B rather than C."

3. Horn, *Ships of Desire*, p. 311.

4. I will use *value* loosely throughout this discussion, so that it can stand either for a general value or for some particular bearer of a more general value. Participation in some ways of life might blind a person to certain general values: membership in a conservative, tradition-based religious community, for instance, might make it impossible to value pluralism, at least for its own sake. More frequently, commitment to one particular value bearer can prevent one from fully responding to the very same value, as instantiated in other value bearers; see the case of Antony's appreciation of Cleopatra's beauty, which causes him not to notice or respond to the beauty of other women.

5. Cf. Frankfurt:

> To care about something differs not only from wanting it and from preferring it but also from judging it to be valuable. A person who acknowledges that something has considerable intrinsic value does not thereby commit himself to caring about it. Perhaps he commits himself to recognizing that it qualifies to be desired for its own sake and to be pursued as a final end. But this is far from meaning that he does actually desire it or seek it, or that he ought to do either. Despite his recognition of its value, it may just not appeal to him; and even if it does appeal to him, he may have good reason for neither wanting it nor pursuing it. Each of us can surely identify a considerable number of things that we think would be worth doing or worth having for their own sakes, but to which we ourselves are not especially drawn and at which we quite reasonably prefer not to aim. ["On Caring," p. 158]

6. Perhaps what we want to say is that a person who does not judge x to be valuable may sometimes experience some of the symptoms of valuing x but cannot value x in the fullest sense. What I mean by the "fullest sense" will become clearer as the chapter progresses.

7. What we might want to say is that coming to appreciate the force of those considerations is within her power—she could achieve this, should she choose to try—but that because she is perfectly virtuous, choosing to try is not within her power. When Martin Luther said, "Here I stand, I can do no other," we all understand that he could have done otherwise had he so chosen. Given who he was, he simply could not have chosen to do a certain thing that, in itself, was well within his power to do.

8. Martin, *The Life of John Clare*, pp. 33–34.

9. "In a real sense" because there are two senses in which a reason may be silenced. In this case, while Sam's reasons for saving Daniel are silenced—they do not enter his mind, he does not feel their force—he would still acknowledge them, after the fact, as real (though insufficiently strong) reasons. In the case where the silenced reasons are immoral, however, an agent might quite reasonably refuse to acknowledge them as genuine reasons at all. In the former case, the reason is acknowledged as legitimate but judged to be irrelevant; in the latter case, the reason is simply ruled out as illegitimate before the question of relevancy is even broached.

10. See, for example, Watson, "Free Agency."

11. I do not mean to suggest that every value in the world is such that it must be a part of one's projects, commitments, or concerns in order to be relevant and thus give rise to reasons for that agent. Some values—agent-neutral moral values, for instance—might be such that they give rise to reasons for everyone—though it is still possible that the strength of the reason might vary from one person to another, depending on the nature of their other commitments, etc. Nor do I mean to propose being part of one's projects, commitments, or concerns as an exhaustive account of the notion of relevance; other sorts of facts (facts about causal relationships, for instance, and in particular facts about an agent's causal inability to affect the situation of a certain value) might render some values irrelevant, at least for practical purposes. I will have more to say about the notion of relevance in later parts of the chapter, though I will not attempt to provide an exhaustive account.

12. Of course, cases in which the evaluator is separated from the value bearer will frequently fail to constitute cases of full value responsiveness.

13. Indeed, it may well be, particularly with respect to works of art, that a full appreciation requires the presence of the object and that imagination can provide, at best, a somewhat pale simulacrum.

14. Cf. Joseph Raz:

> How then does the personal meaning of attachments and their objects relate to their (impersonal) value? Simply: our attachments appropriate (impersonal) value, and make it meaningful for us. They go well beyond the recognition of the value of their objects, and of the attachments themselves. They endow it with a role in our lives, make it relevant to the success or failure of our life. I may recognize the merits of

my city, and the value of engaging in civic activities, but only my actually embracing that good by caring about and becoming actively involved in the civic life of my city makes the life of my city, and my engagement with it, important for the success of my own life. [*Value, Respect, and Attachment*, pp. 19–20]

15. Forster, *Passage to India*, p. 197.

16. There are obvious relations between the type of individual I am describing here and the type Frankfurt refers to as a "wanton"—a person who has first-order desires but no second-order volitions. See "Freedom of the Will and the Concept of a Person," in *The Importance of What We Care About*, pp. 16ff. Indeed, it will be apparent to anyone familiar with his work that the discussion that follows is deeply shaped by Frankfurt's views.

17. Of course, the possibility of acting on external motivations without pausing to fully appreciate the reasons for those actions has a downside: if we get too used to acting in this manner, we can find ourselves on "automatic pilot," living distractedly and absently, finding ourselves alienated from our experience. (It is possible, after all, to be so distracted that one fails to notice how good the cake tastes even while one is eating it.)

18. This quote can be found in numerous places on the Internet, but the original source is obscure. It can also be found in the following work, which omits the word "particularly": Elizabeth Venstra, *True Genius: 1001 Quotes That Will Change Your Life* (New York: Skyhorse Publishing, 2008), p. 125.

19. Whether it is enough depends, in large part, on how strong an agent's will is. To say that an agent has a strong will is to say that she is able to choose to perform the action she judges herself to have the best reason to perform, even when she finds herself unable to appreciate that reason, and even when she is gripped by a vivid appreciation of the reasons in favor of some other course of action.

20. Dancy, *Ethics without Principles*, p. 41.

21. There are other categories as well. A disabler eliminates a reason one would otherwise have, and an attenuator does the opposite of an intensifier, i.e., decreases the strength of one's reason without eliminating it altogether. (Ibid., p. 40.)

22. Bratman, *Intention, Plans, and Practical Reason*, p. 35.

23. I suspect that we should say "relationships" here, rather than "commitments to relationships," but it might be best to leave the issue open. What is clearly true is that at least in some cases, a relationship will generate reasons only if there is a relevant sort of commitment; one cannot be someone's friend, for instance, without performing at least some voluntary actions that constitute commitment to the friendship. Family relationships, on the other hand, may perhaps generate reasons, possibly even obligations, whether or not one chooses to commit oneself (which is not to say that there might not be voluntary actions by means of which one could cancel or dissolve such a relationship). Even in the friendship case, though, it seems plausible to say that if framework reasons exist, it is the relationship that generates them, though it does so by virtue of the commitment.

24. Michael Bratman, "Planning and Temptation," in *Faces of Intention*, pp. 52–53. Bratman's discussion, it should be noted, is focused specifically on instru-

mental reason, so that he concentrates more on the sorts of plans and intentions that are formed in the process of satisfying one's desires and reaching one's goals than on the sorts of long-term commitments and relationships that loving agents generally form.

25. See especially "The Importance of What We Care About" (in *The Importance of What We Care About*) and "On the Usefulness of Final Ends" (in *Necessity, Volition, and Love*). The idea of the beloved as a final end is also emphasized by Neera Kapur Badhwar, "Friends as Ends in Themselves," pp. 1–23.

26. Alice Munro, "Runaway," in *Runaway*, pp. 34–35.

27. Frankfurt, "Reply to Susan Wolf," p. 250.

Chapter Six. Valuing Persons

1. I will discuss the fourth problem, inconstancy, later in this chapter.

2. Of course, to speak of justification necessarily involves the possibility of failure, and one might object that it is not clear that the vision view, as I have developed it, can allow for this. But there is a type of failure that is possible, which I briefly touched on in chapter 1: the sort of love directed toward persons would be quite unjustified if directed toward mere objects. Thus, the father who loves his sports car as other people love their children (and more than he loves his own children) is making a serious error, part of which is that he cannot justify loving a mere object in that way. The vision view does not, then, imply that love is never unjustified, even if it holds, in agreement with what I take to be common sense, that most cases of love for persons are in fact justified.

3. Which is not to say that the justification must be easy to articulate. See the discussion of Green's "my Bill" example in chapter 1.

4. McTaggart, *The Nature of Existence*, vol. 2, pp. 153–54; cited in Lamb's "Love and Rationality," in *Love Analyzed*, p. 35, n. 19.

5. Grau, "Irreplaceability and Unique Value," p. 112.

6. Cf. Neil Delaney: "The ideal of romantic love involves a relation between persons, not between a person and a set of qualities. . . . When someone issues a complaint like 'he only loves me for my body,' this is best interpreted as that person's observation that her lover's love is focused on qualities that she herself regards as peripheral." ("Romantic Love and Loving Commitment," p. 343.)

7. Kant, *Lectures on Ethics*, p. 155.

8. McTaggart, *The Nature of Existence* vol. 2, pp. 151–52.

9. This is not to deny that people sometimes fail to understand themselves from the first-person perspective and in some matters are better understood by others; nor, of course, is it to deny that a person can in some respects be her own worst critic. But the general claim is true, notwithstanding the interest and importance of certain cases that run contrary to it.

10. Frankfurt, "On Caring," p. 170.

11. Pascal, *Pensées*, pp. 217–18.

12. Velleman, "Love as a Moral Emotion," p. 365.

13. Ibid.

14. Ibid., pp. 371–72.

15. Ibid., p. 370.

16. On Frankfurt's view, love is a matter not of decision but of volitional necessity: such commitments of the will are not under our control. But this view does not guarantee love's continuation and indeed may heighten our worry: the fact that such commitments are not under the control of our will means that they may terminate themselves on their own, and without our permission.

17. Of course, there may be cases in which the values that do come to be there, and come to replace the values that were previously there, will not be the sort that the lover can appreciate. Not everyone can appreciate or even recognize every value, after all. But this is, obviously (if sadly) enough, something that really happens: people grow apart and fall out of love, and relationships end. It is no objection to an account of the nature of love that it allows for this sad possibility; indeed, it would be an objection if such an account did not allow for it.

18. A number of philosophers have suggested that love can be grounded in historical rather than present properties. But because this is frequently seen as a way around the universality, promiscuity, and trading-up problems, the properties cited are typically of the wrong sort; they are nonrepeatable relational properties—the fact, for instance, that A and B were together on a certain occasion and shared a certain memorable experience, etc. Since no one else shared this experience with A, B's having done so constitutes a nonrepeatable property that no one else can possess; so if it generates a reason for A to love B, then A has reasons for loving B that he will not have for loving anyone else (not even an exact replica of B). The problem, though, is that although such historical facts may play a causal role in A's loving B, or perhaps may function as enablers for the reasons that ground A's love, they do not seem capable of generating favoring reasons for love themselves—at least not without being supplemented by the more ordinary sort of consideration provided by personal qualities that are, by their very nature, repeatable. (After all, it was presumably not merely the fact that A and B were together on the occasion in question, but that B was particularly charming, funny, or pretty, in a way that A noticed and appreciated, that gives the real explanation; and the second sort of fact seems much more pertinent to the actual justification of his love for her.)

19. Proust, *Swann's Way*, pp. 19–20.

20. Edyvane, "Against Unconditional Love."

21. "Rather than wanting to be loved unconditionally, what you really want is for your lover to be strongly committed to you. This commitment should draw your lover to you even in circumstances wherein some, most, or even all of the properties that figure in her grounds for love are diminished or absent." (Delaney, "Romantic Love and Loving Commitment," p. 350.)

Chapter Seven. Love and Morality

1. Plato, *Symposium and Phaedrus*, p. 113.

2. Ben-Ze'ev and Goussinsky devote a considerable portion of *In the Name of Love* to the issue of "wife-killing"—that is, the murder of women by their husbands or romantic partners. See especially chapter 4 in that work.

3. Martha Nussbaum, "Steerforth's Arm: Love and the Moral Point of View," in *Love's Knowledge*, p. 344.

4. At least, this is the case in the film version (written and directed by Anthony Minghella). In the novel it seems clear that Katharine is already dead as the result of an airplane crash; his attempt here is not to save her but to return to her body, which he promised to do before leaving her.

5. Hurka, "The Moral Superiority of *Casablanca*."

6. In "Beauty, Evil, and *The English Patient*" (*Philosophy and Literature* 28, no. 1 [April 2004]), Sharon Barrios and I argue that the film does not clearly endorse Almásy's decision; indeed, it can be read as making precisely the point that the fact that an action is romantic does not require us to admire or endorse it.

7. Ben-Ze'ev and Goussinsky, *In the Name of Love*, p. 67.

8. Robert Ehman, "Personal Love," in *Eros, Agape, and Philia*, ed. Soble, p. 260.

9. Banville, *The Sea*, p. 168.

10. Lewis, *Four Loves*, p. 60.

11. Leopold, *Sand County Almanac*.

12. Nussbaum, *The Fragility of Goodness*, p. 365.

13. Murdoch, *The Sovereignty of Good*, p. 59.

14. Ibid., p. 92.

15. Ibid., p. 37.

16. Ibid., p. 34.

17. Ibid., pp. 90–91.

18. Murdoch, "On 'God' and 'Good,'" p. 51.

19. See Velleman, "Love as a Moral Emotion," especially pp. 360–61.

20. Ibid., p. 373. That Velleman's account runs into trouble at this point becomes clear, I think, in his attempt to explain where the husband's reasons for saving his wife should come from.

> The grounds for preference in this case include, to begin with, the mutual commitments and dependencies of a loving relationship. What the wife should say to her husband if he hesitates about saving her is not "What about me?" but "What about us?" That is, she should invoke their partnership or shared history rather than the value placed on her by his love. Invoking her individual value in the eyes of his love would merely remind him that she was no more worthy of survival than the other potential victims, each of whom can ask: "What about me?" [P. 373]

It is at the very least odd for Velleman to claim that the husband's reasons have "nothing essentially to do with love," and then go on in the very next sentence to locate those reasons as arising from the circumstances of "a loving relationship." But the inclusion of "loving" is no accident, for the modifier is essential: a nonloving relationship, even a marriage, would give rise to reasons of a very different nature. At any rate, what I take to be the crucial error is revealed in the last sentence: despite the fact that Velleman has recognized, earlier in his essay, that loving is a type of valuing that does not involve and even precludes comparison, he appears not to have taken this recognition to heart. If he had, he would be able to see what a loving husband would clearly see: that the fact that his wife is "no more worthy of survival than the other potential victims" is simply irrelevant in this context, and not something that needs to influence his deliberations at all.

21. Fromm, *The Art of Loving*, p. 46.

22. Perhaps it is not even so pleasant. As Nietzsche remarks, "'Pity for all'— would be hardness and tyranny toward you, my dear neighbor!" (*Beyond Good and Evil*, aphorism 82, p. 271).

23. Or, as W. S. Gilbert put it, "When everybody's somebody, nobody's anybody."

24. James, "Moral Philosopher and Moral Life," p. 204.

25. Murdoch, "On 'God' and 'Good,'" p. 50.

26. Ibid., p. 66.

27. Taurek, "Should the Numbers Count?" pp. 307–8.

28. Wittengstein, *Culture and Value*, p. 46; Greene, *Quiet American,* p. 183. Compare Lewis, *The Problem of Pain*, pp. 103–4: "There is no such thing as a sum of suffering, for no one suffers it. When we have reached the maximum that a single person can suffer, we have, no doubt, reached something very horrible, but we have reached all the suffering there can ever be in the universe."

29. Boyd, *Any Human Heart*, p. 278.

30. Lewis, *Four Loves*, p. 60.

31. Pope Benedict XVI, Encyclical Letter (Libreria Editrice Vaticana, 2005), p. 11; quoted in Ben-Ze'ev and Goussinsky, *In the Name of Love*, p. 37.

32. There is a rich literature here; some places to start include Gregory, "Against Couples"; Halwani, *Virtuous Liaisons*; Lemoncheck, *Loose Women*; McMurtry, "Monogamy"; Richard Taylor, *Having Love Affairs*; Vannoy, *Sex without Love*; and Weaver and Woollard, "Marriage and the Norm of Monogamy."

33. "The perfect friendship I speak of is indivisible; each one gives himself so entirely to his friend, that he has nothing left to distribute to others." Montaigne, "Of Friendship," p. 192.

34. See Ben-Ze'ev, *Love Online*, pp. 230–32.

Afterword. Between the Universal and the Particular

1. Murdoch, *The Sovereignty of Good*, p. 96.

REFERENCES

Adams, R. M. *Finite and Infinite Goods: A Framework for Ethics*. New York: Oxford University Press, 1999.

Armstrong, John. *Conditions of Love*. New York: Norton, 2003.

Ashbery, John. *Self-Portrait in a Convex Mirror*. New York: Viking, 1975.

Austen, Jane. *Pride and Prejudice*. Norwalk: Easton Press, 1991.

Badhwar, Neera Kapur. "Friends as Ends in Themselves." *Philosophy and Phenomenological Research* 48, no. 1 (1987): 1–23.

Banville, John. *The Sea*. New York: Knopf, 2005.

Baron, Marcia. *Kantian Ethics Almost without Apology*. Ithaca, NY: Cornell University Press, 1995.

Bartels, A., and S. Zeki. "The Neural Correlates of Maternal and Romantic Love." *Neuroimage* 21, no. 3 (2004): 1155–66.

Ben-Ze'ev, Aaron. *Love Online: Emotions on the Internet*. New York: Cambridge University Press, 2004.

Ben-Ze'ev, Aaron, and Ruhama Goussinsky. *In the Name of Love: Romantic Ideology and Its Victims*. New York: Oxford University Press, 2008.

Boyd, William. *Any Human Heart*. New York: Random House, 2003.

Bratman, Michael. *Intention, Plans, and Practical Reason*. Cambridge, MA: Harvard University Press, 1987.

———. "Planning and Temptation." In *Faces of Intention*, 35–57. New York: Cambridge University Press, 1999.

Brentlinger, John A. "The Nature of Love." In *Eros, Agape, and Philia*, edited by Soble, 136–48.

Broome, John. "Incommensurable Values." In *Well-Being and Morality: Essays for James Griffin*, edited by Crisp and Hooker, 21–38.

Brown, Deborah. "The Right Method of Boy-Loving." In *Love Analyzed*, edited by Lamb, 49–63.

Broyard, Anatole. *Kafka Was the Rage: A Greenwich Village Memoir*. New York: Carol Southern Books, 1993.

Buber, Martin. *I and Thou*. New York: Scribner, 1970.

Buss, Sarah, and Lee Overton, eds. *Contours of Agency: Essays on Themes from Harry Frankfurt*. Cambridge, MA: MIT Press, 2002.

Camus, Albert. "The Myth of Sisyphus." In *The Myth of Sisyphus and Other Essays*, translated by Justin O'Brien, 1–138. New York: Vintage, 1991.

———. *Notebooks, 1942–1951*. New York: Paragon House, 1991.

Chang, Ruth. *Incommensurability, Incomparability, and Practical Reason*. Cambridge, MA: Harvard University Press, 1997.

Cocking, Dean, and Jeanette Kennett. "Friendship and Moral Danger." *Journal of Philosophy* 97, no. 5 (May 2000): 278–96.

Coetzee, J. M. *Youth: Scenes from a Provincial Life*. New York: Viking, 2002.

Crisp, Roger, and Brad Hooker, eds. *Well-Being and Morality: Essays for James Griffin.* New York: Oxford University Press, 2000.

Dancy, Jonathan. *Ethics without Principles.* New York: Oxford University Press, 2004.

Delaney, Neil. "Romantic Love and Loving Commitment: Articulating a Modern Ideal." *American Philosophical Quarterly* 33, no. 4 (October 1996): 375–405.

Dilman, Ilham. *Love and Human Separateness.* New York: Blackwell, 1987.

Edyvane, Derek. "Against Unconditional Love." *Journal of Applied Philosophy* 20, no. 1 (2003): 59–75.

Ehman, Robert. "Personal Love." In *Eros, Agape, and Philia,* edited by Soble, 254–71.

Eskapa, Shirley. *Woman versus Woman.* London: Heinemann, 1984.

Forster, E. M. *A Passage to India.* Harmondsworth: Penguin Books, 2000.

Frankfurt, Harry. *The Importance of What We Care About.* New York: Cambridge University Press, 1988.

———. *Necessity, Volition, and Love.* New York: Cambridge University Press, 1998.

———. "Some Mysteries of Love." The Lindley Lecture, University of Kansas, 2001.

———. "Reply to Susan Wolf." In *Contours of Agency,* edited by Buss and Overton, 245–52.

———. *The Reasons of Love.* Princeton, NJ: Princeton University Press, 2004.

———. *Taking Ourselves Seriously and Getting It Right.* Palo Alto, CA: Stanford University Press, 2006.

Fried, Charles. *Right and Wrong.* Cambridge, MA: Harvard University Press, 1978.

Fromm, Erich. *The Art of Loving: An Enquiry into the Nature of Love.* New York: Harper, 1956.

Glück, Louise. *Proofs and Theories: Essays on Poetry.* New York: Ecco, 1994.

Goodman, Nelson. *Languages of Art: An Approach to the Theory of Symbols.* Indianapolis, IN: Bobbs-Merrill, 1968.

Grau, Christopher. "Irreplaceability and Unique Value." *Philosophical Topics* 32, nos. 1 and 2 (2006): 111–29.

Green, O. H. "Is Love an Emotion?" In *Love Analyzed,* edited by Lamb, 209–24.

Greene, Graham. *The Quiet American.* New York: Viking, 1956.

Gregory, Paul. "Against Couples." *Journal of Applied Philosophy* 1, no. 2 (1984): 263–68.

Hall, Judith, and Shelley Taylor. "When Love Is Blind: Maintaining Idealized Images of One's Spouse." *Human Relations* 29, no. 8 (1976): 751–61.

Halwani, Raja. *Virtuous Liaisons: Care, Love, Sex and Virtue Ethics.* Chicago: Open Court, 2003.

Hampshire, Stuart. *Morality and Conflict.* Cambridge, MA: Harvard University Press, 1984.

Hass, Robert. "Looking for Rilke." In *The Selected Poetry of Rainer Maria Rilke,* edited and translated by Stephen Mitchell, xi–xliv. New York: Vintage International, 1989.

Hirsch, Edward. *How to Read a Poem: And Fall in Love with Poetry.* New York: Harcourt, 1999.

Horn, Kate. *Ships of Desire.* New York: Cassell, 1909.

Hurka, Thomas. "The Moral Superiority of *Casablanca* over *The English Patient.*" *Globe and Mail* (Toronto), January 25, 1997.

James, William. "The Moral Philosopher and the Moral Life." In *The Will to Believe and Other Essays in Popular Philosophy; Human Immortality.* New York: Dover, 1956.

Jarrell, Randall. *Pictures from an Institution.* London: Faber & Faber, 1954.

Jollimore, Troy, and Sharon Barrios. "Beauty, Evil, and *The English Patient.*" *Philosophy and Literature* 28, no. 1 (2004): 23–40.

———. "The Psychology of Exclusivity." *Les ateliers de l'éthique* 3, no. 1 (Spring 2008): 52–60.

———. "'Like a Picture or a Bump on the Head': Vision, Cognition, and the Language of Poetry." *Midwest Studies in Philosophy* 33 (2009): 131–58.

Kant, Immanuel. *Lectures on Ethics.* Edited by P. Heath and J. B. Schneewind. New York: Cambridge University Press, 1997.

Kekes, John. *Facing Evil.* Princeton, NJ: Princeton University Press, 1990.

Keller, Simon. "Friendship and Belief." *Philosophical Papers* 33 (2004): 329–51.

———. *The Limits of Loyalty.* New York: Cambridge University Press, 2007.

Kolodny, Niko. "Love as Valuing a Relationship." *Philosophical Review* 112, no. 2 (April 2003): 135–89.

Krauss, Nicole. *The History of Love.* New York: Norton, 2005.

Kristjánsson, Kristján. "Casual Sex Revisited." *Journal of Social Philosophy* 29, no. 2 (1998): 97–108.

Kundera, Milan. *Identity.* Translated by Linda Asher. New York: HarperCollins, 1998.

Lamb, Roger. "Love and Rationality." In *Love Analyzed,* edited by Lamb, 23–48.

———, ed. *Love Analyzed.* Boulder, CO: Westview, 1997.

Lear, Jonathan. *Love and Its Place in Nature.* New York: Noonday, 1990.

Lem, Stanislaw. *Solaris.* New York: Houghton Mifflin Harcourt, 2002.

Lemoncheck, Linda. *Loose Women, Lecherous Men: A Feminist Philosophy of Sex.* New York: Oxford University Press, 1997.

Leonard, John. *This Pen for Hire.* New York: Doubleday, 1973.

Leopold, Aldo. *A Sand County Almanac.* New York: Oxford University Press, 1949.

Lewis, C. S. *The Problem of Pain.* London: Collins, 1957.

———. *The Four Loves.* New York: Harcourt, Brace, 1960.

Little, Margaret Olivia. "Seeing and Caring: The Role of Affect in Feminist Moral Epistemology." *Hypatia* 10, no. 3 (Summer 1995): 117–37.

———. "Virtue as Knowledge: Objections from Philosophy of Mind." *Nous* 31, no. 1 (March 1997): 59–79.

Locke, John. *An Enquiry Concerning Human Understanding.* Various editions.

Martin, Frederick. *The Life of John Clare.* London: Macmillan, 1865.

McDowell, John. "Virtue and Reason." *The Monist* 62 (1979): 331–50.

———. "Incontinence and Practical Wisdom in Aristotle." In *Essays for David Wiggins: Identity, Truth and Value,* edited by Sabina Lovibond and S. G. Williams, 95–112. Cambridge, MA: Blackwell, 1996.

McDowell, John. *Mind, Value, and Reality*. Cambridge, MA: Harvard University Press, 1998.

McMurtry, John. "Monogamy: A Critique." *The Monist* 56 (1972): 588–600.

McTaggart, John. *The Nature of Existence*. 2 vols. New York: Cambridge University Press, 1927.

Mill, John Stuart. *On Liberty and Utilitarianism*. New York: Random House, 1993.

Mills, Ralph J., Jr., ed. *On the Poet and His Craft: Selected Prose of Theodore Roethke*. Seattle: University of Washington Press, 1965.

Montaigne, Michel de. "Of Friendship." In *Other Selves: Philosophers on Friendship,* edited by Michael Pakaluk, 185–99. Indianapolis, IN: Hackett Publishing Company, 1991.

Moran, Richard. "Seeing and Believing: Metaphor, Image, and Force." *Critical Inquiry* 16 (Autumn 1989): 87–112.

Munro, Alice. *Hateship, Friendship, Courtship, Loveship, Marriage*. New York: Knopf, 2001.

———. *Runaway*. New York: Random House, 2004.

Murdoch, Iris. *The Sovereignty of Good*. London: Routledge and Kegan Paul, 1970.

———. *Existentialists and Mystics: Writings on Philosophy and Literature*. New York: Penguin, 1997.

Murray, Sandra L., John G. Holmes, and Dale W. Griffin. "The Self-Fulfilling Nature of Positive Illusions in Romantic Relationships: Love Is Not Blind, but Prescient." *Journal of Personality and Social Psychology* 71 (1996): 1155–80.

Nehamas, Alexander. *Nietzsche: Life as Literature*. Cambridge, MA: Harvard University Press, 1985.

———. *Only a Promise of Happiness: The Place of Beauty in a World of Art*. Princeton, NJ: Princeton University Press, 2007.

Nietzsche, Friedrich. *Basic Writings of Nietzsche*. New York: Modern Library, 1992.

———. *Beyond Good and Evil*. In *Basic Writings of Nietzsche,* edited by Walter Kaufmann, 179–436. New York: Random House, 2000.

Nozick, Robert. *Anarchy, State, and Utopia*. New York: Free Press, 1975.

———. *The Examined Life: Philosophical Meditations*. New York: Touchstone, 1989.

Nussbaum, Martha. *The Fragility of Goodness: Luck and Ethics in Greek Tragedy and Philosophy*. New York: Cambridge University Press, 1986.

———. *Love's Knowledge: Essays on Philosophy and Literature*. New York: Oxford University Press, 1992.

———. *Upheavals of Thought: The Intelligence of Emotions*. New York: Cambridge University Press, 2001.

Nygren, Anders. *Agape and Eros*. Translated by Philip Watson. Philadelphia: Westminster Press, 1953.

Ondaatje, Michael. *The English Patient*. New York: Knopf, 1992.

Ortega y Gasset, José. *On Love: Aspects of a Single Theme*. Translated by Toby Talbot. Cleveland, OH: Meridian Books, 1957.

Overall, Christine. "Monogamy, Nonmonogamy, and Identity." *Hypatia* 13, no. 4 (1988): 1–17.

Pascal, Blaise. *Penseés*. Translated by A. J. Krailsheimer. New York: Penguin, 1995.

Plato. *The Symposium*. Translated by Alexander Nehamas and Paul Woodruff. Indianapolis, IN: Hackett Publishing Company, 1989.

———. *Symposium and Phaedrus*. Translated by Tom Griffith. New York: Everyman's Library, 2000.

Proust, Marcel. *Swann's Way*. Translated by Lydia Davis. New York: Viking, 2003.

Rawls, John. *A Theory of Justice*. Cambridge, MA: Belknap Press of Harvard University Press, 1971.

Raz, Joseph. "Incommensurability and Agency." In *Incommensurability, Incomparability, and Practical Reason*, edited by Chang, 110–28.

———. *Value, Respect, and Attachment*. New York: Cambridge University Press, 2001.

Sandel, Michael. *Liberalism and the Limits of Justice*. New York: Cambridge University Press, 1982.

Scarry, Elaine. *On Beauty and Being Just*. Princeton, NJ: Princeton University Press, 1999.

Scruton, Roger. *Sexual Desire: A Moral Philosophy of the Erotic*. New York: Free Press, 1986.

Seidman, Jeffrey. "Two Sides of Silencing." *Philosophical Quarterly* 55, no. 218 (2005): 68–77.

Shaw, George Bernard. *Getting Married*. New York: Brentano's, 1920.

Singer, Irving. *The Nature of Love*. Vol. 1, *Plato to Luther*. 2nd ed. Cambridge, MA: MIT Press, 2009.

Smith, Adam. *Theory of the Moral Sentiments*. Edited by Knud Haakonssen. New York: Cambridge University Press, 2002.

Soble, Alan, ed. *Eros, Agape, and Philia: Readings in the Philosophy of Love*. New York: Paragon House, 1989.

———. *The Structure of Love*. New Haven, CT: Yale University Press, 1990.

Solomon, Robert C. *About Love*. Indianapolis, IN: Hackett Publishing Company, 2006.

Stendhal. *On Love*. Translated by Gilbert and Suzanne Sale. 1975. Reprint, New York: Penguin Classics, 2004.

Stocker, Michael. "The Schizophrenia of Modern Ethical Theories." *Journal of Philosophy* 73, no. 14 (1976): 453–66.

Stroud, Sarah. "Epistemic Partiality in Friendship." *Ethics* 116 (2006): 498–524.

Taurek, John. "Should the Numbers Count?" *Philosophy and Public Affairs* 6 (1977): 293–316.

Taylor, Charles. "Iris Murdoch and Moral Philosophy." In *Iris Murdoch and the Search for Human Goodness,* edited by Maria Antonaccio and William Schweiker, 3–28. Chicago: University of Chicago Press, 1993.

———. *A Secular Age*. Cambridge, MA: Harvard University Press 2007.

Taylor, Richard. *Having Love Affairs*. Buffalo, NY: Prometheus Books, 1982.

Teilhard de Chardin, Pierre. *On Love.* New York: Harper and Row, 1972.

Tennov, Dorothy. *Love and Limerence.* New York: Stein and Day, 1979.

Vannoy, Russell. *Sex without Love.* Buffalo, NY: Prometheus Books, 1980.

Velleman, David. "Love as a Moral Emotion." *Ethics* 109 (1999): 338–74.

Watson, Gary. "Free Agency." *Journal of Philosophy* 72, no. 8 (1975): 205–20.

Weaver, Bryan R., and Fiona Woollard. "Marriage and the Norm of Monogamy." *The Monist* 91, nos. 3 and 4 (2008): 506–22.

Weschler, Lawrence. *Vermeer in Bosnia.* New York: Pantheon, 2004.

Williams, Bernard. "Ethical Consistency." In *Problems of the Self,* 166–88. New York: Cambridge University Press, 1973.

———. "Persons, Character, and Morality" and "Moral Luck." In *Moral Luck,* 1–19, 20–39. New York: Cambridge University Press, 1982.

Wilson, A. N. *Iris Murdoch as I Knew Her.* London: Hutchinson, 2003.

Wittengstein, Ludwig. *Culture and Value.* Translated by Peter Winch. Chicago: University of Chicago Press, 1980.

Wright, Robert. *The Evolution of God.* New York: Little, Brown, 2009.

INDEX

accidie, 100, 106, 108–9, 110, 113
acknowledging (vs. appreciating) value, 107, 110–11, 121, 123
Adams, R. M., 43
Adam's Rib (Cukor), 174n.26
agape, xiii, 176n.2
agent-relative values, 104
akrasia, 100, 109, 113
Armstrong, John, 1, 2, 49, 71
antirationalism, 13, 15, 16,18 ff., 23, 52, 68, 71, 95–6, 99, 118, 121
appreciating (vs. acknowledging) value, 72, 107, 110–11, 121, 123
attenuators, 183n.21
Augustine, 3
Austen, Jane, 2, 10, 127
awe, 83–4, 88, 93, 98

Badhwar, Neera Kapur, 184n.25
Banville, John, 149–50
Baron, Marcia, 31–2
Barrios, Sharon, 186n.6
Bartels, Andreas, 49
Beatles, 69
beauty, 44, 70–2
Ben-Ze'ev, Aaron, 148
Berkeley, George, 89
Berryman, John, 84–5
Boyd, William, 160
Bratman, Michael, 114–15, 119, 183n.24
Broome, John, 86–7
Broyard, Anatole, 1
Buber, Martin, 3, 43, 90

Camus, Albert, 28, 95
Casablanca (Curtiz), 91, 148
Chang, Ruth, 91
Christianity, 2, 163
Clare, John, 100
Coetzee, J.M., 2, 3, 71
commensurability. *See* comparability.
commitment, 101, 108, 111–22
comparability, 76, 77, 92
comparative, evaluative reasoning as, 76, 77, 78

comparisons, permissibility of, 43, 91
comprehensive comparative survey view, 76–82, 85, 87–8, 93, 123
comprehensiveness, 76, 77
contemplation, 82–8
continence, 38
Cooke, Alistair, 111
cosmic force, love as, 2–3
courage, 38, 53

Dancy, Jonathan, 113, 175n.42
Dante, 2
Delaney, Neil, 11, 142, 184n.6, 185n.21
Descartes, René , 76
detachment, 76–8, 79–80, 82–3, 87, 90, 180n.10
determinations of relevance, 117–18
Dilman, Ilham, 4
disablers, 183n.21
disinterestedness, 128–9, 180n.10
Drowning Wife (example), 30–34, 35–6, 43, 101, 106, 114, 154, 158, 160

Edyvane, Derek, 141
The Elephant Man (Lynch), 70–1
Empathy, 160
The English Patient (Minghella), 148
enablers, 113–15, 125
endorsement (of a value), 107–8
engagement (with a value), 107–8
epistemic partiality, 52
ethically ideal relationship, love as, 90, 151
exclusivity in love relations, 162–7
external motivations, 106, 111, 116

favorers, 113–15, 125
final value, 104
Forster, E.M., 108
framework reasons, 114–15
Frankfurt, Harry, xiv, xvi, 11–13, 14, 21–22, 32–4, 43–4, 67–8, 114, 118, 119–21, 131, 135, 176n.3, 181n.5, 183n.16, 185n.16
Fried, Charles, 30
Freud, 2, 153